The RISE ~of the~ IRISH WORKING CLASS

The RISE ~of the~ IRISH WORKING CLASS

The Dublin Trade Union Movement
and Labour Leadership
1890~1914

Dermot Keogh

APPLETREE PRESS

First published in 1982 by
The Appletree Press Ltd
7 James Street South
Belfast BT2 8DL

British Library Cataloguing in Publication Data
Keogh, Dermot
The rise of the Irish working class.
1. Trade-unions—Ireland—History
I. Title
331.88'09415   HD 6664

ISBN 0-904651-75-4

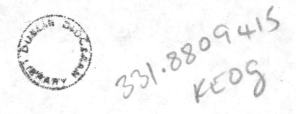

Printed in Northern Ireland by Appletree Press Ltd

Contents

Acknowledgements

I would like to express my gratitude to the History Department of University College Dublin, and in particular to Professor Dudley Edwards and Dr Fergus D'Arcy for the encouragement, useful advice and helpful guidance given to me while researching this work. Dr D'Arcy has had a profound influence on it and in recent years, Professor Joseph Lee has been of great assistance.

I would also like to thank the Archbishop of Dublin, Most Rev. Dermot Ryan, for allowing me access to the Walsh papers, and to the arch-diocesan archivist, Fr Kevin Kennedy, for his helpfulness in this aspect of the research.

It would be impossible to mention all the many trade unionists who went to endless trouble to help the writer and extend to him the hospitality of crowded offices while consulting union files. In particular, I want to thank Mr Donal Nevin, of Congress, Mr MacGrath and Mr Tony Sherlock of the Irish Graphical Society, Mr Brennan of the Plumbers' Union and Mr Gerry Duffy of the Plasterers' Union. I am also greatly indebted to Mr Seamus McGonagle and Mr Larry Quigley for their invaluable help. My profound gratitude is due to the veteran labour historian, Mr Brian O'Niall whose advice and knowledge has proved of immense help. (He wrote in the Ireland of the 1930s when such a venture was neither 'popular nor profitable').

I would also like to thank Mrs Vanek of Wicklow who gave me access to her grandfather's papers, the printer, journalist and labour leader, Adolphus Shields—a man whose contribution to the growth of the Irish trade union movement has not yet been given due credit.

My gratitude also to Charlotte Wiseman and Veronica Fraser of UCC who kindly prepared the manuscript for publication.

I would like to thank my colleagues in the Department of Modern History, UCC, and Dr P. J. McGrath of the Philosophy Department who gave me access to valuable papers, and all members of the library staff, in particular, Ms N. Browne, Ms A. Collins, Ms Una McCarthy, Mr P. O'Connell, Mr N. Fahy, and Mr J. Murphy.

My gratitude to Janet and John Banville who were a particular source of intellectual support during the research and writing of this book.

Finally, I would like to thank Ann, Eoin, Niall and Aoife for their tolerance, patience, friendship and encouragement.

Dermot Keogh
Dept of Modern History
University College
Cork

Abbreviations

ASC&J	Amalgamated Society of Carpenters and Joiners
ASRS	Amalgamated Society of Railway Servants
AST	Amalgamated Society of Tailors
DAA	Drapers' Assistants Association
DCC	Dublin Chamber of Commerce
DMOA	Dublin Municipal Officers Association
DMP	Dublin Metropolitan Police
DTC	Dublin Trades Council
DTPS	Dublin Typographical Provident Society
ICA	Irish Citizen Army
ILP	Irish Labour Party
INTO	Irish National Teachers Organisation
IOO	Independent Orange Order
ISRP	Irish Socialist Republican Party
ITGWU	Irish Transport and General Workers Union
NLI	National Library of Ireland
NUDL	National Union of Dock Labourers
NUOP	National Union of Operative Plumbers
NUR	National Union of Railwaymen
PRO	Public Records Office, Dublin
RIC	Royal Irish Constabulary
STA	Scottish Typographical Association
TA	Typographical Association
TCD	Trinity College, Dublin
UCD	University College, Dublin
UTA	United Trades Association

Preface

In the neglected field of Irish labour history, writers and historians have tended to concentrate their research on the first two decades of the twentieth century. The reason for such a preoccupation is obvious, for these years witnessed the arrival in Dublin of the militant and mercurial James Larkin, and the return from America of the revolutionary socialist, James Connolly. It was also a time of unprecedented trade union expansion. The foundation and rapid growth of the Irish Transport and General Workers Union to a strength of over 10,000 in four years provoked a fierce reaction from employers, and led to one of the most bitter industrial struggles ever experienced by Irish labour.

According to legend and learning, the main architects of this development were Larkin and Connolly. For many historians both bestride the past like the Colossus of Rhodes dwarfing the work of less charismatic trade union personalities. Even in the most detached accounts of the growth of the labour movement, Larkin is a hero, a promethean figure fighting the good fight against almost insuperable odds, and in harness and harmony with his colleague, James Connolly, he continues to cast an ideological spell. By implication, those who followed in the wake of these two great men were leaders of stunted political stature, puny vision and gradualist inclinations. In some cases they are also accused of betraying their revolutionary heritage.

What exactly was the Irish labour heritage? The 'betrayed' social revolution has been a receiving theme in the left wing press, and the argument goes something like this: a Dublin working class, radicalised by the founding of the ITGWU and the militant leadership of James Larkin, were led towards gradualism by William O'Brien on the one hand and by the tide of nationalism on the other. In other words, the 'deferred' revolution of 1913 was 'betrayed' by the 'minimalist' approach of moderates like William O'Brien.

When I began to research this subject I was motivated by a dissatisfaction with the approaches of many historians to the researching of Irish labour history in this period. The many 'lives' of Connolly and Larkin, no matter how professionally constructed they might be, have by the very nature of biography tended to set their subjects apart from their trade union colleagues and from the working class rank and file. This book attempts to place both of these men back in their immediate historical context and to redefine that context, and due attention will be paid to the ideology of the 'second line' trade union leadership. In this way, I hope it will be possible to continue the process of separating learning from legend and reality from the entangled web of received truths.

For the moment I would like to adopt the approach to history which relates events of major social significance almost solely to the actions of 'great men'. Constitutional nationalists revere Daniel O'Connell and Parnell; revolutionary nationalists worship at the shrines of Wolfe Tone and the Fenians, while the labour movement looks to Connolly and Larkin for inspiration. Rarely is the influence of the individual understood to have had more impact than in the shaping of the Irish labour movement. In the 1920s J. Dunsmore Clarkson wrote in his classic work, *Labour and Nationalism in Ireland*:

> A. E. (George Russell) relates that one day, as he sat on the top of a Dublin tram, he felt a certain vibrancy in the air, as though he were in the presence of some vast magnetic power. He was irresistibly impelled to look up; his eyes fixed themselves on the masterful bulky figure of a man, seated at the other end of the tram. A few days later he was introduced to that man; that man was Jim Larkin.

By personalising the reasons for the growth of the trade union movement, as Clarkson does, a number of disturbing conclusions follow: is it not then difficult to avoid having to accept the widely-held view that strikes are fomented by agitators? After all, one man's charismatic is another man's agitator. Pushing the argument a stage further, holders of the 'personality theory' are pushed towards supporting a conspiracy view of history.

Such an approach is seriously deficient. It fails to explain why it is that 'agitators' are apparently so much more influential in some industrial situations rather than in others. Why, it might be asked, was Larkin so effective in Dublin before his visit to America in 1914 and such a disaster on his return in the early 1920s?

The answer lies in the fact that widespread grievance is the touchstone for successful agitation; no amount of frenetic manoeuvering by one man, or a group of men, will create widespread social unrest in the absence of acute deprivation. This does not mean that trade union leaders had no significant role to play in formulating and voicing the feelings of their followers. Certainly, they were the articulate spokesmen of a movement, but above all, they were the 'catalysts of conflict rather than the cause'.

In the context of Dublin, Clarkson allowed himself to be dazzled by the definite Larkin mystique and, consequently, he was blind to the profound changes which were taking place in the city's trade union movement prior to 'Big Jim's' arrival in Ireland. The American historian accurately described the behaviour and outlook of the 'old' unions, but he failed to recognise that by 1907 the economic and political world to which many craftsmen belonged was beginning to crumble or had already done so. Out of the uncertainty was emerging a general acceptance by workers of new ideas on the need for trade union, social and political reform. Moreover, the militancy of the newly-formed organisation for drapers' assistants, under the leadership of the talented Michael O'Lehane, helped greatly to accelerate this process. Larkin's arrival in Dublin coincided with, rather than caused, this development.

I will argue that control of the Dublin Trades Council (DTC) was slowly captured by the 'progressives'. Practically all of these men supported the radical nationalist movement: some were revolutionary separatists, a minority were Social Democrats, and an even smaller group revolutionary socialists. Thinking generally was confused and often contradictory, and with the twin forces of nationalism and socialism competing for the support of the trade unionists, many workers simply gave allegiance to both ideologies without recognising any essential clash of interests. The need to choose was not found necessary until November 1913, and then many workers joined the ranks of the Irish Volunteers instead of the Citizen army. A year later, thousands joined the army and transferred their allegiance to wider 'humanitarian' objectives.

In reflecting the feelings of their rank and file, the majority of union leaders were far from being social revolutionaries either of the syndicalist or the socialist camp. The true nature of their radicalism was best revealed when efforts were made by employers to intimidate, cheat, or deny trade unionists their hard-won rights. There existed a growing trade union consciousness, not a social revolutionary one.

It was at the industrial level that the main battle of the period under study took place. And it was as organised workers, defending the principles of combination, that the unions affiliated to the DTC

extended the hand of friendship and comradeship to the beleaguered members of the Irish Transport and General Workers
Union during 1913. From a selfish point of view, apprenticed labour
was defending itself indirectly against possible future attacks on
craft unions. I do not accept that any significant section of the
fledgling ITGWU, and this includes the 'second string' leadership
with the exception of Connolly and Larkin, were either politicised
revolutionary socialists or syndicalists. They were men, in the main,
willing to defend the fundamental principles of trade unionism no
matter what the cost. The following conclusion of Emmet Larkin
will have to be modified:

> The deeper significance of these disputes (a series of strikes in which the
> ITGWU was involved in 1908), though no one realised it at the time,
> was that they were the beginnings of a truly revolutionary working class
> movement in Ireland.

This study attempts to show that trade union militancy should not
be confused with social revolutionary zeal.

1 Dublin: A Tale of Two Cities

When the English journalist, Arnold Wright, came to Dublin to write the history of the lockout in 1913 he seemed singularly unimpressed from the moment of his arrival by the city's 'industrial aspect'.[1] Unlike any leading manufacturing town across the St George's channel where 'chimneys belching forth black smoke' were very much in evidence, the skyline of Ireland's capital was practically free from these ugly symbols of industrialisation. From the top of Nelson's Pillar which offered a commanding view of the metropolis, Wright could only count 'as many factory shafts as you have fingers on your two hands'.[2] These were dotted about the city in isolated positions. The capital had, of course, no distinctive industrial quarter.

In 1912 a prominent young Dublin barrister, William Dawson, made much the same observation as Wright about his native city:

> Dublin has been flippantly defined as 'a large city completely sur-rounded by golf links'. It is, of course, much more than that. One of its chief charms to English visitors, and to natives returning thither from England, is its distinctiveness. Dublin looks like Dublin. It bears no resemblance to Liverpool or Manchester or other English cities. Cork, likewise, possesses this distinctive charm. Belfast completely lacks it.

Charm, it appears, was a quality which most towns and cities lost in the process of industrialisation. Belfast, with its gantries and rows of drab, red-brick, working-class houses clustered around the linen mills and heavy engineering works, was without the elusive characteristic of charm. Her sister city in the south, on the contrary, had charm but lacked the means of providing a decent livelihood for many of its citizens. In short, the social, economic and environmental composition of Dublin and Belfast could not have been more unalike. The latter was a leading industrial centre which could compete with any other manufacturing area in either England or Scotland. The former was a city which, but for a few key industries and the location of government departments there, would never have gained the prominence or notoriety it traditionally enjoyed throughout the British Isles.

Dublin was a capital city. After 1907 the administration was in the hands of the efficient Chief Secretary, Augustine Birrell, assisted by the capable Under Secretary, Sir James Dougherty, until the latter's retirement at seventy, in 1914. The ceremonial head of government operations was the Lord Lieutenant, Lord Aberdeen, a diminutive man ruled by his matronly and overweening wife. There was little doubt in the popular mind who governed the Viceregal Lodge. Lady Aberdeen was domineering, interfering and never out of the public eye. Her work with the Women's National Health Association (WNHA) had made her a well-known, if not a well-loved, figure in working-class areas. But her meddlesome nature, on the political plane, had exacerbated the link between the Viceregal Lodge and Dublin Castle and led to strained relations between Lord Aberdeen and Birrell.[3]

The city where Birrell made his home for part of the year had a population of 290,638 in 1901 and it rose to 304,802 in 1911.[4] Within ten years the number of families had risen from 59,263 in 1901 to 62,364; the density of population per acre had fallen from 69.8 to 68.3 in 1911. The number of houses in 1911 was 35,477, or an average of 8.2 persons per house; and the average size of a family in the city was 4.6 persons.

According to the chief medical officer for the Dublin Corporation, Sir Charles Cameron, the capital had the highest proportion belonging to the poorest classes in the United Kingdom.[5] In 1903, 39.7 per cent of all deaths took place in the workhouses, hospitals and prisons. Out of a total of 9,047 deaths in that year, 1,618 occurred in the workhouses while in the 76 largest towns of England and Wales, only 22.7 per cent of the deaths occurred in similar institutions.

Lancashire had a population of 4,495,409 made up of 913,581 families of whom 14,727 occupied a single room. Glasgow which had a very large poor population, had 24 per cent of its families in one room tenements, while Edinburgh had 14.2 per cent in one room dwellings. However, in Dublin, 21,702 families or 36.6 per cent occupied a single room.

Over a third of the population, living within the boundaries of the Grand and Royal Canals, were in slum dwellings.[6] The poor occupied houses vacated by the wealthy who had moved throughout the nineteenth century to residences in the suburbs. What were the mews of the rich in the past had become the tenements of the poor. The stables adjoining most of these once splendid mansions also gave shelter to families in 1911.[7]

Bad housing conditions took their toll on the poor. The death-rate of children under one-year-old in Dublin was about the same as the average rate for the 76 largest towns in England and Wales. In fact, the rate was much below that of many English towns despite the fact that it was higher than London. But it was the high mortality rate of children of the poor which worried Sir Charles Cameron most. In 1901, the families of the 'independent, professional, and middle classes' numbered 104,624 individuals. Only 273 children belonging to parents from this sector died in 1903, the ratio being 2.5 per thousand. On the other hand, the 'hawkers, porters, labourers' class numbered 95,885 people. Of these, 1,462 children under five died in the same period.

Such a high death rate was caused by both the bad housing conditions and a poor diet. Infants rarely got sufficient milk. Frequently they were fed on 'a bit of everything' used by the family. The majority were breast fed.[8] The menu of the poor rarely included meats, such as mutton, beef or pork, except possibly at Christmas. Rashers and sausages were the only meat commonly used.

Potatoes and cabbage were the most commonly used vegetables while peas and beans were rarely seen.[9] Fruit was too expensive to be widely eaten. Condensed skim milk was used extensively as was tea and cocoa. Fish was also popular. Butter was a luxury. The poor ate bread and dripping. Thus, Sir Charles Cameron concluded: 'I have no doubt that diets greatly deficient in fats render people more susceptible to the attacks of various diseases, especially of tuberculosis.'[10]

Contrary to what Lady Aberdeen and her Women's National Health Association thought, bad diet had relatively little to do with poor education. A pamphlet issued by the WNHA showed how it was possible to maintain a family of seven on 8s–9s per week. The diet recommended by these good ladies was skim milk, oatmeal, red herrings, bacon, dripping and treacle. One prominent trade unionist, however, put his finger on the problem at a meeting of the Dublin Trades Council (DTC) when he said that people were underfed because they were underpaid.[11]

Sir Charles Cameron found that in 1903 there were many thousands of families in the city subsisting on less than 15s per week, while some incomes were as low as 10s or even less. He knew of the case of a tailor who lived with his family in Dame Court on 10s a week. His rent was 2s 6p which left 7s 6d for food, fuel, light, clothing, bedding and tram fares. Their breakfast consisted of dry bread and tea. They had only one other meal which consisted of dry bread, tea and herrings with porridge on occasions.[12] By 1914 the average wage of Dublin's 18,000 labourers averaged about 18s per week.[13] In winter, when a family was in greatest need of good food, it was least likely to get any. Bad weather often hampered outside work and the labourer who was fortunate enough to have regular employment was put on 'broken time' which reduced his take home pay considerably.

The poor were often forced into any number of false economies. Families lived on credit, the source of which was the local pawnbroker. Every Monday or Tuesday, when the household money had run out, bedclothes, Sunday suits and valuables of every description were wheeled to the pawnshop where money was advanced on their value. On the following Saturday, when and if the week's wages were received, the articles were redeemed. The sums advanced on such items were generally small, rarely exceeding 2s. In 1903 alone, 2,866,084 tickets were issued in the city and the loans to which they referred amounted to £547,453, 'or at the rate of £2 4s per head of the population in the city'.[14]

Despite its employment situation and large slumland, Dublin showed many signs of being a relatively prosperous city. Not all the 300,000 population lived at subsistence level. The professional class numbered 18,438, just 206 more than the number of domestic servants returned in the 1911 census.[15] The medical profession numbered 2,358, or 0.77 per cent of the population, while the clergy numbered 1,784 or 0.58 per cent.[16] Besides enjoying better housing conditions, more wholesome food, greater educational opportunities and a well-paid job, the professional class also had one further advantage over the poor: they could expect to live nearly twice as long as most manual workers. In Britain in 1901, people in the upper class could expect to live for nearly sixty years, while those at the lowest income level were lucky not to die before they were thirty. Paupers and vagrants died sooner.[17]

One of the wealthiest men in the city was Lord Iveagh, the owner of the Guinness Brewing empire. Of the 60,000 breweries in existence in 1910, it was estimated that 1,200 of these would have to combine to match the output of the James's Gate works. One fifth of the world's stout was produced there, while one of the company's

150 vats contained enought stout to supply two and a half pints to every soldier in the British Army. Some 10,000 empty casks were returned to the yards daily.[18]

The profits made from this huge empire were enormous. One working day's profit at James's Gate was sufficient to pay a four per cent dividend on an enterprise with a capital of £80,000. Put another way, 5,300 families could have been maintained comfortably on the net profits from the firm, the head of each family being liable to income tax. In 1910, Guinness made £1.33 million profits and paid just under £0.75 million to shareholders.[19]

A staff of 3,500 was employed to run the malt stores, the fermenting house, the huge vat houses, the cooperage, the maltings, the refrigerating plant, the power house, the racking sheds, the internal railway, the drays and the barges which plied the Liffey. These men were the best paid and the best catered for in the city. It was difficult to get into the company and discipline was kept among the men by the knowledge that no one was indispensable. There were literally thousands of men willing to step into the shoes of a sacked employee.

The second largest employer in the city was Messrs W. & R. Jacob & Co., quality biscuit makers who exported to Sumatra, Adelaide, Singapore, Buenos Aires, Seattle and Damascus.[20] They employed over 3,000 workers and were reputed to be model employers.[21] A recreation hall, rest rooms and dispensary were provided for the employees. However, the firm's reputation in this area became a little tarnished as some of the pay rates were made public. Smaller employers ran jam, sugar, chocolate and confectionary works with some success. The numbers they employed rarely exceeded 100.

Dublin was also quite famous for its distilling industry. The Jameson, Power, and Roe families each controlled the city's three famous whiskey-making concerns. Power's employed 300 hands and distilled an average of 900,000 gallons a year.[22] Both the other firms employed a similar number of men. The products of the mineral water of A. & R. Thwaites & Co. Ltd, and Cantrell and Cochrane were well known.[23]

Other industries included match-making, foundry work, soap and candle manufacture, poplin making, the production of fertilisers and paints, clothing manufacture, ship-building, and brush, shoe, and pipe making.[24] These were, in the main, small business concerns catering for a local market. Dublin was in no sense a leading manufacturing centre, it was primarily a port and it was on the docks that thousands of Dubliners found casual employment unloading boats, carting goods or doing warehouse work.

The capital was also the centre of several shipping and railway companies. The British and Irish Steam Packet Co. which made its first run between Dublin and London in 1815 was by far the most successful. Their existing fleet consisted of five passenger boats of about 1,400 tons. The City of Dublin Steam Packet Co., which was established in 1823, was the holder of the prestigious and lucrative government mail contract. It had four steamers, the Leinster, Munster, Connaught and Ulster, which ran between Dublin and Holyhead. There was also a service between the North Wall and Liverpool. Other smaller companies, such as the Tedcastle Line, had links with Merseyside. Boats also plied regularly between Bristol and the North Wall.[25]

The railways were also a great source of employment and profit; the Great Southern and Western, the Great Northern and the South Eastern companies held sway. Moreover, many of the directors of these companies, such as Sir W. J. Goulding, were resident in Dublin.

Employers in Union: The Chamber of Commerce

If Dublin Castle was the centre of political authority in the capital, the seat of economic power resided in Commercial Buildings, Dame Street, where the local chamber of commerce held its weekly meetings. Descended from the Ouzel Galley Society which was founded in 1783, the DCC had 657 members in 1906.[26] No employer could afford not to be a member of an organisation which took decisions regularly affecting the commercial life of the city.

The chamber was dominated by the larger employers. Sir J. Malcolm Inglis held the post of chairman from 1900 for three years. Sir James Murphy was elected the following two years. Marcus Goodbody reigned in 1904 and 1905. He was followed by Laurence Malone who also held the position for two years. John Mooney was elected for three years and he was succeeded by William Martin Murphy who was in office during the crucial years of 1912 and 1913.[27]

Few, if any, members of the chamber harboured a desire to change society. The turn of the century witnessed a satisfactory level of prosperity in their ranks. Many of the more than 600 employers were not excessively wealthy but they had security from their business and investment transactions. In the words of Charles Dickens, 'It was clearer than crystal to the lords (of Irish industry) that things in general were settled for ever'.

When Queen Victoria visited Dublin in April 1900, she was presented with an address by the DCC. The chamber president, J. Malcolm Inglis, and secretary, Marcus Goodbody, 'approached Your Majesty with feelings of loyalty and devotion':

> We recognise in the visit a special mark of your Majesty's favour to this portion of your dominions, and a gracious compliment to the valour displayed by Your Majesty's Irish soldiers on the battle fields of South Africa. We are glad to be able to assure your majesty that the trade and commerce of the country, which we more particularly represent, have participated in the advancing prosperity of the Empire at large, and we are pleased to note the growing disposition of all classes to unite in promoting the best interests of our country.[28]

If any dissent existed at all in the chamber towards the visit of the elderly queen, it was not expressed publicly. Most leading figures of the DCC were committed unionists, wholly satisfied with the wealth which membership of the British Empire brought them. In 1906 the chamber had reason to feel content, and in a letter to Lord Aberdeen this feeling of confidence was clearly expressed:

> We believe that with the approaching settlement of the land question which we hope the government will press forward as quickly as possible and with a revival of trade, such as may reasonably as possible be expected, we may look forward with some confidence to general and continued prosperity in the future of our country. In connection with this we would venture to express the opinion that a royal residence in Ireland would greatly tend towards a better feeling in this country and would be a further bond of union of far-reaching effect.[29]

But if there was one moment when many employers were most likely to lose their reserve and begin twitching nervously, it was at the mention of the words 'trade unionism'. The businessmen and merchants of the city had long since recognised the necessity of combination as far as their own interests were concerned. Master drapers, master bakers, master printers, master carters, coal and timber merchants, ship owners and railway owners, all had their individual protective association. The DCC acted as a sort of unofficial co-ordinating body.

But the mere mention of trade unionism in these circles caused suspicion, and deep-seated hostility, an attitude based mostly on ungrounded fear and only partly on fact. Traditionally, employers regarded unions as disruptive and illegal combinations of malcontents who wished to extort exorbitant rates of pay from hard pressed firms. Often, their wildcat action resulted in destroying the competitive edge enjoyed by an employer by forcing him to pay more, members of the DCC argued. An example of this attitude can be found in the *Irish Times* throughout the nineteenth century where management refused to recognise or deal directly with the Dublin Typographical Provident Society (DTPS). The *Irish Times* argued that it had taken a long time to sweep away the secret privileges of guilds and confraternities to submit themselves to any new form of tyranny. The issue 'was one of liberty and profit'.[30]

The question of profit alone prompted the *Irish Times* to claim that it could save £1,500 a year by not employing 'society' men. The strict ratio of apprentices to journeymen imposed by the DTPS on all employers was sufficient to cause such a loss. But there was another overriding reason for blocking the progress of the printers' union. The employer lost his 'liberty'. He no longer had absolute authority over his men. The right to hire and fire whom he liked, when he liked, no longer applied in a union house. The *Irish Times* added sternly:

> In what are called 'society' offices, the foreman is a complete nonentity. He is superseded by an individual calling himself in the language of trade societies, the 'Father of the Chapel'. It often happens that some pressing matter may require the utmost exertion of the whole establishment in order to 'catch the post'. Should the editor go to the printers' room to see how matters are progressing, he finds the men in solemn conclave, 'holding a chapel' under the dictatorship of the 'Father of the Chapel', while the foreman stands by utterly powerless.

By 1907 trade unions had been legalised, but many of the residual fears concerning worker combination remained. This was particularly true of areas where an employer never had to deal with worker combinations before. I refer particularly to the non-apprenticed labour sectors such as carting and unloading ships. It was generally where employers had little or no personal experience of handling corporate labour representation that the bitterest confrontations took place.

At best, many employers were ambivalent in their attitudes to the principles of trade unionism. Combination was legal after 1870 but for many businessmen a large question mark continued to overshadow the *bona fides* of worker associations, particularly new ones.

At worst, employers declared war on all efforts at combination among their workmen. Sanctions were brought into operation against union organisers, the most effective being the denial of promotion. In other cases, known union sympathisers were dismissed on the slightest pretext. It was not uncommon for a firm to refuse to deal with a delegation of men making a general complaint. Individuals should make their own complaints personally to the management without the necessity of having to shelter and hide behind a union, argued management.

Many firms seemed to believe that their businesses should be run like a family, using a combination of tenderness and tyranny to coax employees to their best efforts. If the employer saw himself in the role of a father, then he had little difficulty in rationalising the additional powers he claimed over his 'charges'. He was not simply a disinterested parent, he was a moral mentor besides, with the responsibility for shaping the character of his staff. Character was formed through discipline and discipline was imposed by working long hours in bad conditions for low wages under the careful supervision and ever-vigilant eye of the owner or foreman.

If a union was introduced into such a firm, the whole hierarchical structure of the organisation was threatened. The employer felt betrayed by his staff for bringing in an extraneous force to meddle in the intimacies of his family. The lesson that employees had rights as well as obligations was often a difficult and costly one for recalcitrant employers to learn.

All employers, even the most progressive, were concerned about the growing power of trade unions. Some accepted reality and lived with the fear while others remained inflexible in their attitudes towards worker organisations. The majority, however, remained strangely ambivalent in their outlook towards unions. They wanted to bend trade unionism to their own image and likeness. If that course of action was not possible, then the organisation in question should be crushed. William Martin Murphy belonged to this school of thought.

William Martin Murphy: Profile of an Entrepreneur

By 1907 William Martin Murphy had established himself as the doyen of Irish businessmen. At sixty-two, he was one of the wealthiest and best respected men in Dublin. He was respected all the more because he was a self-made entrepreneur and a living refutation of the fiction that Irishmen, and especially Southerners, had no business acumen. He was to Dublin what the shipping magnate, William James Pirrie, was to Belfast.

Born in Bantry in 1845, he was educated by the Jesuits at Belvedere College, Dublin. He studied architecture in the office of John J. Lyons who was also the owner of the *Irish Builder*. Murphy got an early taste for journalism in that magazine and on the *Nation,* run in part by friends, the Sullivans, of Bantry. The premature death of his father forced him to take over the family building contracting business at nineteen years of age.[31] A combination of luck and skill made the business prosper under his direction. The railway-building boom in the latter half of the last century gave the young Murphy the opportunity he sought to lay the foundations of a large consortium. Soon he established himself as one of the largest contractors in the country and this allowed him to sell his experience abroad at a later date.

Without leaving London, he organised and profited from the building of railways in Africa. With the arrival of the electric tram Murphy won contracts for his firm to lay tracks all over England. Even Buenos Aires owed her first tramtracks to Murphy. At his death in 1919, an admirer wrote praising his abilities as an organiser:

> His brain was like a searchlight—he would turn it at will on the one subject and illuminate and enlighten every essential detail. Without leaving his office in London, for instance, he envisaged the problem of building a railway on the west coast of Africa and carried it through to the last sleeper.[32]

Murphy's keen sense for a new idea paid rapid dividends and while still in his fifties he became the head of a huge commercial empire. In Dublin alone he owned a big hotel and a large department store and was a director of the United Tramway Company. As proprietor of the *Irish Independent*, which he had bought from a Parnellite management in 1900, he had at his disposal a very strong propaganda weapon.

Murphy was fortunate to possess other talents besides the Midas touch. He had quite a successful career in politics, representing the St Patrick's division of Dublin for seven years up to 1892; he chose to retire from active public life while the pro- and anti-Parnellite factions were fighting bitterly.[33]

In appearance, he was frail and patrician-like. According to the

Dublin correspondent of the somewhat unfriendly *New Statesman*:

> He has an unassumed distinction and seemliness; he wears a black coat, has a neatly-cut beard, and a shapely head; he is a picture of restraint and experience but keen and vigorous for his years . . . nothing disturbs Mr Murphy's equanimity.[34]

At the time of his death, the *Daily Express* wrote:

> If you met him you got the impression of an ascetic kindly man of the diplomatic class, exceedingly well dressed, quiet spoken with a humourous twinkle in his eye and no trace of the Dublin accent. His was a case of the iron hand in the velvet glove. Behind the blue eye dwelt a soul of iron.[35]

This 'iron in the soul' took on a form of rugged individualism. As a self-made man he could not tolerate weakness in others; be they employers or workers, his message to them was the same: You really have yourself to blame if you are not a success. He was quite merciless with his business colleagues when some of them suggested that prosperity in Ireland was unachieveable while the country continued to be ruled and overtaxed from Westminster. As a parliamentary nationalist, he believed Home Rule to be an ideal solution to the political, agrarian and industrial problems particularly besetting the southern part of the country. Prosperity declines whenever a nation is governed by an alien power, he admitted in 1887. Speaking to an audience at the Wood Quay National Registration Club in Dublin, he cited the example of Belgium which had prospered after it had won its freedom from the Dutch in 1830.[36] But a lot could be achieved in the interim, before the introduction of Home Rule, to set Ireland on the path to economic success. He argued that banks should be more willing to make available risk capital to investors, and condemned the attitude prevalent in Irish trade circles that it was less than respectable to devote one's life to making money. He claimed that industry was crippled by the social class who made a fortune and then gave up the business out of a sense of snobbishness or toadyism,[37] and argued that the only answer to the Irish economic question was uninhibited individual enterprise.

Murphy was a recluse. In work as in leisure he preferred his own company:

> Nothing pleased him more than to take the helm of his fine yacht—The Myth—and steering by the back of Whiddy (island off Cork), shape his course for Beare Island and so to the broad Atlantic.[38]

But nowhere was his individualism more manifest than in his relationship with his many thousands of employees. Doubtless, his success as a businessman indicates that he must have had a good understanding with his workers, most of the time at least. In his 1887 speech he refused to bow to the conventional employer wisdom which blamed the workers for the ills of Irish industry:

> I am not going to say that the workingmen of Ireland are any more perfect than any other class in the community . . . but surely we have all heard of difficulties between employers and workingmen in other countries, where trades have flourished notwithstanding. But I entirely deny that it (unrest) is all the fault of the workingmen, or that the Irish workman, in Ireland, is more difficult to deal with than workingmen elsewhere. My own experience, extending over 20 years, is that by meeting workingmen fairly and by treating them as possessing equal rights, I have never failed to make reasonable and amicable arrangements.[39]

Murphy was speaking here as a politician and perhaps the criticism could be levelled that he was striving for popular effect rather than revealing his true feelings on this subject. Nonetheless, as president of the DCC some twenty-five years later, he advanced certain liberal views designed to lower the tension between workers and employers. Nor did he hesitate to use his position of respect to lecture his colleagues, some of whom still believed that they had a choice as to whether they should treat their workers well or badly:

> Apart from its justice, the policy of looking after the conditions of your labour, particularly low paid labour, without waiting to be asked, will be found to pay from a business point of view. A voluntary advance of wages to meet the increased cost of living will be far more highly valued than anything extracted in times of social warfare. Above all, such acts are evidence of the personal sympathy of the employer with his men, which goes further in preserving good relations than most people imagine. It is not possible in large undertakings that employers can come into personal contact with many of their workmen, but the latter are quick to discern when they are looked upon as something more than mere machines, and where an interest in them and their welfare exists beyond the mere exchange of labour and wages.

In practice, Murphy lived out his philosophy of industrial relations to only a certain degree. He was honest in his dealings with his men, but the terms of employment were often harsh. That is not to say that he did not give every man his due. His treatment of his personal staff at the time of his death will illustrate this point.

In his will, Murphy left a personal estate of £264,005, of which death duty was £36,185. Two thousand pounds was left to charity, and a sum of £200 was to be spent on Masses.[40] His typist got one year's salary, his housekeeper £70, his butler £50, the gardener £25 plus a 'prospective' pension of £1 a week; and each of his domestics was paid three months wages. Nobody could accuse him of being mean or thoughtless towards his staff.[41] His action may have been considered generous by many of his fellow employers who would not have acted quite so benevolently towards their servants. Murphy demanded strong personal loyalty and got it.

This same attitude permeated his entire business career and coloured his attitude towards his employees. They were hired under certain conditions and if anyone deviated from the correct path he risked dismissal or demotion. All outside interference, on the side of the men, was resented and reduced to a minimum. Trade unions, the main source of such interference, were barely tolerated. While Murphy often claimed, like most of his colleagues, that he had nothing against worker combinations,[42] in fact the reverse was the case. Neither was it true, as he had told the DCC, that there had been no major strikes in any of his businesses in over fifty years. Writing to Archbishop Walsh of Dublin in November 1913, the trade unionst John E. Lyons contradicted this view:

> At the recent inquiry, (Board of Trade inquiry into disturbances in Dublin in 1913) Mr Murphy stated that he was always in favour of trade unionism and never had a dispute with a trade union. When he was confronted with the fact that the *Independent* had a long conflict with the stereotypers society, he wriggled his way out of the position by saying that it was only a dispute between the men, and that the firm had nothing to do with it. I know from personal acquaintance with the facts of the case that his presentation of the matter is incorrect as I was one of a deputation from the trades council to Mr Murphy representing the *Independent*, who tried to affect a settlement between the society and the firm. My knowledge of the facts is shared by every delegate of the trades council, by every member of the stereotypers society, and by a very large number of other tradesmen, who consequently consider that Mr Murphy's statement was not to be taken as literally true.[43]

Despite these charges, Murphy's industrial relations record was almost trouble-free and his claim concerning a clear strike record was not entirely untrue. But the real reason which lay behind this success was not his ability to live with the reality of trade unionism; it rested on his not inconsiderable ability to avoid employing workers belonging to trade unions. Lyons again explains:

> In the execution of contracts in the past, Mr Murphy avoided coming
> into conflict with trade unionism by employing non-union labour,
> wherever possible. At the time trade unionism was not as well organised
> as it is now, and Mr Murphy's efforts are directed towards a
> perpetuation of the oppressive conditions which trade unionism seems to
> remove.
>   A member of the brick and stonelayers society told me recently when
> we were discussing Mr Murphy's evidence at the inquiry that the
> mortuary chapel in Glasnevin cemetery was erected by Mr Murphy with
> non-union labourers and that these were drawn from various sources
> outside Dublin, no Dublinman being employed on the job.[44]

While Murphy could afford to get away with employing men 'on the
lump' in the building trade, he was not able to avoid having to deal
with craft unions such as printers, stereotypers and lithographers.
Here he made his peace with such societies. But where most unions
were concerned, he never missed an opportunity to assert his
dominance over them. Thus his attitude towards trade unionism
was both antagonistic and ambivalent. Like his business colleagues,
he tended to stress the rights of capital to the near exclusion of the
rights of labour. Perhaps the *Freeman's Journal* summed up the
situation best when it wrote of Murphy after his death:

> Like most energetic and successful men, he had strong views as to the
> rights and duties of the employer and the capitalist. He was the leading
> figure of 1913 (the lockout). Perhaps his peace was too much of the
> victor's peace and a less sweeping victory might have had more satis-
> factory results in the years that have followed. But it is due to him to
> acknowledge that it was not so much the pecuniary profits of the success
> that interested him as his desire to safeguard these powers of inde-
> pendent management which he regarded as indispensable for the
> prosperity of Irish industry. His views on this point belonged, perhaps,
> to a world that is passing away; but they were as honestly held as they
> were triumphantly enforced.[45]

Murphy accepted the structure of society and argued that economic
progress could only be achieved through free enterprise and
personal initiative. Any force, or body of men, which resisted the
uninhibited interplay of market forces was a threat to progress and
had to be resisted. Trade unionism was such a force when it became
militant and aggressive rather than docile and pliable, and its
advancement had to be resisted, since no compromise was possible

with restrictive institutions. However, to understand the nature of the conflict between capital and labour it is necessary first to look back to the 1860s and the setting up of trade unions on a regular basis.

2 The Old Unions

In 1863 an influential section of the skilled workers of Dublin decided to set up a corporate organisation 'for the protection of the rights of labour', membership of which was to be confined to tradesmen. Each craft was circularised and urged to join. The silkweavers joined and, within two years, twenty four other crafts had followed their example. The United Trades Association (UTA) proved modestly efficient and almost adventurous in its objectives. A labour newspaper was published for a short time.[1] But besides propaganda work, the association also provided practical assistance in times of industrial unrest. When the printers of the *Irish Times* were locked out in 1865 the UTA placed a special levy of a halfpenny per week on each member to support the men.[2] Little else is known about the activities of the forerunners of the Dublin Trades Council except that it was dominated entirely by local craft unions and did not last for more than six years. Yet it had proved successful during its short life, and demonstrated the effectiveness of corporate action to sectionally-motivated trade associations. The lesson, however, was not strong enough to keep the trades together.

Over forty years later, in 1907, many of the same locally organised trades formed the backbone of the Dublin Trades Council. The Ancient Guild of Brick and Stonelayers had a steady membership of about one thousand. The Dublin Typographical Provident Society had about the same number. There were just over 500 members in the coopers' union and 300 in the plasterers' union. The Dublin Metropolitan House Painters had fewer than 200 members, while the silkweavers were down to about 160. The bakers had a very active union with over 500 members. Yet many of the local unions had been in decline since the middle of the last century and a lot of the old trades had practically disappeared. There were hatters, chandlers, pewterers, basket makers, organ makers, leather dressers, skinners, silkdyers, tanners and weavers in the city but they were no longer sufficiently strong or numerous to form a protective organisation.

In spite of this, many old unions managed to linger on. Associations affiliated to the trades council represented: bottle makers; carpet planners; confectionary and sugar boilers; bleachers and dyers; stationary engine drivers; fire brigade men; glaziers and lead sash makers; farriers; marble polishers; mineral water operatives; paper cutters; smiths; stonecutters; saddlers and harness makers; tinsmiths and sheetmetal workers; tile and mosaic fixers; wagon and cart builders; and waterworks employees.

Dublin seemed to have an excessively high number of diminutive, locally based unions, despite the inroads made by the powerful English-based unions into Ireland in the latter half of the nineteenth century. Outside the capital, and particularly in Belfast, the larger engineering, building and printing trade unions made rapid progress. The Amalgamated Society of Engineers came to Ireland in the late 1860s and set up branches in all leading Irish towns.[3] The United Operative Plumbers Association also set up in Dublin in the mid-sixties, completely eclipsing the local association. The plumbers' annual delegates meeting was held in the city in 1870.[4] The Amalgamated Society of Carpenters and Joiners set up in Dublin in 1866, and took over part of the local society in 1891.[5] Other large unions also recruited men in the city with comparative ease. By 1907 the Amalgamated Society of Tailors had two local branches, the Emerald and the Progressive, each with a membership of about 300. The United Society of Brushmakers was about 200 strong. The Amalgamated Society of Cabinetmakers was a bitter rival to the local union, while the Amalgamated Society of Painters faced the same problem. There was overlapping and duplication in other areas also. But the English unions did not have it all their own way. The trend throughout Ireland in the late nineteenth century was towards total absorption into larger trade units, generally with a head office in England. All the financial arguments, and they were very persuasive, pointed to the need for mergers. Most Dublin-based unions were incapable of supporting their members from their own funds during a protracted strike. For example, the Operative Butchers' Trade Union had receipts of £215 in 1894 and an expenditure of £198.15s leaving only a balance of £17.15s to carry forward.[6] It would be quite impossible to fight a strike with such a pittance at the disposal of the executive. In contrast, the British railway workers' unions which came to Ireland in the 1870s were well equipped in both finances and personnel to combat the strongest group of employers. In 1907, the Amalgamated Society of Railway

Servants had 3,999 Irish members falling to 3,219 in 1914.[7] Between 1900 and 1914 the ASRS spent £43,673 and only received £27,919 in this country. Some £15,000 of this sum was used to fight two Irish railway strikes in 1911.[8] The railway drivers' union, ASLEF, and the Railway Clerks Association to a lesser extent, had large memberships and correspondingly large bank balances.[9] Few locally-based unions could possibly have matched the financial strength of their cross-channel rivals.

Perhaps the best example of local independent-mindedness and organisational strength was to be found in the printing trade. Here three English societies, the bookbinders, the engravers and litho artists, and the stereotypers, controlled some of the key areas. The Dublin Typographical Provident Society controlled printers exclusively and would not entertain the thought of absorbing any ancillary trades such as the stereotypers and engravers. Not unlike the exclusive London Society of Compositors, the DTPS claimed undisputed suzerainty over a twenty-mile radius of the city.[10] However, the Typographical Association, the British-based rival of the DTPS, was no respecter of traditional rights. Several efforts to merge the two societies in the nineteenth century had failed after a few trial marriages. Since the 1860s, the TA had set up 'chapels' or branches in Belfast, Galway, Carlow, Cork, Kilkenny, Derry, Newry and Wexford. In 1893 one Hugh McManus was appointed full time organiser for Ireland. He was determined to destroy the sovereignty of Dublin printers and get them to join the TA, even if it meant a bitter trade war. After sounding out the Dublin printers in 1908, he seems to have found some positive response to his scheme, and in March 1909 he felt strong enough to make his first move in public and called a meeting in the Mansion House.

The DTPS, however, had friends in high places and they sought their help with alacrity. A letter was sent to the Lord Mayor who replied by return post:

> I am directed by the Lord Mayor to inform you that immediately on receiving your letter this morning he wrote to Mr McManus in Belfast, withdrawing permission for the use of the Mansion House on Easter Monday for the holding of the conference of the Typographical Association, and I am also to send you the enclosed copy of a letter forwarded to Mr McManus this evening. The Lord Mayor desires me to assure you that he would not be a party to anything detrimental to the interests of your society and perhaps in view of the fact that the permission has now been withdrawn, the deputation referred to in your letter may not find it necessary to call.[11]

McManus did not give up easily, and the dispute between the two printing unions went on for two years. Finally, a peace conference was arranged for October 26, 1911, between the TA, the DTPS and a third party, the Scottish Typographical Association under the auspices of the Printing and Kindred Trades Federation.[12] The opening exchanges at the conference were less than cordial. One DTPS delegate described the men who had resigned from his society as 'rats' and he refused to withdraw the remark when challenged, 'stating it was their proper designation'.[13] The Scottish delegates claimed that their members working in the city were being victimised. Under DTPS rules, the STA were subject to a three year probationary period before they were entitled to full benefit from the local society. The reciprocal arrangement was much more in favour of DTPS men who came into benefit in Scotland only one year after lodging their cards with the STA. Moreover, the DTPS man was also entitled to remove money when leaving. The TA saw amalgamation as the quickest and best solution to such a series of intractable problems. Although the STA wavered at the proposal and were inclined to favour it when pressurised, the DTPS were adamant in their refusal. The Printing and Kindred Trades Federation later quietly dropped the unity proposal at the behest of the DTPS. A new reciprocity agreement was worked out which all three unions agreed and the old difficulty of double subscription was cleverly overcome by the introduction of 'associate' membership. Under this clause, a member who moved into the area controlled by another society needed only to pay 2d per week as an 'associate' member. He also had the option of becoming a full member. If he chose the former course, he retained full membership of his own society but paid his subscriptions and received benefits through his adopted society.[14] The DTPS had beaten off the threat to its autonomy.

Workers in the building trade suffered most from the struggle between rival unions. The Stucco Plasterers were challenged by the National Association of Operative Plasterers in 1899. Initially, the English union met with a measure of success because on one occasion 'Mr Joseph Duffy charged the secretary, Mr James O'Neill, in the presence of several members who were in the room on the occasion, with being a member of the National Society of Plasterers'.[15] But the challenge was not sustained and in the local plasterers' annual report for 1901 the secretary, P. Malone, went out of his way to say he hoped 'that the same fraternal feelings and good fellowship may continue to exist amongst the members of the only plasterers' trade society in the metropolis of Ireland'.[16] However, the local unions of carpenters, cabinet-makers and painters all had longstanding and bitter rivals in cross-channel unions.

Disputes between 'regular' and 'amalgamated' carpenters were as acrimonious as they were protracted. The former tended to look down on the latter as inferior workmen, but the 'amalgamated' man often retorted by belittling and making fun of the antiquated structure of the 'regular' man's union. In 1876 Thomas Parker, a former 'regular' carpenter who had transferred to the new society, wrote:

> The society is rotten to the core. Within the last twenty years half-a-dozen attempts have been made to reform it but all to no purpose; it got into the groove again. These few years past its decent members have abstained from taking part in its proceedings, they not being ambitious of returning to their homes with a black eye or torn habiliments. The society has outlived its time; it is out of place just now; it is not required. Some years ago a necessity existed for every man who wished to get the value of his labour to belong to the 'regular carpenters' when there was a glaring discrepancy between the wages of society and non-society men. This is no longer the case. The members of this body are living on the name made for them by their fathers and grandfathers, not upon their merits.[17]

The debate continued between rival societies in the same destructive tone. Instead of devoting their full attention to matters of pressing importance, officials bickered and fought among themselves over grievances which were more often imaginary than real. It was often difficult enough to resolve the perennial demarcation disputes which arose between related trades, but to keep rival unions apart who might be working on the same building site or in the same workshop often proved quite impossible. The overall effect on the trade union movement was far from beneficial.

Were the Dublin unions either one hundred per cent English or fully controlled locally, the effect might not have been so demonstrably retarding. But to have wasteful overlapping and duplication was really to inheirit the worst of both worlds. Peaceful co-existence was quite impossible in such a tangled web of tradition and intransigence. Basically, the majority of unions in the city in 1907 was introverted, sectionally-motivated and thoroughly self-interested. It was this sectional selfishness which gave a distinct character to the unions. Yet behind all the rivalry and the jostling for the upper hand over the other unions, members of the DTC, with few exceptions, were tradesmen. Knowledge of a certain technique and set of skills and the freedom to practice them through membership of a selective society set them among the 9,000 artisans of the metropolis.

Labour Aristocracy

In the nineteenth century there was little difficulty defining a Dublin craft society as a group of workers who attained their status through serving a prescribed period of apprenticeship. Such a scheme's implementation required the enforcement of restrictive conditions, the exaction of premiums, rigid limits of servitude and a strict regulation of the number of apprentices permitted to each employer. By 1900 this system had come under severe strain in England due to rapid industrialisation and the destruction of traditional patterns of production:

> In the late nineteenth century a secure body of highly-paid artisans, protected by apprenticeship restrictions enforced by their trade unions was only to be found in a few industries and there only in some centres of industry; in printing, engineering and shipbuilding . . . and for the rest in a few small and static trades such as silk hat manufacturing, brush-making, and coachmaking and some, but by no means all, of the glass trade. The building trade trembled on the edge of the aristocracy; their members frequently dropped out of benefit and they suffered from the competition of the semi-skilled. Neither was there any real labour aristocracy in the staple export trades, coal and the main branches of textile manufacture.[18]

Whether this controversial view is accurate or not is not at issue here. But what can be said with accuracy is that whatever about the rest of the British Isles, the craft union structure continued to dominate the life of industrial Dublin as late as 1907, even if it continued to do so with decreasing effectiveness. The apprenticeship system was rigidly adhered to even by the weakest of trades. A boy began to 'serve his time' when he was about fourteen years of age. The indenture form signed in Dublin was standard; a boy pledged to serve his master honestly, fairly and diligently:

> He shall not waste the goods of his said Master or give or lend them unlawfully to any. He shall not commit Fornication, nor contract matrimony within the said term . . . He shall not play at cards, dicetables or any other unlawful games . . . Without licence of his said Master he

shall not buy or sell. He shall not haunt or use taverns, alehouses, or absent himself from his said Master's service day or night.

The more indelicate references in the indenture were discreetly omitted in the case of girls. But they were also forbidden to marry during their 'time'. A good example of the procedure and thinking behind the system can be found in the Silkweavers' minutes for May 7, 1860:

That all weavers taking apprentice to the silk trade be supplied with an indenture by the trade gratis and that any man binding a boy, not having an indenture from the trade, that the boy be not acknowledged by the trade. And that there be four of the committee and chairman at least present with the secretary acting for the time when an indenture be given. And that all boys bound apprentices within the last seven years, that their masters be requested by the secretary to bring or send their indentures to the committee.

The Silkweavers' union was particularly harsh on men who used their sons as cheap labour:

And that all weavers having sons (eldest excepted) at the trade that they bind their sons the same as if they were strangers and if any man keeps his son or any one else longer than one month for a boy that has been at the business before and two months for a boy that has not been at the trade before without indenture that the master be considered employing an illegal hand (and that he be expelled from the trade) for so doing or subject to a fine of not less than ten pounds and not be allowed an apprentice for the next seven years.

If entrance to the trades was controlled sharply then the sons of craftsmen were given preference. This form of patronage or nepotism was as respectable as it was universally practised. Reference to such preference often appeared in the rules of a society.[19] In 1913 a DTPS resolution before the council urged that 'apprentices shall serve seven years at the trade; preference shall be given to sons of printers'.[20] At Bricklayers' meetings the younger members of the trade were often identified by referring to their fathers. For example, at one meeting, one John Murphy was referred to as 'James's son' and a Patrick Barry was identified to the members as 'Whistler's son'.[21] Not surprisingly, it was not uncommon for trades to run in families and extend for generations.

For printers, bricklayers, silkweavers and plasterers, the apprenticeship lasted for seven years. For tailors it was five years, and four years for most other trades. While many English unions had been forced to reduce the length of the apprenticeship to facilitate the demands of industry and the pressure from their members, the Dublin unions withstood the pressure to dilute their standards. The TA was forced to reduce the traditional seven-year training term to five years in 1911, after a collapse in discipline to the old practice. The DTPS did not take the two years off the apprenticeship until the 1940s. The duration of training is an important factor because it generally helped settle the status of a society in the social hierarchy of the trades. The longer the apprenticeship, the greater was the importance attached to the trade and the more the respect extended to its members.

A large subscription rate was one of the most striking characteristics of the 'old unions'. The Regular Society of Glasscutters, Glaziers and Lead Sash-makers, which was by no means a wealthy union, insisted upon an entrance fee of 2s 6d, and 8d per week 'subs'.[22] In 1862, the Regular Operative Carpenters charged 1s per week; and members of the local painters union had to pay the same amount.[23] At the time, these tradesmen were earning 30s a week. The glasscutters were probably not earning any more than that sum in 1907. In contrast, the general workers' unions which came to Dublin in 1908, such as the National Union of Dock Labourers and the Workers' Union, charged 3d per week.[24] However, even if the cost of membership was high to the craft unions, the benefits which a man could look forward to were considerable. This was all the more so at a time when no social services or out-of-work benefits were available from the state.

The majority of Dublin trade unions were registered as friendly societies. Their general objectives can be summed up in the words of the preamble to the rules of the regular carpenters in 1876:

> The glory of God, the honour of our Queen, the well-being of our neighbours, the support of each other in distress, provision for our members in old age, and decent interment, and to provide for the children of our deceased members.[25]

In 1862, the Regular Operative Bakers' Society had as its object:

> To provide out of general funds, a weekly allowance to such of its members as by age or illness respectively are incapacitated from earning a livelihood, to secure employment for the unemployed at the same time guaranteeing their fidelity to interring becomingly the deceased and assisting their widows and orphans.[26]

The bakers were true to their word. In the early 1900s an

unemployed member was paid 7s 6d for the first twenty-six weeks and 4s 6d for the following twenty-six weeks. When a member, or one of his family, died, the bakers provided:

> three linen sheets and a table cloth, six candlesticks, a snuffer's tray, and such other articles that were deemed necessary for the decent laying out of the dead.[27]

When the wife of a member died, £8 was given by the union 'to provide a respectable funeral'. The Glasscutters and Lead Sash-makers paid £5 on the death of a member or a member's wife towards the obsequies.[28] All members of the trade were bound to attend the funeral if it took place on a Sunday. Members absent without written excuse were fined 6d. The carpenters even had their own beautifully handcarved bier in which the coffin was carried by members to the cemetery.

The importance laid on funeral benefits by members was not exaggerated. It was an expensive business burying a relative in Edwardian Dublin. In 1909 a leading trade unionist and a member of the DTPS, William Richardson, claimed that it cost £1 to bury a seventeen-day old baby in Glasnevin cemetery.[29] He described such a charge as 'legalised robbery'. It certainly was quite expensive when, as we shall learn later, a general labourer would be fortunate to take home a weekly wage of that amount. The burial of an adult would presumably cost more. Nor did this figure include the hiring of a hearse or the purchasing of a coffin.

The importance attached to a decent burial by the unions can only be understood if the Dubliners' disgust at the thought of burial in a pauper's grave is fully appreciated. As far as the craft unions were concerned, the funeral of a member was a great social occasion when the society had an opportunity of advertising the dignity and good etiquette of the trade. Were a member to be buried without all the trimmings attached to a socially acceptable funeral, it would reflect badly on the standing of the trade in the eyes of the public. No effort was spared to do the job properly.

The other benefits were paid with the same regularity. Out-of-work pay was a major consideration in a city which often saw large numbers of tradesmen almost permanently unemployed. Bakers, bricklayers, carpenters, printers, etc., could command between 30s and £2 for a fifty-four hour week. Compared with the wages of a labourer, the tradesman was much better off. But this really depended upon whether he could get work regularly. Many tradesmen, with the exception of printers, were unable to work an uninterrupted year. In the building trades work halted almost completely in winter. Many tradesmen lived in poverty but with the terror of starvation removed.

The DTPS provided the best example of an efficiently run union with a healthy balance at the end of most years. Through the careful handling of funds it was able to lodge a considerable sum of money each year which helped towards providing additional benefits:

> DTPS balance at the end of 1902: £1,479-15-10
> DTPS balance at the end of 1903: £1,681-2s
> DTPS balance at the end of 1904: £1,313-9-6
> DTPS balance at the end of 1909: £2,031-12-4[30]

However, the majority of Dublin-based unions could not claim as healthy a balance sheet. What was promised members by way of benefits were sometimes hollow promises. If, for example, a union which represented the men of one factory had a strike on its hands, literally every member on the books would be claiming pay at the one time.[31] In 1876, the rules of the Regular Carpenters provided for 8s 6d weekly unemployment pay and 7s 6d per week to members 'on reaching an age past their labour'.[32] A member's next of kin were supposed to receive £4. But financial difficulties seemed to make the payment of all benefits problematical. In fine, very few Dublin-based unions could withstand a major industrial disaster such as a lock-out of the whole trade. Most of the unions were capable of paying the friendly society benefits to its members but lacked the resources to fight any widespread protracted strikes.

In spite of this paucity of resources, membership of a craft union meant far more to a man than a source from which to draw welfare benefits. There was a pride in the trade which left a stamp on a man. The activities and interest of the union often dominated a man's life. When he was unemployed the union headquarters provided a shelter and source of activity. Each working day the idle book had to be signed if a man was to qualify for benefits, so even if a man wanted to, he could not avoid passing a few hours a day at headquarters. There he was at least assured of a fire and daily papers. Band practice also provided another outlet for energy and frustration. In 1907 there were over ten trade union bands in the city. If they sounded well it was no wonder because the musicians had plenty of time to practise.

The men who ran the Dublin-based unions were amateur administrators and part-time officials trying to operate organisations which badly required professional, full-time staff. Although some unions were quite obviously inefficiently run, a surprising number operated as smoothly as if they were controlled by professionals. Ability, dedication and commitment on the part of the elected committee often transcended the obvious disadvantages and difficulties of part-time administration. Books were kept in good order, accounts and all money matters were handled with scrupulous honesty and all meetings were minuted in varying degrees of literacy. Perhaps the best example of this can be found in the records of the Dublin Trades Council which were kept by a carpenter named John Simmons for over twenty years. The printers and the bricklayers minutes also provide a good example of care and accuracy.

The man with the power in a union was the general secretary who was elected annually by a ballot of paid-up members and generally held the post for a number of years if he proved effective and efficient. The president was second in command although many unions did not bother filling the post. But if these were the men with powers, they were also the men who were expected to carry the burden of the work load. Administrative duties and the need to attend meetings often made deep inroads into a man's time. Officials were expected to attend two meetings of their union a week, a committee and a general meeting. If an active official was a delegate to the DTC he also had to be at council meetings on a Monday night. If he sat on the DTC executive committee he also had to go to the trades hall in Capel Street on Thursday nights.

Besides being hard workers, union officials had often to be diplomats. The handling of a union meeting required delicacy and firmness. Drunkenness often presented a real problem, and the handling of such cases was provided for by rule:

> Any member appearing intoxicated or cursing or conducting himself in a disorderly manner, shall, on complaint being made to the secretary, be brought before the committee of management and . . . be fined not less than ten shillings.[33]

The glasscutters made the same provision:

> If any member enters the trade union room during the time of business in a state of intoxication, he shall be requested by the president to withdraw, and if he uses insulting language to the president, he shall be

fined two shillings and sixpence, and shall be conducted out of the room by order of the president.[34]

Such rules were frequently invoked against unruly members. A bricklayer named John Lyons proffered a charge against one Augustine Duffy junior for striking him in the face 'cutting him severely and putting him out of the hall calling him and his people "coults" '.[35] Duffy later admitted the charge, stating that he had been drunk at the time. Physical force had rarely to be resorted to in order to restore peace but there were occasions when union officials had to eject troublemakers. At a lodge meeting of the Operative Plumbers' union in 1868, the following altercation took place:

> '. . . a disgraceful uproar—caused by some drunken members in which the GMP, Mr Forster (with great provocation caused by Mr Maguire) took a prominent part with Mr Maguire when the GMP and Mr Maguire had some hot words which ended in (—?). Mr Forster exhibited a sample of pugilistic power never before imparted by any delegate in striking Mr Maguire between his skylights (*eyes?*) and nasgal (*sic*) organ causing a confusion of blood. The chair ordered those gentlemen to be removed down to the bar or any other place to settle the dispute so as not to interfere with the business of the board.[36]

Union meetings were generally not quite so eventful. Normally, the union official's task was mundane, routine and very unrewarding. Yet he persevered with a persistence and a tenacity of purpose which might mistakenly indicate that he was being paid a large retainer. In fact the general secretary usually received no more than two pounds a year and expenses. Pecuniary rewards were not among the motives which compelled men to do so much for their fellow workmen and receive so little in return; what drove them to undertake such humdrum work was a certain pride in their respective trades. They were proof of the traditions and practices associated with their crafts, and they were determined to preserve the high standards expected of them. But they were also prepared to take every measure necessary to prevent the erosion of their rights and customs. They were members of an aristocracy, even if many of them were penniless peers.

The 'Bowler Hat' Tradition

No tradesman in 1907 would feel properly dressed without his bowler hat. It was both a symbol of his prosperity and his thorough-going respectability. Moreover, it differentiated him from the ordinary labourer who wore the customary cloth cap. Behind the symbol there lay a certain air of superiority over the ordinary 'five-eight', an expression generally used to describe the labourer. The inequality of society was an undisputed and accepted fact in craft circles. Indeed, many tradesmen would have had little difficulty accepting the sentiments expressed in the lines of Alexander Pope, quoted in the rules of the British National Association of Operative Plasterers: 'Order is Heaven's first law, and this confessed some are and must be greater than the rest.'[37] Egalitarianism aside, no effort was spared to preserve the good name of a trade and woe betide any individual who might bring it into disrepute. An alcoholic tailor named Ring caused the AST real concern in 1906. Brought to court, Ring was charged with desertion by his wife and family, leaving three of his children to be cared for in the North Dublin Union. It was stated that the defendant could earn two pounds a week. According to his wife, Ring had left her repeatedly during the last six years. Whenever he chose to work it was usually only for a week. However, if his wife asked him for her allowance her husband would refuse, claiming that he owed money because he had been 'on the cod'. For the benefit of the judge, this expression was explained as meaning that the defendant had been out drinking with other tailors. The relieving officer told the court that he had heard that expression all too frequently:

> Tailors give us more trouble than all other classes of men in Dublin. They earn good wages, but the most of them spend their money on drink. The ordinary labourers were much better towards their families. We have the families of from ten to twelve tailors living on the rates from year's end to year's end—all through drink. The system of drinking in the tailors workshops in Dublin is scandalous. They drink all their wages. I have repeatedly gone to workshops to follow a man up, but as soon as I arrive he disappears, and trots from one shop to another. They are the worst class of tradesmen I am aware of.[38]

Happily the judge took a more lenient view of Ring's transgressions. The defendant was given a chance, provided he agreed to take his children out of the 'union' and take 'the pledge'. This Ring promised to do, provided his wife, who was described in court as 'a hard-working poor woman', also agreed to abstain from drink. Both were contrite and accepted the judge's terms.

However, the matter did not end there as far as the AST was concerned. The evidence of the relieving officer which cast doubts on the sobriety of the whole trade infuriated the tailors of the city. A special plenary meeting of both the Emerald and the Progressive branches was held within days of the court case. Nothing less than a public retraction of the relieving officer's 'gross, libelous and misleading statements' was sought in the press by a union which represented over 700 Dublin tailors who paid £6,000 in friendly society benefits per year.[39] Ring was not even a member of the AST.

The matter was never really satisfactorily resolved. However, the tailors' reputation seems to have recovered despite the incident. Yet it serves to illustrate how tetchy craft unions were about their public image. The AST was far from being an exception. A broader based attack on workmen was liable to produce a unified response from the unions. While lecturing on the medieval guilds at Maynooth, Fr P. J. Dowling commented that the future industrial progress of Ireland was being impeded because 'some workers will not give an honest day's work for their pay'.[40] The lack of productivity in Ireland stemmed from the fact that many employers 'think more of sport than of industry', wrote trade unionists, William Partridge and E. L. Richardson in reply to such conventional wisdom.[41] Despite these random attacks on the character and performance of the trades, the craftsmen had achieved a decided air of respectability by 1907 although the spectre of irresponsibility continued to haunt them. They had a past to live down, a past which continued to crop up and be held against them. This accounts for the jealous way in which they defended their name and never missed an opportunity to enhance it. When the Irish Trade Union Congress held its inaugural meeting in Dublin in 1894, there was no indication that the city's employers regarded the unions with suspicion. On the contrary, every courtesy was paid to visiting delegates. The congress was wined and dined by Charles Brennan, the owner of the Phoenix Brewery, and William Martin Murphy 'kindly granted to delegates and their friends free passage for three days over the entire system' of the Dublin United Tramway Company.[42]

Attitudes Towards General Labour

Some trade unionists suffered from such an excess of 'respectability' that they refused to associated themselves publicly with their fellow workers. The president of the bricklayers union, Richard O'Carroll (who was killed in the 1916 Rising), was forced to admit in 1915:

> That certain of our members who have profited largely by the activities of trade unionism are to be seen walking in the ranks of the organisation

which has improved their condition and protected their interest. This is the class of individual who belongs to his union because he can't help it. He seldom, if ever, attends a meeting of his trade, takes no interest in its affairs and subscribes to its funds through compulsion.[43]

However, the tradesman's quest for status and his hostility towards the general labourer was based on more than snobbery, having firm economic motives. Skilled labourers were often forced out of a job by the willingness of general workers to take up employment regardless of traditional demarcation lines.

Craft unions, with the possible exceptions of the printers and allied trades, the silkweavers, the goldsmiths and the coopers, suffered greatly from the unwelcome competition. The Metropolitan House Painters' Union was beleaguered with complaints about non-society men doing an apprenticed worker's job. On July 3, 1912, they had before them the applications for membership of six men. All were rejected on the following grounds:

> Frank White for scabbing; James Yule for taken (*sic*) up on a job on the Great Northern Railway wherein a member was employed and left same on trades' principles. The information of the matter is as follows: Mr Peter Macken got a job on the Northern Railway, having to work with unskilled workmen, he left the job, reporting himself to the engineer beforehand and stated that he could not work with such men; Louis J. Hunt for not being a painter. It was explained to the committee that he never worked at the painting trade until recently. Previously to him taking up the painting trade he was a jockey; Andrew Archer for scabbing; Thomas White his case not entertained, to-bad (*sic*) to relate, rejected immediately his name was called out.[44]

The highly principled painter in this list who refused to work with 'unskilled' men was Peter Macken, better known as Peadar Maicín, killed while fighting as a volunteer in the 1916 Rising. Members of the Stucco Plasterers were also dogged by the challenge from cheap, casual labour. From the scant records of the society available there emerges a clear picture of a small group of apprenticed workmen striving to impose union rates and standards on recalcitrant builders.

The trade unions associated with the clothing industry fared even worse. The silkweaving industry was in decline in the city, but because of the skilled nature of the work there was never any fear of a challenge from non-society, domestic source. Tailoring and dressmaking trades were less fortunate. By the turn of the century clothing factories were well established in Britain. New inventions, such as button-holing and blind-stitching machines made it possible to improve the quality of factory production. Yet despite such technological advances, the out-worker and the workshop system were not replaced by the factory. All three methods of production continued side by side, while the new machinery only went to step up the challenge to the more traditional forms of working and intensify exploitation and sweating in the process.[45]

Traditions died harder in Edwardian Dublin, with its sluggish economy, than in most other centres in the British Isles. By 1911 there were 2,989 tailors and tailoresses in the city, 1,296 seamstresses and shirtmakers. Of these, not more than 800 were members of the AST. Yet this select group of bespoke tailors controlled a surprising number of the best clothing shops in Dublin. Out of a list of 180 tailoring businesses in the city in 1913, about 130 were listed as 'unfair' houses. The remaining fifty were 'fair' shops and also happened to be among the most important businesses in the city.

The bespoke tailors, despite the comparative strength of their position, exhibited yet another facet of the general antipathy among apprenticed workers towards general labourers. The AST was hesitant and openly hostile towards working with new clothing workers' unions which, it was feared, constituted a potential threat to their own organisation. The founding of unions in Britain to cater for lower grade clothing workers was to induce greater intransigence from the AST: although quite unprepared themselves to open ranks to the outworkers and sweated labourers of the backstreet workshops, the bespoke tailors of Dublin resented the intrusion of other unions despite the protestations of organisers that their area of recruitment in the industry in no way threatened either themselves or the prosperity of their society.

In 1894 the Amalgamated Union of Clothing Operatives was founded in Britain to serve non-apprenticed labour in the industry. Among its early organisers were Emmanuel Shinwell and an ex-clerical student born of Irish parents in Leeds named Andrew Conley. By 1900 it had opened its ranks to women and in 1905 had 1,400 members. Seven years later there were over 12,000 in the union, 8,000 of them women.[46]

In 1903 the AUCO made an effort to organise the Dublin clothing workers only to be stymied by the opposition of the AST. A member of the AUCO's executive, T. D. Hollinshead of Blackburn, made a strong case for his union in the Irish papers. The society he represented was 'a *bona fide* union', composed of any number of workers (of both sexes) who have united together for the purpose of collectively bargaining with the employers for better wages and higher remuneration. The AST and AUCO were kindred but not the same trades, he explained:

> The tailoring trade, like many others, has undergone, and is undergoing, many changes. The introduction of machinery and the consequent sub-division of labour, has radically altered the conditions in this trade. To a large extent the old system of one or two men completing all the processes by which a garment is made has vanished. Large establishments employing many hands are now the order of the day. Each person has one certain process to perform. This sub-division of labour cheapens the cost of production, and naturally lowers the selling price. The tailors society which contains many of the old craftsmen, naturally objects to the way in which the members are being deprived of work. But though it may be deplorable, it is inevitable; and the tailors, instead of blindly opposing the system, should try to understand the changes that are taking place and adapt themselves accordingly.[47]

But the AST was not in an adaptable mood. It did not agree with the division of labour. Neither did it want to encourage the growth of an organisation in the city which did. The AUCO's case did not receive a sympathetic hearing and, despite the need for such an organisation among the most depressed sections of the clothing industry in the city, its fledgling branch died out rapidly.

It is quite possible that the local impetus for organising the AUCO may have come from a section of the Jewish *diaspora* in the city. The small community of Jews was later strengthened greatly by the influx of refugees fleeing the Russian pogroms of 1903. The 1901 census lists the occupations of Jews born abroad as follows: 261 drapers; 223 pedlars; 200 students and scholars; 88 commercial travellers; 66 domestic servants; 64 general dealers; and 72 tailors.[48] Most of the occupations cited are linked, in one way or another, with the clothing industry. In 1909 the International Tailors, Machinists and Pressers Trade Union was formed and Jewish operatives played a major part in the foundation.[49] But like the AUCO it also incurred the wrath of the AST. The DTC refused it affiliation on the principle that where one society existed to cater for the members of a trade, a second was superfluous if not mischievous. The union stumbled on for eight years with a membership of less than fifty and merged finally with the Irish Garment Workers Industrial Union when it was formed in 1918.[50]

In this case the lines of demarcation between the AST and the new union was not entirely clearcut and this is where the difficulty arose. But where the spheres of influence were more accentuated between craft and general worker, the former seemed to subjugate his antipathy towards the latter and allow non-apprenticed labour to join the executive ranks of the DTC. In many instances the craft unions had no grounds for rejecting affiliation requests from such quarters. At a meeting of workers in the Mechanics Institute in 1864, an attempt was made to set up a general labourers' union 'for the purpose of taking steps to associate in the amelioration of their conditions'.[51] A labourer called Michael Hogan took the chair while members of the United Trades Association, such as brassfounders, bricklayers, carpenters and plasterers, were in the audience. A Mr M. Corry of the Bricklayers Union opened the proceedings and praised the labourers for the key role they played in society:

> The Labouring class of this country as well as all others are the prop and stay of societies. Without them all commercial pursuits were annihilated. The army and the navy depend upon them for the maintenance of their ranks. The stubborn soil yields to the supreme force of their giant arm. In tillage, in cultivation, in collecting together the ripened corn, their utility is manifest. In all corporal and manual exercises they are ever ready, whether for remuneration or for the expression of gratitude, to render themselves incomparably useful, and hence they are entitled to appreciation of service, as also to full value for that commodity on which they depend—namely, labour, manual labour, the work of the hands.

Corry was fulsome in his compliments:

> In point of intellect also they rank as high as the most aristocratic in the land. Their genius is naturally as bright and brilliant (though not cultivated nor educated) as the most accomplished of our modern orators—they have susceptibilities, but they lack the means to acquire the necessary impressions to signalise themselves in science, in art, and all other polite acquisitions.

He urged the labourers 'to concentrate, to identify, to amalgamate, and if possible to raise themselves in the estimation of their fellow-men by battling with the poverty that now stares them in the face.[52] But there was absolutely no question of the planned society gaining affiliation with the UTA, although by 1907 the situation had changed in favour of non-apprenticed labour and it was no longer unconstitutional for general workers' societies to join the DTC, the successor to the UTA. Yet a certain element of snobbery remained and the 'bowler hat' tradition was taking a long time to die.

'Buy Irish': Protectionist Economics and the DTC

One of the forces which drove craft and unapprenticed labour together was their rising perception of the growing threat from imports. Between 1894 (the earliest date from which DTC records are available) and 1907, a subject which monopolised the minds of trade unionists and monopolised meeting time in Capel Street was the question of combating the growing threat of foreign goods facing the skilled labour of the city. Hardly a trade could afford to rest easy over the challenge from British-made goods. However, there was relatively little that they could actually do to prevent or even neutralise the challenge from abroad. Traditional methods of production, circumscribed by a web of customs and practices imposed on employers by the unions placed many local firms in an unenviably weak position. But despite the serious threat to employment in the city, the DTC failed even to take full advantage of their position, which offered some limited opportunities for progress. The campaign against foreign goods was based on prejudice. While it was often argued that English goods were inferior and were produced by non-union or 'unfair' labour, generally the reverse was nearer the truth. English goods did meet a high standard, were often produced by 'fair' labour under factory conditions, and were also cheaper.

The weight of the trade union argument for preference of home produced goods rested on a direct appeal to the practical patriotism of the consumer. People were urged to 'buy Irish', not because an article or commodity was good value, but because it was made in Dublin by fair labour. The foundation of the Industrial Development Association (IDA) in 1905 to further the interests of local manufacturers was welcomed by the unions.[53] About 700 firms were soon issued with licences which allowed them to use the IDA trade mark.

The IDA supported the production of high quality goods and implicitly agreed with the hiring of high cost labour. The trade unionists supported the association and their demands did not go unrequited. In no sense did the IDA champion union rights, but its philosophy afforded a type of protection when translated into action. Moreover, the burgeoning nationalist movement advanced a protectionist solution to Ireland's economic ills.

The 'buy Irish' campaign was sometimes taken to the most bizarre lengths. At one DTC meeting Maurice Canty of the

Corporation Workers Union brandished a roll of toilet paper in his hand. The paper, he said, had 'made in Norway' clearly printed on it and was being used extensively in Dublin's public toilets. He had complained of the matter to the cleansing department of the corporation. In another incident, the plumbers' delegate caused uproar in the hall when he innocently told delegates that the Right to Work committee, which had been set up to combat unemployment, was intending to hold a mass meeting and had received offers, free of charge, of posters printed in London by fair labour for the occasion. When order was restored, it was agreed that all printing work, without exception, should be done in Ireland, on Irish paper and with Irish labour.[54]

One of the most indefatigable champions of the 'buy Irish' campaign was the carpenter, John Simmons. In 1900, he was pointing out indignantly that 'English ale was being palmed off on the Irish by removing the label from the bottle', and at another meeting claimed that German and Belgian matches were being sold in Dublin to the detriment of the local product.[55]

However, the sheer ineffectiveness of the anti-foreign goods campaign can be judged by the repetition and multiplicity of the complaints brought before the DTC. Carpenters tried in vain to halt the importation of ready-made joinery and shop fronts;[56] the brushmakers vied against the sellers of English, convict-made brooms; the tailors opposed giving contracts, awarded by public tender, to 'unfair' British houses;[57] in 1911 the bottlemakers complained that 65,000 gross of bottles were imported into the country at a cost of £33,000 to the detriment of their trade; in the same year, the newly elected Lord Mayor came in for severe criticism from the vehicle builders and harness makers' union because he bought an imported coach and second-hand harnesses.[58]

Perhaps of all the vocational groups in the city, the people to offend the trade unionists most often were the clergy. Complaints centred around the building, furnishing and maintenance of church property. When Clongowes Woods college imported an altar from Italy the loss to skilled labour in the city was considerable. The marble cutters alone estimated that they had lost £500 over the Jesuits decision to purchase from abroad.[59] St Michael's church in Kingstown, according to the DTC, imported an organ costing £2,000 which 'should have been made in Ireland'.[60] The DTPS was the union with the greatest grievance against the clergy. Priests and nuns, according to the printers, seemed to insist upon using imported prayer books which could have been printed in any jobbing house in the city. And the clergy added insult to injury when, according to the DTPS, religious magazines and papers were produced by unfair labour.[61]

What the trade unions were asking consumers to do, in many instances, was to pay a higher price for goods because they were home-made. Workmen were seeking a concealed subsidy from the public for the luxury of having articles made by the craft unions, an approached taken to extreme lengths by the printers in the 1860s:

> Those operative printers of Dublin who belong to trades unions have published, through the medium of the *Freeman's Journal*, a modest request to THE PEOPLE, that they should pay threepence for those newspapers which employ society men, rather than pay a penny for those which do not; or they request a Protestant and Conservative community to patronise newpapers in direct opposition to their own opinions, rather than an organ which endeavours to represent them, but which employs non-society men and boys. The address in the *Freeman* of yesterday morning, for the society of printers, is evidently pointed against us and other journalists who, in this nineteenth century actually do not choose to subject themselves to the arbitrary dictation of Trades Unions with the very agreeable alternative of a strike.[62]

However, the DTPS were as unsuccessful then as most other unions in 1907. People would buy what they considered to be good value even if, in marginal cases, the consumer might have given the benefit of the doubt to Irish-made goods. In a free enterprise economy the trade unions had to either compete or perish and no amount of pleading with the public to buy certain goods for reasons of sentiment could succeed.

The Archbishop of Dublin, William Walsh, gave one of the most balanced critiques of this campaign in 1896. In a letter to the DTC, which had urged him to prevail upon his clergy to support the 'buy Irish' campaign, he wrote:

> I should trust that it is unnecessary for me to seek to impress upon them (the clergy) the duty of giving a preference to Irish goods when they are to be had as good and as cheap as those imported from England or from abroad. But it would, I fear, be utterly futile if I were to suggest anything beyond that. I have long since come to the conclusion that it is mere waste of time to ask people either to purchase inferior articles or to pay a higher price for goods for the sake of encouraging Irish manufacture. I have, however, no doubt that in many departments of trade there is

sufficient business capacity in Ireland to enable purchasers to get what they want as good and as cheap in Irish manufacture as in anything that is imported into the country.[63]

This was the attitude of many towards home-made goods. Yet while many trade unionists persisted in asking the impossible from the public, not every one in the DTC was looking over his shoulder for an answer to this apparently intractable problem.

3 The Winds of Change

The Foundation of the Irish Trade Union Congress

One of the most significant and formative steps in the history of the Irish labour movement was the establishment of an independent Irish Trade Union Congress (ITUC) in 1894. Since the setting up of the British TUC twenty-six years earlier, delegates of local combinations had crossed the channel to attend the annual meetings of the 'labour parliament', yet dissatisfaction with the arrangement grew. Frustration accumulated because of the natural tendency to place Irish motions at the end of a long agenda, and even if Congress found time to discuss some of their problems, the remoteness of such issues for most members generally ensured that they were given short shrift. Matters came to a head in 1893, and early the following year the local congress held its inaugural meeting in Dublin attended by 119 delegates from all parts of Ireland.[1]

At the time, trade unionists failed to comprehend the full significance of their action. This was borne out when Congress held its second annual meeting in Cork in 1895. The president, J. H. Jolly, explained to delegates that the new organisation was meant to supplement, not to supplant, the British congress. Local unions could not compete with the big amalgamates by sending adequate representation to Britain, and even when locally-based unions undertook the not inconsiderable cost of sending one of their members to the BTUC 'the advantages accruing to the unions of Ireland have scarcely been commensurate with the expense incurred', argued Mr Jolly.[2] But if the president's line of reasoning received unqualified acceptance from the 121 delegates, representing fifty-three unions of which twenty-four were amalgamates, the British congress was quite annoyed by the move. In retaliation, the standing orders which provided that one Irish delegate must be elected to the parliamentary committee of the BTUC each year were revoked.[3] There was a feeling that the breakaway ITUC had been set up in competition with her British rival. Although this was not quite accurate, English trade unionists believed this to be the case and the gulf between the two organisations widened considerably. In the succeeding years, representatives of Irish trade unionism ceased almost entirely to attend British congresses and the Dublin labour movement become more isolated than ever.

The amalgamated unions did not remain aloof from the fledgling ITUC but while subscriptions remained voluntary the parsimonious attitude of the British-based union executives resulted in very poor financial support for congress from that quarter. In 1895 only two amalgamateds contributed: the Typographical Society subscribed £5 and the General Union of carpenters handed over £2.[4] In an effort to put congress on a stronger financial footing a penny-a-head was introduced in 1906. Under this system, the amalgamateds still bore the brunt of fees. Out of total affiliation fees, of £74.4s.8d collected, English executives paid £30.19s. The previous year, British-based unions had contributed £29.4s under the voluntary system. But if these unions subscribed the most money, they also had the most power in congress. The skilled trades, largely represented by cross-channel unions, controlled and dominated most posts of responsibility. Between 1894 and 1906 the presidency of congress was held by the AST twice, by the Typographical Association twice, and by the carpenters twice. The bakers, saddlers, bootmakers, ASRS, butchers, plasterers and pork butchers each held the post once. The all-important post of secretary was held by John Simmons of the ASC & J from 1894 to 1899. Hugh McManus of the TA took over for 1900 and E. L. Richardson of the DTPS held the post from 1901 to 1911.[5]

Congress was governed throughout the year by a part-time executive known as the parliamentary committee. Membership of that body showed much the same tendencies in representation as the presidency and the secretaryship. Amalgamated men were in the majority while many Irish-based union members were also strongly represented, although while the balance of power favoured the cross-channel unions, there were growing signs that the smaller and weaker local organisations were gradually making their presence more strongly felt. The break from the BTUC had, if anything, been of greater benefit to them. At national level, the combined force of local unions from a centre such as Dublin or Belfast, could act as a highly significant power bloc in congress. Despite the grandiose plans harboured by congress in the early days of its existence, the organisation was quite disappointing in its performance. Hampered by insufficient funds, unable to employ full-time officials, and reduced to only meeting in committee four times a year, congress exercised little or no power. As a lobbying force, it was not as effective as it might have been. The annual congress meeting itself was something of a social occasion and a talking-shop which at least provided a common platform for trade unionists of different views to meet each year, and that in itself was not a hollow achievement.

There was, however, one obvious draw-back in such a scheme. While severing the British link may not have been the sole cause of the sense of isolation experienced by Irish trade unionists, it did nothing to cure it either. Denied any direct annual contact with outsiders, Irish trade unionism was all the slower to respond to the growth of labour radicalism in Britain. A corollary of this was that if Irish Labour was more cut off from outside influences, it was more susceptible to the impact of domestic forces. Were nationalist sentiments to gain dominance in trade union circles, this would threaten the unity of the congress in view of the very large Protestant membership from the north. Tensions inside congress were numerous: there was conflict between amalgamated unions and Irish-based organisations; there was rivalry between craft and general labourer unions; and perhaps most explosive of all was the growing 'political' fissure.

Another crucial difference of opinion was caused by a conflicting understanding over the nature of society and the role of trade unionism. The one group, and initially they formed a majority, wanted to make their peace with capitalism while others sought to undermine the system which divided capital and labour. The former were in the ascendant for the first ten years of the existence of congress. In 1901, a Belfast flaxdresser, A. Bowman, was elected president at Sligo. In his opening address, he told delegates:

We then as organised workers can say to those who have the capital. Let us join hands. You have the capital, we have the muscle and skill and by a judicious blending of capital and labour this land of ours . . . shall blossom as the rose and her sons and daughters shall be fully employed.

Four years later a saddler from Dublin, named Joseph Chambers, was president and he spelled out the implications of Bowmann's remarks in greater detail. In 1905 he told congress:

I should, therefore, like to make it absolutely clear that our mission is essentially one of peace as between employers and employed, provided always that both elements which go to make up the industrial life of the nation obtain their respective rewards.

Chambers deprecated movements of a disruptive character between employers and workers 'born of ulterior motives of interested and self-elected agitators'. The only trade union demands he supported were those

> that tend to secure to the workers at least a living wage, a just percentage of the profits of his toil—in short, a fair day's pay for a fair day's work, whether that work be for state, the local authority or the private employer.

Although the president's attempts to assuage the fears of employers by demonstrating the conciliatory tone of unions were welcomed by the majority of delegates, an articulate and influential minority were opposed to letting the lion of capital lie down with the lamb of labour. This group was led by a Derry tailor, James McCarron, a staunch member of the Labour Representation Committee. He had urged congress, for many years, to be more forthright and assertive in its demands for better pay and working conditions for all affiliated union members. As president of congress in 1907, he argued that there could never be industrial peace without class war.

> It cannot be concluded that there is either equity or justice in a law which entitles a few men, who neither sow nor reap, to appropriate the wealth of creation . . . by the energy and industry of the whole community. How long is this iniquitous system to continue.[6]

Slowly the tide was beginning to change in favour of the labour-orientated minority. The previous year at Athlone a Limerick baker named Stephen Dineen had made a scathing attack on the injustices of 'our present-day industrialism'.[7] According to the canons of capitalism, he argued, man was treated as an inanimate, integral component of production:

> Being in business to make money, the firm or company first endeavours to find out how much of any given kind of work a man can do at his greatest capacity. That becomes the standard of production. Wages are fixed on that basis. But production largely exceeds the demand, and wages start on the down-grade until the labour of the husband cannot maintain the family. The wife helps in any way she can, and the children are eventually pressed into service. After a time the husband is squeezed out by the compelling forces of the competitive system operating upon the youngest members, perhaps of his own family and he joins the dismal ranks of the unemployed.

The failure to place production and distribution on an organised basis was the direct cause of unemployment; 'in place of this necessary organisation there is gambling in futures, rigging of markets, and continuous financial and political manipulation—all of which have as counters the lives and happiness of the common people', he said.

Dineen claimed that it was up to the government and local authorities to find a remedy for 'the economic disease of unemployment'. He wanted special departments set up and kept in a state of readiness to deal with recurring periods of depression and distress. But such measures were only palliatives. 'The unemployed problem will still be with us until the workers' party becomes the dominant force in the state, and the evils of the capitalist system, under which nineteen out of every twenty go down to the grave of poverty, is finally got rid of by the substitution of public for private control of industry', he urged. Finally, Dineen defended the labour movement from the more traditional criticism concerning restrictive practices:

> Much has been said of the tyranny of trade unionism and some of us can recall the time when we were regarded as conspirators and revolutionaries, and when the Church also sought in various ways to discountenance the movement. But with all its deficiencies and sins, I claim that trade unionism has a title, both of what it has accomplished, and even a Christian movement. The Founder of Christianity, the Carpenter of Nazareth, opposed Himself of the doctrine, prevalent then as now, of the survival of the fittest. So, likewise, in the stress and struggle of modern, commercial and industrial life, trade unionism interposes on behalf of the weak and the helpless.

Three or four years before such a speech might have caused a furore on the floor of congress, but by 1906 trade unionists had not alone become more tolerant of another man's views, there was a general drift in the direction of parliamentary socialism.

In Belfast two years later, a printer named James Murphy was elected president of congress. He went even further than Dineen in castigating those who condemned a socialist-trade union alliance:

> The air is full of rumblings and threatenings and disruptions, as to the alliance between the trade unions and the socialists, and dark and malignant prophecies are being uttered as to the future of British industry if this alliance should not be dissolved . . . The socialists have analysed the human misery connected with our industrial conditions and have proposed a remedy. Until a better plan is suggested, we may reasonably refuse to be drawn aside from the pursuits of a scheme which, while not perfect is at least comprehensive, and appeals to all that is best in our hearts and minds.[8]

Murphy was a Belfastman and a supporter of the Labour party. He, like many of his colleagues, could not but have been influenced by the success of the Labour Party in England where they won twenty-nine seats in the 1906 general election.[9] The lesson was not lost on these men who saw the necessity to channel trade union energies in a specific left-wing political direction. Neither of the traditional parties satisfied these men, for the Liberals and the Conservatives were not seen to be friends of the working man.

If northern trade unionists were questioning the traditional allegiance of workers to Unionist ideology, there was also growing scepticism in the south over the *bona fide* character of the Nationalist Party. The parliamentary party, led by John Redmond after 1900, was extremely vulnerable when scrutinised by an urban electorate. The ambivalent attitude of the MPs towards social reform caused most concern to trade unionists. Redmond's reticence to seek the application of remedial legislation to Ireland rested on the belief, which was shared and pioneered by John Dillon, that social palliatives merely weakened the people's resolve to the central objective of the home-rule party.[10] Moreover, many MPs had cause to fear the wrath of the Catholic church if they were to interfere in this area.[11] The clergy treated with suspicion the encroachment of the State into hitherto untouched areas, their opposition to the Medical Insurance Bill of 1911 being a case in point. Ostensibly the Church turned down the Bill on the grounds that it was not suitable to rural Ireland. The bishops wanted to retain the Poor Law system, no matter how repugnant it was to its recipients, instead of a dispensary system as proposed under the Bill. The bishops also felt that the payment for such a service would place too much of a burden on the small employer, who was expected to pay a certain amount for his workers. It was then demanded that Ireland be excluded, not only from the medical clauses, but from the entire workings of the new Bill. The bishops did not win this battle outright, for a portion of the Bill was actually extended to Ireland. Yet its most significant clause on medical benefits was not applied, and quite possibly this was really what the bishops were seeking all along.

Besides the deficiencies of the Irish parliamentary party, the idea of a labour party in itself appealed to workers more and more. A further reason why it was necessary to put politics in congress on a strictly labour or working class plane was that delegates were usually hopelessly divided on a nationalist-unionist axis. The only possible way to transcend such differences was to establish a sort of working class popular front with a basic agreement on the necessity to fight for social objectives. Labour might thus hold the middle ground between unionism and nationalism.

Many delegates, however, refused to see the wisdom of this course and clung tenaciously to traditional beliefs. In 1907 a Dublin brushmaker, William Murphy, urged the setting up of links with the Labour party because the Nationalists had proved a dismal failure. This remark brought delegates to their feet; a former printer and delegate to congress for the Paviors' union, P. T. Daly, wanted the motion urging men to join the labour party dropped; a Dublin coachmaker named Milner claimed that the nationalist party was 'in reality a labour party'.[12] Indeed, the very same point had been made a year earlier by the Lord Mayor of Dublin, J. P. Nannetti, MP (a member of the DTPS):

> With reference to the organisation of a separate labour party a good deal could be said on both sides, but he thought they in Ireland were in the happy position that they had a labour party . . . the Irish Parliamentary Party and he asked them to take advantage of the party. There was the necessity of setting up new parties. The platform on which he was proud to stand was broad enough for any workingman. They could make the parliamentary party do everything they wished. They required no spur in that direction, he assured them. They were purely labour as well as nationalist and he as a worker could not be with them on the platform that day were it not that he was a nationalist.[13]

Despite the bitter opposition from the floor, the original motion seeking an alliance with the labour party was carried by thirty-six votes to twenty. It was a singular triumph for the growing left wing lobby and salutary warning for the nationalists. The resolution symbolised a radical change in trade union tactics, and if the trend were to continue, it seemed that a growing number of trade unionists would no longer be content to stand on the political sideline and watch conservative MPs represent their views in a half-hearted fashion. The idea of proxy representation was losing ground rapidly and many trade unionists considered it of vital importance for labour to become directly involved in parliament. While this was by no means a unanimous viewpoint, and others continued to support the nationalists and unionists, a large question-mark now overshadowed the sagacity of such a strategy. Congress no longer found it possible to ban the discussion of politics.

Even in Dublin where industrial stagnation had for so long thwarted the growth of the trade union movement, men were beginning to take greater note of the need for radical social reform. By 1907 workers in the capital were discovering that it was no longer possible for organised labour to remain politically neutral towards the questions of poverty, exploitation and deprivation of every variety. Direct trade union involvement in politics on a nationalist-socialistic basis, both at local and national levels, was gaining more credence as a practicable idea.

The general change in attitude experienced was certainly encouraged by the growth in Catholic social thinking which came about in the pontificate of Leo XIII. At the end of the nineteenth century the Churches of western Europe were faced with a mass exodus of workers to more secular philosophies. It was partly in an effort to block this haemorrhage of the faithful that Cardinal Gaspart Mermillod founded the Fribourg Union in 1885. The school aimed at developing and refashioning Catholic social thinking, which was so hopelessly out of date, to meet the needs of Christians living in industrialised society.

In 1891 Leo XIII published the encyclical Rerum Novarum, or the Workers' Charter as it was popularly known, and Cardinal Mermillod and his school exercised a great influence over the contents of the work. The encyclical also reflected the views of Cardinal H. E. Manning on the labour question. Many Dublin trade unionists had great respect for the Pope and took his teaching seriously. In token of the appreciation for the work he had done for the poor, the DTC passed a resolution on the occasion of Leo XIII's silver jubilee:

> On behalf of the skilled and unskilled trade unionists of the city and council of Dublin, may we offer Leo XIII our hearty congratulations upon attaining the twenty fifth year of his pontificate and our fervent wishes that Divine Providence may spare His Holiness's health and strength to continue his beneficial and valuable work in the interests of the human race.[14]

A year later, in 1903, the Pope was dead, and in a resolution of condolence, the DTC praised him as 'a man singularly remarkable for the manner in which during his pontificate he commanded the respect of mankind and, above all, of the workers of Christianity'.[15]

Most Dublin trade unionists unhesitatingly considered themselves members of the Christian fold. Contemporary Catholic social thinking which influenced them so much was explained by a

Maynooth professor, Dr P. Coffey, in 1906. Echoing the words of Leo XIII, he wrote:

> It is an undeniable fact that the wealthy and titled classes are inclined to boast of their abundant wealth and to feel proud of their inherited titles and lineage . . . It is equally undeniable that they have a tendency to look down loftily on the masses of the people as a common crowd of inferior beings . . . of course they deny and resent this charge, and imagine they can triumphantly refute it by pointing to poor law and philanthropic institutions and state-aided charities of all sorts. But how many of those payers of poor rates bear the burden of supporting the poor simply because they have to bear it, and cannot get rid of their millions of workers in pretty much the same spirit as they support their horses, or pretty much the same motives as they pay for the upkeep of their machinery; regarding their workmen in the light of materialistic economy, as a sort of rolling stock, 'as so much muscle or physical power . . . like chattels to make money by'.[16]

For Dr Coffey, as for another clerical champion of the poor, Fr Aloysious, OFM, Cap., the solution to the problem of labour was to be found in 'Christian socialism'.[17] This consisted in a programme for better housing and extended education. The workers' personal contribution to this process was listed as sobriety, thrift, and other forms of self-help. Many members of the Dublin labour movement would not have disagreed with this view of their role. The main object of trade unionism, argued Dr Coffey, was to enable the united labour movement to secure by every fair and lawful means, just and equitable treatment so as to live in contentment and peace with the employer class. However, the success of such an outlook was contingent upon the goodwill of the employer, who was exhorted as a Christian to mitigate the burden of his employees and respect their rights:

> The employer is bound to see that the worker has time for his religious duties; that he is not exposed to corrupting influences and dangerous occasions; that he be not led away to neglect his home and family, or to squander his earnings . . . The employer must never tax his work-people beyond their strength or employ them in work unsuited to their sex and age. His great and principal duty is to give everyone a fair wage. The salary ought to be sufficient to allow the workman to exist in a sober and honest manner.[18]

A just wage, fair working hours, no 'sweating' and no exploitation of boy labour were hardly features of the Dublin employer-labour ethos in 1906. Yet basic as these conditions actually were, they would have been sufficient to satisfy many local trade unionists. Where just conditions of employment were not provided, the worker had to resort to the only remaining weapon at his disposal—the strike.

Dr Coffey felt that industrial action should only be used as a last resort and only as an extreme attempt to remedy intolerable grievances after the gravest consideration. 'To start an unprovoked or unnecessary or unjustifiable strike is a no less terrible crime on the part of the workman's leaders than is the crime of provoking a necessary one on the part of a cruel and heartless employer', he added.[19] In Dublin, however, such a high-minded concept of strike procedure was not adhered to by either side.

The workers of Dublin were never in the main social revolutionaries. They concurred with much of the teaching of Leo XIII and the writings of many Christian social thinkers. In so far as a document such as *Rerum Novarum* helped pin-point areas of abuse in the industrial sector, it drew attention to the flaunted rights of labour. Workers were sensitised to the need for concerted action as a means to overcome and defeat unrequited grievances. The trade union movement was equipped with an orthodox and thoroughly respectable analysis of industrial society and was thus furnished with the intellectual backing to stand up firmly to any employer in a straight fight involving clearly defined cases of injustice.

James Connolly and the Influence of Radical Socialism and Fabianism

Socialists were never really very popular in Dublin yet that did not prevent men from attempting to advance various schools of left wing thought in the capital. The printer, Adolphus Shields, attempted to preach Fabianism in the city in the 1890s, without much popular success. In 1889 he anticipated what Dr Coffey was to write on the social order, by arguing:

I have often wondered that there should be any question as to the attitude the church should take on this question—whether or not we shall continue to maintain the present social system, under which we are comfortable and many are miserable, or whether we shall try a change of plan which promises an equal chance to all. Surely the ghastly facts are known, there ought to be no discussion anymore, only one united, passionate endeavour to mend the cruel wrong. We know that competition means living death to the many that the few may be enriched. Why do we cling to competition? 'The earth is the Lord and the fulness thereof'; it was given to man not to a few men. Why are the few, calling themselves landlords, i.e. landthieves, permitted to rob the people of a gift of God which is as essential to their existence as is the water or the air? Can there be a doubt in any unprejudiced mind as to what Christ would say were He on earth now?[20]

Shields was quite critical of the role played by the Church in Irish society, yet he was not in any doubt about what side the Christian ought to take. There was no evading the preferential option for the poor. He was conscious that a change was taking place in the consciousness of the workers in Dublin in the 1890s. He dated the breaking down of class divisions between workingmen from 1889 and the London dock strike (see Chapter 5), but he had much more faith in the reforming political power of a united trade union movement than the Marxist James Connolly, who had little time for Fabianism.

The Scots Irishman, James Connolly, attempted a more revolutionary solution. Arriving in Ireland in 1896 and aided by a small coterie of Dublin left-wing activists, he set up the Irish Socialist Republican Party (ISRP). With tireless energy he helped build up the nucleus of a Socialist movement in the capital, but despite the caution with which he chose his steps, it was like walking in a minefield where sooner or later he was liable to touch off an explosion. Even though the platform he chose to advance deliberately underplayed the role of revolution, his reception from the populace of Dublin was decidedly frigid. In fact, Connolly probably only ever came to prominence when he was involved in such escapades as protesting against the visit of Queen Victoria and pro-Boer demonstrations.

While working as a labourer he was probably encouraged to join the United (building) Labourers Union and he rose to become its delegate to the DTC. The fact that he was a poor attender might indicate the contempt in which he held the leaders of organised labour in the city. Commenting on the presidential address, delivered to the ITUC by Dublin plasterer, George Leahy, in 1900, Connolly wrote sardonically:

What to expect from the gathering? . . . We know what we have received in the past—much talk and many schemes whereby we might through combination improve our lot as slaves, but never a suggestion on the point how we might proceed to abolish our status as slaves and elevate ourselves to the dignity of freedom . . . for what, after all, are the various nostrums of technical education, fair wages . . . to employment liability acts, etc., what are they in essence but a device to modify the severity of the slave drivers' lash whilst still expressly recognising the right to apply the lash.[21]

Connolly expressed his repugnance to ameliorative and reformist action more clearly in another article:

> We are trade unionists, but we are more than trade unionists. The trade unionist who is only a trade unionist is to the socialist what the believer in constitutional monarchy is to a republican. The constitutional monarchist wishes to limit the power of the king, but still wishes to have a king; the republican wishes to abolish kingship and puts his trust in the people; the trade unionist wishes to limit the power of the master; but still wishes to have done with masters and pins his faith to the collective intelligence of democratic community.[22]

Connolly made very few converts with his revolutionary doctrines. And with such slow progress being made in the socialist field, tensions grew up within the ISRP. A feud in 1903 between the members, over the misappropriation of funds from the club bar among other things, impelled Connolly to emigrate with his family to America. Very few in Dublin either noticed or mourned his passing from the local political scene.

While Connolly's personal impact on the course of Dublin's labour history at that point had been slight, he left behind him a number of disciples who seemed to spend more time fighting among themselves than furthering the cause of socialism. However, there emerged from their divided ranks a young man who was to play a decisive role in shaping the character of the Irish trade union movement. His name was William O'Brien and he was to combine many traditions, the craft unionist, the nationalist, the Fabian and the 'cautious' revolutionary socialist. He was a good example of the conflicting and contradictory consciousness found in the Dublin labour movement.

William O'Brien

John William O'Brien was born on January 23, 1881, in Ballygurteen RIC barracks, near Clonakilty, Co Cork, the youngest son of a policeman who was later transferred to Carrick-on-Suir where the family lived for seven years.[23] In 1896 the family settled in Dublin where William's two elder brothers were already working, Tom as a clerk in the revenue department of the Customs House and Daniel as a temporary sorter in the post office.[24] William's father died soon after the move to the capital and his mother opened a boarding-house at 43 Belvedere Place, Mountjoy Square, to help support the children.

Both O'Brien's elder brothers were committed socialists and members of the ISRP. At an early age, William became used to hearing both Dan and Tom discussing party matters in the house. In an effort to satisfy his curiosity, he was given *An Appeal to the Young* by the Russian anarchist Kropotkin. While his political education was continued in the home, O'Brien attended school at St Patrick's, Drumcondra, where he quickly earned the nickname 'Socialist Bill' for himself by his precocious references to left-wing ideas.

However a telling indication of his home background can be found in an early conversation he had with his brothers:

> I continued to listen to their talk and there was mention continually of somebody named Connolly. Connolly says so and so. Connolly does not agree with that. Connolly's point of view is this, and so on. Then when I had an opportunity I asked who was Connolly. 'He is a very smart fellow,' I was told. 'Where does he come from?' 'From Edinburgh.' 'And what is he?' 'Just a labourer.'

O'Brien was sceptical:

> 'A labourer,' said I. 'How could a labourer know all these things?' 'He went to the national Library and studied.' This was not very convincing to me. I could not understand how a labourer should be so important as all that. The labourers I was acquainted with were people who drifted around the roads and took up casual jobs and were almost entirely illiterate. However, I had to accept what was stated.[25]

Bill O'Brien was to harbour these lingering doubts about the ability of labourers for some time, though later he joined the ISRP and worked tirelessly to politicise the general workers.

O'Brien suffered from a physical disability; he had a clubbed foot which led to his being called by the nickname 'Hoofie'. This physical defect probably forced him to look for work which did not involve much movement. On August 1, 1898, he was apprenticed to John Harris and Son, Tailor, of 17 Talbot St, for a period of five years.[26] He learned the trade well and in 1904 was appointed master tailor of the North Dublin Union at 30s a week.[27]

As a socialist, O'Brien felt compelled to play an active role in trade unionism. As a delegate to the DTC for the Amalgamated Society of Tailors in 1909, his talents as a politician were soon noticed. He had the tenacity to attend practically every meeting, get to know everyone, and build up a whole chain of valuable contacts who would come in useful, particularly at election time. It was at such a time that O'Brien was at his best. He lobbied votes with determination and never left the success or failure of any vital issue to be decided on the floor. His determination and meticulous attention to detail brought him success in most areas. Wherever there was a committee, O'Brien was sooner or later elected to it and it was not long before he had himself made chairman. At twenty-three, he was secretary of AST branch; at twenty-nine he was on the DTC executive and was appointed temporary secretary in 1911 when John Simmons took ill; in 1913 he was made vice-president of that body and president the following year. He operated with the same degree of effort at Congress level where he was elected to the parliamentary committee in 1910; four years later he was elected president.

O'Brien's quest for power did not drive him to neglect the interests of his trade at council meetings. He complained bitterly, like other delegates, over the various 'injustices' being done to tailors by, for example, granting corporation clothing contracts to firms in England or to 'unfair' houses in the city.[28] On at least one occasion his determination to champion the cause of his trade brought him into conflict with some of his socialist colleagues.

The International Tailors, Machinists and Pressers Trade Union, with headquarters at 44 York St, were set up in 1909 to safeguard and promote the interests of everyone engaged in the clothing trade. It stood for a more radical form of industrial action than that represented by the AST, yet O'Brien opposed this progressive move because it conflicted with the sectional interest of his own union. He even threatened to resign from the DTC if the new union was not refused affiliation.[29] This is a clear instance of where O'Brien allowed his sectional interest as a trade unionist to override his broader commitment as a socialist to the advancement of the working class. More significantly, in later years he allowed his strong nationalist feelings to demote the cause of socialism to a secondary place. From 1908 onwards, this young tailor had come under the influence of the writings of the talented journalist, W. P. Ryan. He subscribed to both the *Irish Peasant* and the *Irish Nation*, read Arthur Griffith's *Sinn Féin* and other nationalist journals. However, the balanced, socially-progressive thinking of Ryan appealed to him most. While he abhorred the aristocratic nationalism of Griffith, he seemed to hold the view that socialism would be the product of national independence, not national sovereignty the fruits of socialism; yet he never really developed a clear idea of how the twin ideologies of nationalism and socialism could be harmonised. He was both a revolutionary socialist and a nationalist at the same time. While such a contradiction normally remained hidden, it swiftly rose to the surface in an hour of national conflict, and invariably the allegiance to nationalism proved the stronger. O'Brien was not alone in reconciling this twin commitment in favour of an independence struggle. It was characteristic of the majority of young trade union activists who were coming to the fore in the 1907 period. They were committed to the achievement of social justice but sceptical of England's ability to deliver such sweeping reforms. Scepticism later turned to conviction and channelled men's energies away from trade union politics towards the paramilitary camp of revolutionary nationalism.

If O'Brien and many of his colleagues were confused on the ideological plane, it did not impede them from working hard for the advancement of trade unionism in the city. Connolly was kept well briefed about the developments in the Irish situation by O'Brien who, in December, 1907, wrote enthusiastically to New York about the growth of the Labour movement in Dublin:

> Lumsden who is now president of the DTC is chairman of the Dublin ILP and our friend. McLoughlin who is vice-president of DTC, is treasurer. It has attracted the bulk of our followers, including the irrepressible McKenna, an individual that Bradshaw styled 'the living illustration of the Darwinian theory'. They are bringing over a bevy of MPs, including Hardie, Ramsey McDonald, Peter Curren and Victor Grey, to speak for them, and considers we are already wiped out. A local LRC has just been formed in Dublin, and it has adopted, by a big majority, a rule admitting 'Socialist Societies'. Although we do not intend having anything to do with it, we think it shows that things are beginning to move here, as such a thing was undreamt of a few years ago.[30]

Things *were* 'beginning to move', owing to people like O'Brien, W. Carpenter (railway union), Peadar Maicin of the Dublin Metropolitan Painters and the Brushmakers' leader, William Murphy. These men were pushing for greater commitment and the need for greater involvement by the trade union movement in society. They were helped to formulate policy and clarify their ideas by left-wing thinkers such as the civil servant, R. J. Mortished, a former English schoolmaster, E. Dudley Edwards and the journalists Francis Sheehy Skeffington and W. P. Ryan. And while trade unionists had been somewhat intimidated by certain pieces of industrial legislation in the past they were given all the protection they required to act militantly in 1906 by the new liberal government.

Legal Protection: Trade Disputes Act, 1906

When the Liberal Government was returned to power in 1906 it was pledged to unshackle the trade unions from the effects of a number of adverse court decisions. In 1900 a dispute had arisen over the alleged victimisation of a signalman by the Taff Vale company. Contrary to the directions of the ASRS, the men came out on strike in sympathy. When the union offered to arbitrate, the manager, Mr Beasley refused, stating that 'the risk of a strike would be preferable to the settlement of a dispute by outside arbitration'. The company had secured a number of 'blacklegs' to maintain a service and the union retaliated by placing pickets on railway stations and offices.[31]

The strike had lasted eleven days and the case brought against the ASRS by the Taff Vale Company for trying to stop the 'blacklegs' from working during the strike took two years to settle and ended in disaster for the union. The court had found that the ASRS was responsible for damages caused by the action of the officers in the strike; under the ruling a trade union was found to be neither a corporation nor an individual, nor a partnership between a number of individuals. It was an association of men which almost invariably owed its legal validity to the 1871 and 1876 Acts. It was also ruled that the funds of the society were apportioned to the purposes of the society and their misappropriation could be restrained by injunction. The acts complained of were performed by an accredited agent of the association, and the case cost the ASRS £41,892.14.9, and had the effect of crippling effective strike action for all unions in the future.

Hardly had the result of the Taff Vale case time to sink in when the Quinn versus Leathem case re-emphasised the liability of union funds for damages. The following are the facts: a Lisburn butcher named Leathem employed assistants who were not members of the butchers' union. Quinn, who was the treasurer of the Belfast Union of Butchers' Assistants, urged Leathem to dismiss these men, which he refused to do, but he attended a union meeting and offered to pay fines and dues provided his employees were allowed to join the association. Quinn refused the offer unless some of the dissident employees were laid off work for twelve months. Leathem would not agree. The union then prevailed upon some of his men to leave his employment and succeeded in inducing one to do so in breach of contract. Further action was taken when another butcher named Munce was approached and told not to buy any more meat from Leathem on threat of having his staff brought out on strike. When Munce acquiesced to the demand, Leathem practically went out of business. An action was then brought against union officials on the ground that they had conspired together to injure Leathem, who won his case and was awarded £250 damages. The union appealed the case, first to the Divisional Court in Dublin and then to the Irish Court of appeal; and finally Quinn appealed to the House of Lords where the original decision was upheld:

> As a result of the case it was established by the House of Lords that if two or more persons combine together, without legal justification or excuse, to injure a man in his trade by inducing his customers to break their contracts with him or not to deal with him their conduct is, if it results in damage to him, actionable as a tort in a civil court.[32]

These two decisions of the House of Lords left trade unionism in a quandry. The modest security won by the Trade Union Acts of 1871 and 1876 and by the Conspiracy and Protection of Property Act of 1875 was eroded completely. Workers were faced with the proposition of either giving up the use of the strike weapon, which would render trade unionism impotent, or risk possible bankruptcy, for while no longer faced with imprisonment for participating in a combination, union officials were liable to have heavy penalties, such as damages which might involve the sequestration of home and belongings, imposed upon them.

The Liberal Government was pledged to reverse these decisions when they were returned to power in 1906, and they introduced a Trade Disputes Act as rapidly as possible; the result was a revolutionary change in union law. Officials were now immune from liability for damages when they were judged to act 'in contemplation or furtherance of a trade dispute'; also prohibited by law were actions of tort against unions. But perhaps of equal significance was Section 2 which allowed peaceful picketing:

> It shall be lawful for one or more persons acting on their own behalf or on behalf of a trade union or of an individual employer or firm, in contemplation or furtherance of a trade dispute, to attend at or near a house or place where a person resides or works or carries on business or happens to be, if they so attend merely for the purpose of peacefully obtaining or communicating information, or of peacefully persuading any person to work or abstain from working.[33]

Trade unions now had the legal protection they required to conduct a militant campaign for labour rights without fear of prosecution, and they took advantage of this in Dublin.

The Dublin trade union movement was entering a new and more decisive phase in the period 1906–8. One of the more obvious manifestations of this growing sense of self-awareness and confidence was reflected in the revival, after a lapse of thirteen years, of the traditional May Day demonstration. The organisers of the event in 1908, the first year of its re-establishment, were quite conscious of how important the demonstration had been to labour throughout the world. At a special meeting of the DTC, the president, William McLaughlin, told delegates how the event 'in former years had been a powerful instrument for strengthening the position of the Labour cause in the city.[34] J. T. Duignan, who had previously helped organise the event, was glad 'that the good work was about to be continued'.[35] While he felt that circumstances had changed since the previous demonstrations and that some trades might no longer be able to provide bands and bring out their large banners, he encouraged every union to at least carry a streamer with the name of the society inscribed upon it.

The whole idea met with the hearty approval of delegates and it was agreed to set up a provisional committee to organise the event. Handbills and posters were printed for the occasion, and on one such notice which contained the list of speakers was inscribed the following quotation: 'Workers unite. You have nothing to lose but your chains, and a whole world to gain'.[36] The demonstration took place on the first Sunday in May and most local trade unions participated in style and force:

> The weather could hardly have been more favourable, and the result was that the procession through the streets prior to the meeting in the Park was of very imposing dimensions. Stephen's Green was the place of muster, and there a big crowd assembled to watch the start of the procession . . . The first contingent to arrive was that of the Coal Labourers Society, with their fine banner and band. Shortly before the time arrived for starting, the Operative Butchers arrived making a big display, with three banners and a band . . . the executive of the trades council led the way, and were followed by the coal labourers, who headed by their banner, made a very fine show. Next came the boiler-makers and coachmakers, both of which bodies were strongly represented. The coachmakers' magnificent banner, twelve feet by nine has on its front the arms of the society surmounting a figure of Justice with the date of the society's incorporation, May 31, 1677. On the reverse side

is the figure of Erin, with harp and wolfhound, and portraits of several distinguished Irishmen. The Operative Butchers were succeeded by the Drapers' assistants who turned out in large numbers, many of them carrying cards in the shape of bannerets bearing the words, unity and self-reliance. Members of the Workers Union, mineral water operatives, coffinmakers, and paper cutters came along in order and were followed by the operative tailors, with their splendid banner. The big banner of the Stationary Engine Drivers was borne in front of the contingent of that society. After the Independent Labour Party came the Bakers with their banner. The railway servants formed a large contingent, as did also the corporation labourers. These were followed by the tin smiths, stone-cutters and slaters, each body being well represented. The Amalgamated Society of House Painters brought several banners and passed in front of the brick and stonelayers, hairdressers and brushmakers, who were succeeded by the united labourers, brass founders, members of the socialist party, bootmakers, ironfounders and carpet planners.[37]

The police kept a vigilant eye on the proceedings, and when the marchers arrived at the Phoenix Park, 'detectives moved about the crowd, but everything was absolutely harmonious and orderly'.[38] Politicians from major parties, Nationalist, Sinn Féin, and Labour, were represented on the platforms from which the 7,000-strong crowd was addressed. Fraternal greetings were sent to the workers of every country who were striving for the emancipation of their class. It was also resolved that Irish people should have complete control of the internal affairs and resources of their country. Workers were called upon to support the industrial revival by buying Irish goods and produce provided they were made under 'fair' conditions.

Further resolutions affirmed the right of every human being to work and live in peace; demanded the recognition of a universal 48-hour week; the payment of a minimum wage; and the excessive use of boy-labour was condemned. A final resolution declared it the duty of the state to provide proper food and clothing for children whose parents were unable or unwilling to maintain them. The state was also called upon to deal with the vast question of unemployment by readjusting the relations between capital and labour, abolishing excessive overtime and giving work to all willing to undertake it. Pensions were also demanded for the elderly.

The day was one of labour pageantry, reminiscent of similar colourful celebrations which took place throughout the nineteenth century. The trade banners of an earlier age were carried with confidence and obvious pride, yet the inconography of those banners reflected allegiance not to trade unionism but to Irish nationalism; the historical figures on the banners were not the friends of labour either, Daniel O'Connell being the most prominent. These were the relics of an age when the name of trade unionism was tarnished with the stigma of illegal combination, and when the painted canvas was designed both to impress and allay the fears and suspicions of onlookers. The situation had changed totally by 1908, and the unfurled banners reflected a new awareness among Dublin trade unionists of their rights as workers and citizens. No longer were the banners carried simply as symbols of loyal respectability in an effort to impress employers and onlookers, for the good name of trade unionism mattered little when to achieve it workers had put their dignity and rights in pawn. The labour movement, stagnant for decades, was beginning to evolve slowly as the campaign for universal labour rights gathered momentum. Defensiveness and the 'siege mentality' gave way to a new spirit of independence and impatience. The backlog of work confronting organised labour placed Dublin at least two decades behind their English colleagues, and employers, who had never before been confronted by a concerted challenge from trade unionism in the capital, might have been forgiven for thinking that their workers were going too far, too fast.

The new-found unity and determination exhibited by Dublin unions did not put organised labour in a cautious mood. Workers were in a hurry because, by comparison with their cross-channel colleagues, they had squandered the past. They did not seek revoluton but recognition of basic rights such as the freedom to combine, etc. Paradoxically, the language often used to put forward reformist demands was revolutionary in tone, a change which looked all too suspiciously like a conversion of convenience to many employers. The rapidity with which workers moved into the twentieth century left many Dublin businessmen stranded in the mentality of the nineteenth century, harbouring prejudices and fears associated with the halcyon days of illegal trade combinations.

The tone in which demands were often to be put forward exacerbated the degree of ill-feeling between both sides of the industrial divide. Many workers seemed no longer to be interested in enjoying the largesse of parsimonious employers. The emphasis was on rights. After 1906 trade unions could make free use of the strike weapon without fear of facing a court action and the financial ruin of their organisation. Both sides now spoke the language of confrontation; strikes and lock-outs were to eclipse almost totally reasonable negotiation as a means of settling disputes, yet therein lay the recipe for industrial chaos and disaster.

4 The Drapers' Assistants Show the Way

Michael O'Lehane: The Early Years

The changing temper of the city's trade union movement owed much to the contribution of Michael O'Lehane, the founder of the Drapers' Assistants Association (DAA). As will be seen in the succeeding pages, workers employed as clerks, barmen and counter-hands, etc., were as vulnerable as general labourers to exploitation and harassment. In fact, the intolerable encroachments made on their privacy by the 'living-in-system' often made the burden harder to bear. Their plight was made even more extreme because for long they had lacked an association to fight for their rights. Prejudice against 'vulgar' combination coupled with the vigilant opposition of employers invariably hindered the growth of trade unionism in this sector.

However, by the end of the nineteenth century, the National Amalgamated Union of Shop Assistants, had managed to gain a foothold in Belfast and a toehold in Dublin.[1] In the former, the union made progress because it had the services of dynamic union officials, among them being Tom Johnson, the future leader of the Irish Labour Party. But in Dublin a wayward member of the ISRP, E. W. Stewart, was the organiser and he made as little progress in recruiting members for the union as he did in converting Dubliners to the cause of socialism when Connolly was in Ireland.[2] By 1911, Stewart had managed to fight with all the leading members of the trade union movement in Dublin, including James Larkin. As he was pushed into the political wilderness by the force of his own vituperative attacks on his enemies, his work as a union organiser took on less and less importance until it almost ceased to exist. Finally, his trade union career culminated in an unseemly scene on the floor of congress in 1911 when he was accused of not being a properly accredited delegate. Throughout the rest of his public life he allowed his poisoned pen to turn out a series of attacks on leading progressive labour leaders.[3] His contribution to the development of trade unionism in the city was both negative and disruptive.

Fortunately, the drive needed to undertake the massive job of organising the 'black-coated' members of the distributive trade was supplied from another quarter. In 1855, a temporary and wholly spontaneous combination of drapers' assistants won a six o'clock closing hour from six firms in Dublin. However, when one of the firms decided to break the agreement, the assistants were quite powerless to bring pressure to bear on the erring employers. In an effort to combat this weakness, the Dublin Drapers' Early Closing Association was formed four years later, although it failed to function effectively.[4] The Shop Assistants' Industrial League, founded in Cork in the 1890s to encourage the buying of Irish-made goods, was the only other organisation on which counter-hands could rely for protection prior to the establishment of the DAA.[5]

Michael O'Lehane, the DAA's founder, was born near Macroom in 1873. After attending secondary school at North Monastery he was apprenticed to the drapery trade and served his time with Cash and Co in Cork city. Later, he worked in the London House (now Roche's stores) and the Queen's Old Castle. He received his early political education as an active member of the GAA and he remained a staunch nationalist throughout his life. In 1898 he moved to Limerick where he worked for Cannock and Co where due largely to the harsh and primitive living conditions provided by the shop, he contracted typhoid fever along with other colleagues. After some months recuperation, he moved to Dublin to work for Arnotts in Henry Street.

O'Lehane was not long in the city before he came into contact with a group of fellow assistants who saw the necessity of forming an association to protect assistants, even if it meant risking their jobs by being denounced to the employers as active members of a 'combination'. Secret meetings were called and sparsely attended. Finally, on August 21, 1901, the DAA was formed and O'Lehane appointed general secretary with a wage of £2 per week. By the end of September there were 22 members, three being women.

O'Lehane proved a capable leader and a popular and resourceful organiser. When he died in 1920, he left behind an organisation representing more than 7,000 members. In his short life he had been president of the DTC, and a member of the corporation for the Kilmainham Ward from 1905 to 1915; he also served on the public health committee and the technical instruction committee; from

1909 to 1911 he was a member of the South Dublin Board of Guardians; at the Galway TUC, in 1911, he was elected chairman of the parliamentary committee and the following year he was made president of congress—the year the Irish Labour Party was founded.[6]

O'Lehane was quite typical of the new breed of trade unionists. His political background was nationalist and he stood on the Sinn Féin platform in municipal elections, yet he was not unmoved by the teachings of socialism. After an executive meeting of the DTC in 1909, O'Lehane confided in William O'Brien that 'he was becoming a more convinced socialist every day' as a result of his trade union experience. There was not, he said, a firm in the city which did not practice 'downright jobbery in their ordinary course of business'.[7] Nonetheless he was confused in his thinking and like many of his contemporaries, had no clear idea of the political path the labour movement should pursue in the context of the struggle for national self-determination. He did know that without a well-organised trade union movement there would be no hope of setting up a successful and disciplined labour party and as a result, devoted much of his considerable energy to putting union organisation on a firm foundation.

He required all his skill as an organiser to dispel the apathy and overcome the hostility of the shop-hands to the idea of joining a trade union. Assistants served a seven-year apprenticeship with poor pay but many felt socially superior to craft or general workers and were repelled by the idea of combination. On the foundation of his union, O'Lehane wrote:

> Many of them (drapers' assistants) did not know at the time the difference between the term trade unionist and anarchist. They were steeped in false notions of respectability, and, as John Burns at the time so epigrammatically described them: 'they have to be eternally young and infernally civil, had to dress like dukes on the wages of a dustman and had to maintain the polish of a cabinet minister on the salary of a footman'.[8]

This false notion of respectability and confused understanding of the basis of trade unionism often turned the shop assistant into a willing strike-breaker:

> Many instances can be given amongst the few outbreaks of labour troubles in this country during the final ten years of the last and first few years of the present century where shop assistants and all kinds of clerks voluntarily and religiously became strike-breakers.[9]

Even after the DAA was firmly established many of the most ardent members were not wholly familiar or in accord with the dogmas of trade associations. Neither were they weaned from the 'inherited prejudice against the common man'.[10] One Belfast branch secretary of the DAA, when asked by a member was he a trade unionist replied vehemently: 'I am not and never will be.'[11]

O'Lehane's task was made even more difficult by the friction and jealously between different sections of the distributive trade:

> The drapers' assistant affects a certain superiority over the grocer's assistant; the grocer's assistant has his own idea about the draper's assistant; the ironmonger's assistant is criticised by both, and in his turn is alive to the merits of his own position; whilst the chemist's assistant looks down on all; and the banker's clerk will no doubt feel a little characteristic disquiet at anybody alluding to him at all.[12]

It is not unlikely that many difficulties presented by such prejudice forced O'Lehane to confine his attention to the drapery shops and 'monster houses' of the cities.

He has a skilled propagandist and an engaging speaker and he was not slow to exploit both these talents to further the interests of his union, or association, as he diplomatically chose to call it in the beginning. Mass meetings were held in every major town. At the inaugural meeting of the DAA held in the Mansion House, Dublin, on October 29, 1901, O'Lehane sketched the objects of the new organisation. They were as follows: to provide a weekly allowance for members when sick or unemployed; to secure a minimum wage; fixed hours and payment for overtime; and to abolish the living-in system and do away with the system of fines, imposed by all employers for minor transgressions of discipline.

The DAA also aimed at promoting early closing and the securing of a weekly half-holiday; the aboliton of the 'present arbitrary system of instant dismissal'; and the provision of free legal aid for members.[13] O'Lehane also sought to support legislation for the benefit 'of our class', and have every DAA branch represented on the trades council in its respective locality, and send delegates to congress. Clearly it was O'Lehane's intention to bring the drapers into the mainstream of the trade union movement regardless of the opposition he was sure to encounter from the more 'respectable' elements of his trade, but gentleness was the hall-mark of his approach. He was prepared to exercise patience and wean potential members of the DAA away from their social prejudice towards 'vulgar' trade associations by degrees.

Nowhere was his tact and diplomacy more evident than in his inaugural speech in the Mansion House. He began by commending the drapers for their industry and respectability. The men of the 'profession' throughout the country were 'foremost in every movement that was good, benevolent and patriotic', he added. Indeed, he wondered why such a body of men had not thought of combining before this 'for the protection of their individual interests and for the elevation of their class'.[14] Coupled with the assurances of the Lord Mayor, who addressed the meeting before him, the audience received the idea well. Recruits to the DAA came forward slowly but at least it was a steady trickle.

O'Lehane pressed home the initiative. Buoyed up by the qualified success in Dublin, he set out on a national promotion tour in early 1902. Again he showed his strong leadership qualities, principally by not neglecting the need for caution. At a meeting in Galway, he assured his audience that the DAA was never unnecessarily aggressive; it aimed at making men and women better, healthier and more self-reliant. Any action taken in future would be carefully and thoughtfully weighed, the meeting was assured. At a crowded meeting in Waterford, a few weeks later, he retained his emphasis on elevating the dignity of the trade; in Irish society, he added, the drapers' assistant was often the butt of jibes and jeers; and in Limerick he appealed to nationalist sympathies:

It is true there was an effort made by another organisation which had its centre in England, but it failed in Limerick first because it was an English association and the bulk of Irishmen would not fall in with it, and secondly it embraced all sections of shop life and the drapers were sufficiently numerous in themselves and intelligent enough to work out their own salvation.[15]

In Derry, people were also urged to join the DAA because it was essentially an Irish organisation, 'financed, governed and managed by Irishmen and women'.

But this tactic, although highly successful in the south, had a major drawback; emphasis on nationalism alienated the Northern Unionist and prevented any mass support for the new organisation from that quarter. However, even if union officials were sensitive to these feelings, it was difficult to avoid the temptation of utilising the dominant nationalist ideology to attract recruits. O'Lehane was keenly aware of the drawing power of this force and exploited it to the full.

The recruiting drive paid quick dividends. In 1902 all the leading drapery stores in Dublin had been infiltrated by the DAA. Eight country branches of the union were formed in 1903, three more the following year, and six were set up in 1905.[16] In 1906 five more branches were founded, bringing the total effective membership from 51 in October, 1901 to nearly 3,000 in 1906.[17]

DRAPERS' ASSISTANTS ASSOCIATION RETURNS 1902-14[18]

Year	New Members	Members Lost	Effective Members Dec. 31	Total Income	Total Expenditure
				£	£
1902	1250	159	1091	774	253
1903	912	288	1715	1766	1028
1904	780	225	2270	2280	1827
1905	865	385	2750	2800	2311
1906	934	518	3166	2977	2166
1907	524	408	3282	2908	2622
1908	629	457	3454	3164	2396
1909	484	398	3540	3299	2573
1910	784	623	3601	3539	2902
1911	751	891	3461	3789	3045
1912	1444	624	4281	4772	4432
1913	522	801	4002	4395	3912
1914	797	903	3896	4114	3835

But it was in the DAA's preparedness to recruit female members for his organisation that O'Lehane showed himself to be most clearly liberated from the prejudices of his trade union colleagues. Generally the more traditional unions such as AST, the book-binders and the silkweavers, opposed the idea of taking women onto their books. For example, in 1863, the silkweavers' society was involved in a curious case:

> The case of Michael Boland, having a sister as a journey-woman, being laid before the meeting. Mr Michael Boland claimed the right from the time the silk trade was first established down to the present. There was a long discussion on this question, for and against, when it was proposed that in as much as journeywomen weavers are contrary to the rules and customs of the silk trade, Boland be denied this unprecedented privilege. (passed unanimously).[19]

The question of Miss Boland's skills and competence at her trade were not discussed. Prejudice took over completely and her application to join the society was turned down purely on the basis that she was a woman. The silkweavers' attitude premeated the whole of the traditional trade union movement.

O'Lehane enjoyed a strong advantage over many craft union members; he had worked with unorganised workers of both sexes and had witnessed the plight of women counter-hands. In the drapery trade all workers suffered equally. His efforts to encourage women to join the DAA met with considerable success: of a total effective membership of 4,000 in 1914, 1,400 were woman.[20] It would appear that no woman ever held a top executive position in the union before 1920, but circumstances rather than prejudice probably accounted for this.

O'Lehane also took a leaf out of other trade unions' books by founding his own trade journal, called the *Drapers' Assistant*, which was published monthly. Common though this practice was in England, no Irish-based union had ever undertaken such a task before. If the general secretary of the DAA had one virtue it was his ability to recognise the significance of a good idea and adopt it to suit his own circumstances. He was in no sense an original thinker or innovator, but an opportunist in the best sense of the word.

The magazine paid dividends. The first issue appeared in 1903 and O'Lehane himself was the editor. Not only was he a good organiser, but also a very capable journalist. The whole purpose of the content of the magazine was geared to change the consciousness of the shop assistant; make him alive to his rights; and stimulate and shame him into actively fighting for the principles of trade unionism. All trade issues were given an airing while, at the same time, the magazine helped mould the national identity of the association and galvanize its members into a united attack on a select number of common abuses. The pseudo-respectability of the older-style assistant with his sense of exalted status and hostility towards the plebeian pursuits of trade unions generally, was mercilessly pilloried. Slowly, such deep-seated and damaging prejudices withered away, thanks, in no small part, to the magazine campaign. O'Lehane's pointed journalism moved right to the heart of the assistants' grievances.

The Living-in System

Many of the difficulties and injustices encountered by drapers' assistants resulted from the practice of forcing staff, as a condition of employment, to live over their work in accommodation provided by the management. If sleeping space was not available over the premises, workers were boarded out in a specially rented house. In either case staff were under constant supervision and subjected to the discipline of the employer for practically twenty-four hours a day.

Inevitably, this meant living in over-crowded dormitories in draughty buildings which were quite unsuited for human habitation. The risk to even a robust person's health and the danger of contracting tuberculosis in such conditions was very real:

> In one large establishment, not a hundred miles from Nelson's pillar, ten young men are compelled to sleep in a room, the cubic measurement of which is only 10,206 feet. In another room there are eight beds and the cubic measurement is 6,600 feet. Again in most of the town and in some of the smaller city houses two persons are compelled to occupy the same bed. Apprentices are huddled together anyhow and the effects of the system, with its surroundings, on their future lives may be better imagined than described.[21]

The larger drapery stores in the city were vulnerable to adverse publicity and sensitive about the 'good name' of their business, the *Drapers' Assistant* exploited this weakness to the full. In April 1908, O'Lehane wrote an editorial:

> The public are not aware of the fact that a bathroom is an unknown luxury in most of the large houses in Dublin. In one of the most 'swell' houses in fashionable Grafton Street where over 100 employees are warehoused, hot water can only be obtained in the kitchen, needless to say not in quantities sufficient for a bath.[22]

The idea of an unwashed and unkempt assistant may have been too much for the patron of Arnotts, Pims or any other of the monster houses. For a number of years, however, such shops were at pains to conceal the truth from their customers rather than remedy the complaints of their staff.

Besides the threat to health, the living-in system often had a more tragic dimension. In some cases, fire claimed the lives of assistants who were forced to sleep under such conditions, while being provided with no emergency exits should a fire break out at night when the shop was under lock and key. In 1891, Arnotts of Henry St was burned down. Todd Burns in Dublin, Rivingstons in Tralee and Duggans in Kilkenny all had large fires in their premises. On each occasion, employees were remarkably lucky to escape with their lives. But the employees of a shop in Camden St, Dublin, and of a store in Limerick were not so fortunate. In 1913, the Limerick blaze claimed three lives.[23]

Early on the morning of July 19, 1905, a fire broke out in the Dublin drapery shop. Seven of the twenty-three girl assistants were taken to hospital suffering from serious burns, two of whom died later in hospital. The body of another girl was located the following day in the burnt out shell of the shop.[24] At the inquest into the blaze witnesses told how the alarm had not been raised until after the fire had taken hold. Panic-stricken, the girls ran to the doors only to find all exits padlocked against intruders. The staff was securely locked in as burglars were locked out and the keys were nowhere to be found. Finally, the girls had to break through a tiny window, squeeze through one at a time and then scramble across the glass-coated roof in bare feet, before jumping one storey to safety.

In evidence, the city architect, Charles McCarthy, said that he had personal knowledge of the building and that the plans of the premises were in accordance with Corporation bye-laws. A lawyer, representing the DAA, asked the architect would it be correct to say that the premises had inadequate fire precautions? The architect agreed that there were not:

Lawyer: Do you consider there was sufficient means of exit in case of fire?

Architect: I think the result has proven there was not.

Lawyer: Would I be expressing your opinion by saying that it is desirable that some steps should be taken to introduce bye-laws which would prevent an occurrence like this happening again?

Architect: Certainly, but any elaborate provisions might make the cost of building practically prohibitive.[25]

The city architect thus implied that employers might find the provision of adequate safety precautions to safeguard the lives of their workers too expensive to implement.

The recommendations of the inquest seemed to support the claim of the drapers' assistants that both the civil authorities and the employers were quite unprepared to take any serious measures to cope with this problem. The central issue raised by the fire was evaded completely. It was recommended that the Corporation be urged to 'take into consideration the necessity of erecting fire alarms throughout the city'. The owner of the shop could afford to repair the damage caused by the blaze with the £16,000 he was to collect from the insurance company. He would have little difficulty finding new staff, but in the event of another fire his workers would be as vulnerable as before.

'Thou Shalt Not Marry'

Curtailment of personal liberty and the infringement of the ordinary rights of the citizen was yet another side effect of the living-in system and nowhere was this more in evidence than in a bizarre case involving Switzers of Grafton Street. In March, 1910, an assistant who had been sixteen years with the firm asked for a week's leave to get married. The manager said he had no objection to the request but would have to bring it before the board as a matter of routine. On March 30, the assistant received a letter from his manager informing him that the company could no longer permit him to continue in their employment, 'as he was getting married to a young lady engaged in the same line of business' as Switzers. In fact, the assistant's fiancee ran a small drapery shop on Lr Drumcondra Rd and, quipped O'Lehane, 'anyone who knows Dublin and its suburbs can readily understand the fierce competition likely to arise between Switzers of Grafton St and this little shop'.[26]

The DAA organised a series of public meetings to draw attention to the case in an effort to have the dismissed assistant reinstated. On 25 August Mrs Sheehy Skeffington addressed a demonstration at Beresford Place, and another meeting was held in the Rotunda where O'Lehane accused the Switzers' management of silencing three Dublin dailies by threatening to withdraw large advertising contracts if they persisted in publishing reports about the affair.

The case was given wide coverage in the English Press. The company was feeling the effect of the campaign and it was forced to telegram Fleet St papers: 'DAA statement issued entirely misleading, largely untrue. Our general policy has always been to encourage marriage amongst our assistants'.[27] To issue such a statement was, in itself, a sign of weakness and a tribute to the DAA campaign and the incident helped underline the degree to which the living-in system could encroach and interfere in a person's private life.

Neither was the Switzers' management exceptional in its severity on employees. Most firms exacted the same unbending obedience from lower executives. The 'thou shalt not marry' case simply extended this mentality to its logical and bizarre conclusion. Indeed, the reason why this type of case did not crop up more frequently in drapery establishments was probably because so few assistants felt financially secure enough to contemplate matrimony. According to O'Lehane, the marriage rate in the trade was well below the national average. An English contemporary corroborates this view:

> From my point of view, writes a drapery manager in the *Economic Review,* 'the greatest objection to this system (living-in) is the barriers it places in the way of matrimony'. Even if any assistant is sufficiently successful to justify him contemplating marriage, the master would unhesitatingly refuse to make an allowance for discontinuing to supply food and lodgings. Besides, masters strongly object to married men; few will engage them under any circumstances.[28]

If the living-in system operated against the best interest of the staff in any monster house, it was a financial boon to employers, for it was cheaper to house staff than provide them with an adequate increase in their annual wages to compensate for a loss in board and lodgings. A DAA breakdown of the cost for keeping an assistant in 1902 is as follows:

> Taking the case of one of the largest and most pretentious of the city houses, the value set upon the living-in provided for the assistants is set down as £26 per head per annum, a modest enough figure, and this added to the £20 salary of many assistants makes a sum of £46 per annum out of which the assistant has to clothe himself in a manner consistent not with his salary but with the reputation of his firm. Taking these figures as they stand it will be seen that the gentleman who has to attend to the 'my ladies' and the 'madames parvenus' in the establishment . . . is not nearly so well off as a full private in the Donegal militia. The cost of keeping an assistant for a day amounts to between 10d and 10^1/$_2$d per head or 6s 1^1/$_2$d per week or £15-18-6 per year. Compared to the militiamam who does not have to dress well or speak politely, he has a clear £18-5s per annum plus the very best properly inspected food.[29]

In England, drapery assistants were a little more fortunate than their Irish counterparts, since the estimated allowance provided by employers to staff living off the premises was £25 to £26 per year and there appeared to be little difficulty obtaining this sum.[30]

Besides being badly paid, housed and fed, the living-in system left the assistants vulnerable to other abuses. In most of the recognised trades where unions were long-established, the number of apprentices allowed to any one employer was strictly regulated. Where a union was weak or had only just been founded, boy-labour was used extensively and this was dispensed with as soon as they became old enough to command an adult wage. The drapery trade suffered greatly from this abuse.

Serving One's Time

The larger Dublin shops usually recruited young assistants from the country and trained them over a seven-year period. Parents paid employers between £40 and £50 to indenture their child and teach him the trade. In an effort to discourage families from sending their sons or daughters to the 'glamour' of the big shop, O'Lehane wrote the following:

> After a visit to the city, a boy is impressed by the mammoth size and brilliant splendour of the shops. Brought inside one of the emporiums of the universal providers he is struck by the magnificence of the place and dreams of the city only to make up his mind to serve his time. For the first couple of weeks, he lives in a whirl of excitement and when the novelty wears off he begins to weary of the long hours and want of fresh air, while he also discovers that some of the suave gentlemen are entirely different to his first impressions. In the living-in shop the food is very often bad and has to be bolted. At the age of 30, he decides to emigrate or remains on as an ordinary assistant at £40 or £50 per year. Or too old at 40, he finds himself unemployed or opens a shop and fails . . . Stop the apprentice traffic.[31]

O'Lehane described this practice of employing boy-labour in committed and colourful language as 'the white slave trade'. There is, however, strong evidence to support his claim that employers took unfair advantage of the younger members of their staff. A drapery shop owner, Myles Lawlor, was prosecuted in 1912 under The Shop Hours Act for allowing one of his young female staff members to work $97\frac{1}{2}$ hours in the one week.[32] Under the Act, the maximum working week was 74 hours. This was only one incident which happened when legislation existed to prevent such abuses, and for most of the first decade of the twentieth century no law was on the statute book to prevent assistants being worked for as many hours as an employer wished.

The Fining System

Yet another trial the assistant had to endure was 'the odious, illegal, and pernicious system of fining'.[33] This system of exacting monetary penalties for minor transgressions of house discipline or protocol also underlined the authoritarian nature of the store regime. Most of the leading Dublin houses were run on military and monastic lines. Even the most punctilious of employees could not avoid transgressing the labyrinth of rules laid down by employers who were as patronising as they were puritanical. Unfortunately, no Dublin fine list has been located by the author but because of the many obvious similarities between Dublin and London, extracts from a British rule book should not unduly misrepresent the local situation.

The necessity to instil a strict code of sexual morality into their charges was implicit in these manuals, yet in one case, if an assistant returned to the premises after eleven o'clock at night, he or she was unceremoniously locked out to roam the streets until morning.[34] The following are a few select rules from various London house lists:

> Every employee is expected in addressing the members of the firm not to omit altogether the customary term of respect. The proper use of the word 'sir' is in no sense derogatory to the self-respect of the person using it, as is proved by the usage of Parliament and the ordinary amenities of society. Anyone habitually disregarding this thing will not be allowed to remain in their employ.

Great importance was attached to neatness of dress. Young women were expected to wear black dresses, 'made to clear the ground, with white linen collars and cuffs and their hair was to be arranged in a neat and becoming manner'. If any assistant allowed a customer to go away unserved without first appealing to the buyer or a superintendent, he was subject to instant dismissal.

Every movement of the assistant was carefully itemised and lists covering behaviour in the shop alone often ran to over 200 rules:

> Customers to be promptly attended to, if not fine—3d; No flowers to be put in water-glasses or bottles; No toilet business or nail cleaning etc., to be done in the shop or showrooms—6d; For unbusinesslike conduct—6d; For using matches or lighting papers—2s 6d; Second offence—dismissal; and for not giving up the docket to the shop-walker before nine the next morning—2s 6d.[35]

An assistant's hours off were made equally intolerable by a similar web of strictures, admonitions and warnings. So detailed were the rules that even in a crowded dormitory, an assistant could not so much as hang a personal picture without risk of fine. Days off necessitated returning to one's shop before eleven, or twelve o'clock on Sunday:

> The gas will be turned out fifteen minutes later. Anyone leaving a light on after that time will be discharged. Assistants sleeping out without permission will be cautioned twice and discharged at the third offence. All bedrooms to be cleared at 8 a.m.; on Sunday, the bedrooms to be cleared at 10.20 a.m. and not entered again till 12.30 p.m. Unnecessary talking and noise in bedrooms is strictly prohibited—6d. Any clothing, boots, etc., left about the bedrooms will be taken away. Servants not responsible for any loss. Each article, 3d. Bedrooms must be left tidy. No pictures, photos, etc., allowed to disfigure the wall. Anyone so doing will be charged with repair. Any assistants making unnecessary noise or disturbance will be discharged. For not turning the gas off in the bedroom at night—1s. Young ladies leaving the shop must remove their boxes the same day.[36]

O'Lehane addressed himself to eradicating the odious system of fining as a priority. By 1910, at least the larger employers in Dublin had ceased the practice under pressure of public opinion. In other areas O'Lehane continued to spotlight the most glaring abuses but not with the same amount of success. After three years in existence, his union had very little to show for its work: the living-in system was as strong as ever in 1906; assistants had to work for between £40 and £50 per year; there was no half holiday in the trade; neither was there a uniform hour for closing, a practice which often forced men to work eighty hours a week.

O'Lehane had succeeded in other ways, however, and it would have been rash and premature of his followers to have expected much more from a three-year-old society. It was a significant enough achievement to have even got the DAA off the ground at all. His ability as a speaker was recognised at Congress when he spoke out against the injustices in his trade, while at local level his contribution to the labour movement earned him the post of DTC president in 1910. He was noted for his desire to wean the Dublin trade union movement away from inter-union rivalry which had so dominated and weakened the DTC over the years. His contribution to the gradual process of change away from the craft consciousness of the past towards the growing spirit of trade union solidarity was significant.

By 1913, O'Lehane's thinking in this area had developed sufficently to put forward the idea of an Irish-based federation of trade unions. Under this scheme each union executive would determine all domestic matters relating to their own members, such as sick benefits, unemployment benefits, superannuation, etc. All unions were to contribute to a central federation fund, in proportion to their effective membership. Unions not complying with these conditions were to be cut off from the central strike fund, and all amalgamated unions were instructed to have suffcient autonomy, if they sought to join the federation.[37] Yet the implementation of such a plan was fraught with difficulties. The biggest stumbling block was a clause in the scheme shifting the authority to declare a strike from the union directly involved to the federation executive. The scheme proved too advanced for contemporary trade unionists; it asked too much, too soon, from men who were just beginning to realise the obligations and advantages of a unified movement.

If O'Lehane's federation plan was over-enthusiastic, it does not detract from his determination to transform Dublin trade unionists from being dominated by craft-centred motives into a broader labour movement with the interests of the majority at heart. By 1907, the DTC had moved quite a distance along the latter path, but the men were cautious and only prepared to make haste slowly. However, O'Lehane's enthusiasm for his own members and his work in the trades council combined to give a new sense of urgency to the proceedings of that body and spur it on to tackle the problems of twentieth century trade unionism.

The quality of O'Lehane's leadership in a time of crisis was given its first real test in October 1906, when a dispute arose between members of the DAA and the management of Boyers, North Earl Street. Although the number involved in the strike was only about thirty, both sides showed a tenacity of purpose and a determination to win at all costs, and it is worth paying close attention to the details of the dispute for a number of reasons. In the field of industrial relations the strike revealed the almost unbridgeable gulf existing between management and workers and the contempt of the former for the latter. From a trade union point of view, it illustrates how mature the DAA had become within a short space of three years. Finally, O'Lehane gave a practical demonstration of his philosophy that a strike was the concern of the whole trade union movement and that a worker's responsibility towards a locked-out colleague could not be discharged simply by paying a levy towards his upkeep; it necessitated active support from the entire labour movement through public demonstrations.

According to the employer, Mr Boyer, the dispute arose over an incident which he considered far from trivial:

> The quarrel is not so much with me as among the employees themselves. It all began about three weeks ago. One of my men falsified figures in stocktaking in order to get another man dismissed. He measured one piece of cloth as $12\frac{1}{2}$ yards instead of $52\frac{1}{2}$. Nine times short measure was taken in a fortnight, and when the matter was pointed out by an assistant the other assistant admitted that they were his figures, and said he had no explanation to give. I told him I did not want a man like that and he left.[38]

However, a diametrically opposed view of the origins of the dispute was given by the staff. Their statement claimed that three weeks after the stock had been taken a wrong ticket was found on a roll of cloth. The writing belonged to the dismissed assistant, the statement said, 'but it did not follow that it was he who had placed it there on the disputed roll of cloth or that he was part of a conspiracy bent on taking the stock wrong'.[39] Mr Boyer takes up the story:

> Two days afterwards, I had a petition presented to me by twenty one of the staff asking for an immediate re-instatement of the dismissed man. I refused and they said that their alternative was to strike on the Saturday morning. I said they could go ahead and that I would have their accounts ready on Friday evening to accelerate them. But on Friday, they returned and said that they were not going out on strike. After some more meetings and deputations I agreed to allow them to remain on getting a full apology. They apologised and consented that a certain number of them would be dismissed—ones which I no longer required, as I had engaged some hands in the interim. I promised to keep them for a week or a fortnight before giving them notice, and this seemed to give satisfaction. I warned them that there were to be no threats used against those of the staff that remained and did not sign the memorial.[40]

But according to the staff statement, some twenty-three of the thirty-five assistants employed by Mr Boyer signed a petition to have the man reinstated and when this was refused, the employer felt that the staff were plotting a strike:

> Previous to that there was not the least intention on the part of the staff to go on strike but Mr Boyer, having put the idea into their heads, one of the deputation fell into the trap and said: 'Well, there may be something to that effect'. Mr Boyer jumped at the idea and said: 'Very well, your accounts will be ready for you tomorrow evening'.[41]

At this stage O'Lehane sought an interview with Boyer and at a meeting of management and men it was agreed that there would be no strike in return for no lockout. However, at this point Boyer demanded on apology from the dissident staff which the twenty-three people involved refused, beyond saying that they would not go on strike. The two factions made their peace but it was a pact both bitterly resented having to honour. According to the staff:

Everything went alright until the 'weeding-out' process began. An assistant, who remained one day extra in the country to bury a close relative was dismissed . . . A few days later another assistant, on leave under doctor's orders, was dismissed. It was then only a question of days, and Mr Boyer admitted that the reason was because some 'were taking too prominent a part in organising in the house'. After nine of those who had tried to get the dismissed man reinstated were gone the others decided to act. Better to fight than be shot down one by one was the principle. An ultimatum was sent to Mr Boyer who still refused to move, and so sixteen men and eight young ladies ceased work, including nine dismissed. All these except one had signed the requisition for the original reinstatement.[42]

The matter was now clear-cut as far as the DAA executive was concerned; an employer had, on the basis of totally insufficient evidence, ruined a young man's character and career by believing that he had deliberately falsified stock-taking figures as part of a conspiracy to defraud the firm. Boyer had then proceeded to victimise members of the staff who had come to the defence of the young man. On available evidence, it would appear that Boyer moved precipitously without any real proof or justification for his action. As charges and counter-charges flew between the pro-tagonists Boyer did little to validate his action; not, of course, that his decisions ever needed to be justified either in his own eyes or before his staff. He was fully convinced that his stand in the matter was quite correct and proper and as conclusive proof of this, claimed to have 'the whole trade in Dublin behind him having put the full facts of the case before them'.[43] He denied that he had ever indulged in a spate of arbitrary sackings. According to the original employees' statement, the death of a close relative had prevented an assistant from returning to work, but Mr Boyer claimed that the said employee 'should have been at work on Friday morning but did not return until Monday'. As regards the assistant who was sacked 'because another employee threatened to resign if he was not let go', he (the assistant) had refused to take instructions from his buyer 'and in a most insubordinate manner told him (the buyer) that he would not be dictated to'. As for the man who was sacked while on sick leave, 'he had not asked for leave of absence'. The remaining dissidents had been dismissed:

> Owing to the continued dissention which still prevailed between the two opposing parties in the house that some of them who took a leading part and would not work smoothly with the other, should be removed . . . in fact, for the proper conduct of the business it was absolutely necessary. We never wished nor did interfere with the right of the assistant to combination.[44]

In fairness, Boyer did have a serious split amongst his staff which affected the smooth running of his business. But he overstated his position somewhat by claiming that he was not concerned by the presence of a union in his shop, particularly since it was the DAA that led the 'move' against him. By the canons of modern industrial relations, Boyer must fare badly after the reconstruction of events, but by the standards of 1906 he was acting perfectly within his rights. He had on his hands a full-scale rebellion by subordinates— even if it was largely of his own personal doing—and he had, by his own standards, an absolute right to dismiss the dissidents and fill their places with assistants of his choice. Moreover, he could count on the full support of his fellow employers in the drapery trade for taking such a righteous stand. Organised labour thought differently, and there lay the basis for a dispute which was grounded on something far more serious than a clash of personality or temperament. For practically the first time, Boyer had to face the unpalatable fact that employees had rights and an organisation to fight for the recognition of those rights.

The number of people actually on strike by mid-October is difficult to estimate. Boyer claimed that there were only 15 out, while 33 remained 'faithful', but in a letter, signed by P. J. McGrath on behalf of the strikers, it was claimed that the Boyer total included workmen, girls, apprentices and some loyal assistants.[45] Feelings were running high on both sides. Boyer, who was followed nightly by assistants hurling abuse at him, was given two plain-clothes policemen as constant companions. Some assistants who left the shop after work to take a walk were also followed and harassed and abused by strikers. One of the girls who continued to work for Boyer after the strike began was a Miss Brigid Andrews. One evening she was harassed by a crowd after she left the shop, hissed, booed and called a blackleg and a scab. A male member of the staff was followed onto the top of a tram by some members and given the same treatment. On another occasion, more than verbal violence was used and an employee, Michael Egan, was kicked once or twice.[46] Some arrests were made arising out of these incidents.

O'Lehane did not allow the situation to deteriorate any further. He immediately set about planning a course of action designed to win trade union support and public sympathy for the strikers. A public defence committee was set up, independent of DAA control, to gather fighting funds. Handbills explaining the origins of the case and advising interested citizens of a series of 'monster meetings' were distributed throughout the city.[47]

On 17 October, 2,500 drapery assistants marched from their shops to a rally in O'Connell St where they were joined by over 2,000 more trade unionists. The Lord Mayor, Mr Nannetti, William Field, MP, and the secretary of the ITUC, E. L. Richardson, all sent letters regretting their inability to attend but expressing their full support for the DAA. At a second public meeting on 20 November, E. L. Richardson spoke and again declared that the labour movement was placing all its resources behind the fight against oppression in the drapery trade. Another speaker, P. T. Daly, described Boyer as 'the second messiah who could do no wrong'.[48]

At the Dublin Trades Council, O'Lehane thanked the meeting for its support and expressed the resolve of the DAA to show more determination than ever to win the strike despite the odds. At a later meeting, he told delegates that Boyer had refused to heed the appeals of the Lord Mayor, Mr Nannetti and other prominent citizens, to bring the dispute to an end. In the light of this rejection, O'Lehane determined to keep the strike 'before the public eye and expose the underhand tactics of the employers'.[49]

But if there was solidarity and militancy in trade union circles the employers were equally determined to crush the strikers, stamp out the spirit of incipient rebellion and teach the fledgling Drapers Assistants' Association a stern lesson in obedience. There was neither the machinery nor the willingness to meet the workers and talk out the problem, and to meet the new threat from organised labour two independent employer bodies, the Drapery Employers' Association and the Merchants Drapers' Association, merged to form a united front.[50]

O'Lehane decided to step up the campaign and a third 'monster meeting' was held on 18 December. After Christmas a significant change in tactics was adopted. Taking advantage of the Trade Disputes Act, 1906, the DAA placed a picket on the North Earl Street premises. Unfortunately, for the picket-line, some of the policemen on duty in the area were less conversant with the subtleties of the Act and an effort was made to bustle the picket out of North Earl St into adjacent O'Connell St, during which two arrests were made.[51] Commenting on the incident, and on the general application of the picketing law in Dublin by the authorities, O'Lehane editorialised caustically:

> Unlike Dublin, the assistant in London is allowed perfect freedom to picket in accordance with the terms of the Trades Disputes Act. In London, there are no police to encourage cornerboys to exasperate the peaceful picketers, and there evidently is no encouragement given to the police to trump up charges of alleged obstruction or intimidation . . . We always had an idea, a somewhat hazy idea to be sure, that the law or rather the administration of the law in England and Ireland were not precisely the same, and the little experience related above convinces us further in this belief. However, let us hope that the time may come, and come soon, when 'His Majesty the Sergeant' shall be more amenable to the public will in the city of Dublin.[52]

The action of the police in harassing a peaceful picket was roundly condemned by the trades council. A vocal minority on the council chided the DAA for taking a stubborn line in the dispute, but on two occasions motions of censure against O'Lehane and his men were rejected and replaced by firm pledges of trade union support.[53] The dispute was now in its third month and showed no signs of being any nearer a solution. The morale of the strikers was high and the skirmish between the police and those on picket duty outside Boyers only helped add to the disputants' confidence of victory. On 22 January, 'the largest trade union show of strength was organised since the '98 celebrations, in Dublin'. According to the *Freeman's Journal*, the bricklayers' band and two other union bands marched at the head of a torch-light procession through the streets of the capital to Beresford Place where a rally was held. The *Drapers' Assistant* estimated that there were about 20,000 in attendance, although this figure seems exaggerated.[54] The interference with picketing rights, recently confirmed in law, incensed many trade unionists and it is likely that they turned out in strength to demonstrate their hostility to the authorities and to give a warning that such action in the future might be met with sterner opposition. The meeting was presided over by the DAA president, M. A. O'Sullivan, who read letters of support from the Lord Mayor and William Field, MP. The DTC president, Mr Lumsden, proposed the following motion which was passed by acclamation:

That this meeting protests against the action of the police authorities in depriving the members of the Irish Drapers' Assistants Association of their legal rights of peaceful picketing and we express our determination for pressing as far as possible the provisions of the Trade Disputes Act and in maintaining the dictum laid down by Parliament in connection with these matters.[55]

Lumsden went on to recommend that all trade unionists should assist the DAA in the peaceful picketing of Earl Street, while another speaker, E. W. Stewart, believed that the employers were merely using this dispute to smash the drapers' union. Certainly, the employers were afraid of the growing power of the DAA and it is not unreasonable to postulate, like Stewart, that they were attempting to break the union financially. More than likely, the master drapers first took Boyer's side because they felt he was correct in his action. It was hoped to end the dispute swiftly and teach the workers a lesson, but as the weeks dragged into months employers may have hoped to over-stretch the DAA's finances and force a settlement favourable to Boyer, not an uncommon way of dealing with unions in the city.

Could the dispute have been avoided? This is most unlikely given the frame of mind of the belligerents. An element of unreasonableness and intransigence was shown by both parties, but the weight of evidence must shift the burden of responsibility onto the employer's side. What O'Lehane was attempting to establish was job security for his members and freedom from the worry of arbitrary or instant dismissal, a problem summed up by O'Lehane himself in a letter to the *Freeman's Journal*:

Some employers are under the impression that employees have no rights to make any demands whatever and even when they do concede, at least, with bad grace that employees have some rights, the spokesmen, the 'ringleaders', are from that hour forward 'marked men'. No matter how capable, how efficient, how honest, they are dismissed on the most flimsy pretext at a moment's notice . . . This arbitrary power of instant dismissal gives the average employer or manager too much scope to gratify his prejudice or satisfy a whim of the moment.[56]

A fundamental right of all employees to 'security of tenure' was at issue in the dispute. The absolute right of the employer to hire and fire whoever he liked, on whatever pretext, also hung in the balance.

Both sides held out grimly until May when a formula for peace was arrived at giving victory to the DAA. Boyer, after eight months, was finally deserted by his fellow employers and a settlement was reached, whether he liked it or not. It is likely that he did not but had little option than to go along with the majority of his colleagues who were tired of fighting a cause that was well and truly lost. Under the terms of the agreement of 13 May the picket was to be lifted from his shop and in return the Merchant Drapers undertook:

> to re-employ in the same houses as before, and in the same or in as good positions as they previously occupied all assistants who were dismissed from firms other than Boyers and Co. owing to being convicted in the police courts in connection with the dispute.[57]

Another clause in the agreement stipulated that the twenty-six male assistants, nine female assistants and six apprentices who were dismissed or resigned from Boyers should not be victimised because of this 'and further that the Merchant Drapers' Association would recommend and encourage in every way the early employment by members of the association of the said assistants'.[58] If any former employees were still out of a job within a week, both parties would meet again to review the position. The final clause said that no obstacle should be put in the way by the DAA to the employment by other firms hereafter of the assistants in Mr Boyer's establishment, to wit loyal assistants or 'scabs' in DAA eyes.

O'Lehane could not have hoped for a more satisfactory outcome to the protracted strike. It was impractical to seek reinstatement in Boyers for the 'dissidents' but the innocence and reliability of these assistants was upheld by the agreement which recommended and guaranteed their immediate re-employment. Furthermore, the respectable master drapers agreed to re-employ staff who had been dismissed for appearing in court on charges of intimidation, obstruction and abusive and insulting language.

The DAA annual report for 1907 confirmed the general feeling in Dublin trade union circles concerning the outcome of the dispute, a 'satisfactory settlement' being its verdict. The conduct of the majority of members during the strike 'could not have been excelled' while the action and general bearing of the assistants 'had placed the DAA in the front rank of organised labour in Ireland', the report added. There was certainly an excuse for adulation, for in its short history the DAA had transformed many of its members from being 'a league of gentlemen', opposed to the labour movement, into a disciplined, well-organised trade union as progressive in its views as it was militant in its methods.

The DAA was not fully responsible for the changes taking place within the DTC during 1907. O'Lehane sprung to prominence when Dublin trade unionists were undergoing a period of intense self-criticism and questioning their traditional attitudes. The DTC had nurtured and preserved many prejudices long after their counterparts in England or even Belfast had mitigated their crippling effects or discarded them completely. It was a time when many Dublin trades felt the full force of competition from mass produced factory articles; realised the deficiences of the Nationalist party; began to question the theory of trade union political neutrality at national level; saw the advantages of popular demo-cracy and, above all, recognised the necessity for the general welfare of the trade union movement to unionise unskilled labour.

The DAA became involved in industrial action at a fortuitous and formative moment in Irish trade union history. It acted as a catalyst, drawing together the threads of the rejuvenated labour movement. Unlike many older unions, it was not afraid to risk the opprobrium of employers by denouncing forcefully and voci-ferously the many glaring abuses prevalent in the trade. Neither was its leadership hesitant over employing the tactics of the mass meeting and of a high-pressure publicity campaign to marshal opinion against the injustices of the living-in system, long hours, boy-labour, the employment of foreign buyers and arbitrary dismissal. Moreover, O'Lehane was willing to run the risk of arrest and deepening hostility of the Dublin Metropolitan Police towards strikers by using the picket to maximum advantage. He never believed in pussy-footing on any issue but neither was he reckless nor a blunt confrontationalist. He was a moderate trade unionist and a good opportunist. Above all, he recognised the value and indispensability of propaganda. The monthly publication of a trade magazine satisfied that requirement admirably.

Many tradesmen who for too long basked in the sun of their own respectability to the detriment of the overall interests of Labour in the city were awakened partially by the shock treatment ad-ministered by the DAA. The traditional *nostrums* and sectional selfishness which for too long dominated and divided the trades in the city were shown to be outmoded and debilitating by O'Lehane and the DAA activities. The chain of apathy had already been placed under severe strain by the many secular and religious ideas on social justice finding support in Dublin at the time, and O'Lehane put ever greater pressure on it. James Larkin finally unfettered many workers later, but much of the groundwork had been well prepared by the industry of a few men equipped with a number of moderate ideas concerning social justice which were to prove almost revolutionary to employers when urged into practice in Dublin.

5 The Rise of the General Workers' Unions

If Edwardian Dublin provided large sections of apprenticed labour with a low and somewhat insecure standard of living, the plight of the city's general workers was far more acute. A series of reports, published before 1914, painted a lurid picture of what life was really like for the poor who lived in the festering slums of the capital. Roughly a third of the population (86,000) occupied the old Georgian tenements situated within the boundaries of the Grand and Royal Canals. This area had to its credit a number of unenviable firsts; the death rate was the highest in the country, while infant mortality was the worst in the British Isles and rivalled Moscow and Paris.

Social deprivation manifested itself in other ways. Malnutrition was endemic and this allowed diseases of all kinds, but particularly the great killer, tuberculosis, to reach 'epidemic' proportions. The poor had no answer to these problems. It is little wonder that many sought relief and escape from the harshness of everyday life by turning to 'the bottle'.

The origins of the social problem had their foundation in the weakness and underdeveloped state of the city's economy. Unlike her sister city, Belfast, Dublin really lacked anything that could be described as heavy industry. Brewing, distilling and biscuit-making concerns gave employment to large sections of the capital's 10,000-strong apprenticed work force.[1] But Dublin was, first and foremost, a port and a commercial centre. Consequently, and of a total male labour force of 40,000 in 1901, the majority were involved either directly or indirectly in the distributive sector. The number of carters, carriers and cabmen in the city rose within ten years from 2,212 to over 3,000 in 1911. In the same period, the number of men employed as coal porters increased by over 20% from 695 to 975. A staggering 17,913 men were general labourers in 1901 and there were over 23,000 in the city by 1911. In the latter category, most of these men could only hope for casual employment. Only the select few, many of whom had served in the army, could hope to enjoy the luxury of a permanent and pensionable job in, for example, the much-coveted Guinness's brewery. The remainder joined the large pool of unemployed, which was sometimes as high as 20% of the work-force, and queued for a part-time job each morning outside delivery yards on the docks.

The lot of the womenfolk was equally harsh. There were no fewer than 13,551 domestic servants in 1911; 4,294 dressmakers and milliners; 1,296 seamstresses and shirtmakers; over 1,000 tailoresses and 1,246 charwomen. A labourer's wage was less than £1 per week while girls employed in Jacob's biscuit factory were lucky if they earned half that amount. There, the lowest paid female workers received as little as 7s per week while senior staff and overseers got 15s. But no matter how little was received by these girls they counted themselves lucky to have a job at all in a city notable for its conspicuous lack of employment opportunities for women. It is not surprising to find that there was a considerable reluctance amongst the operatives to do anything, such as joining a union, which would place their positions in jeopardy. This reluctance and reticence towards organisation was not shared by many male workers, and the level of union achievement in 1907 did not reflect the feeling in the capital amongst unapprenticed labour towards combination. The need was there as was the determination. It only required a force to appear capable of galvanising the vast pool of casual labour into action.

Local institutions exhibited a marked inability to produce personnel talented enough to set such a movement in train. A number of Dublin-based unions catering for general labourers were as sectionally motivated as many of the craft organisations, while the leadership was plodding, conservative and singularly undynamic. The United Builders' Labourers and General Workers' Union was founded in 1889. By 1912, a mere 1,108 men had been recruited and the figure rose to 1,408 two years later.[2] However, contrary to what the name might indicate, this union only recruited builders' labourers and although there was no specific rule to exclude other general workers, little was ever done to encourage them to join.

The Irish Municipal Employees' Trade Union, more popularly known as the United Corporation Workers of Dublin, was founded in the 1890s for the purpose of unifying a specific section of manual workmen. Within the confines of its restricted objective the union was quite successful and by 1913, 1,532 men had joined. The gaslighters and waterworks employees had their own organisations. Other smaller municipal workers' unions were set up in Dun Laoghaire and Rathmines. The Queenstown and District Government Labourers' Union had 120 men on its books in 1912 and over double that number the following year. In 1905 the Rathmines and District Workmen's Union was established with about 50 members: seven years later there were 56 members, but in 1913 membership jumped to 104. Founded in 1907, the Dublin Operative Waterworks Employees' Association made a return of 38 members to the registrar of Friendly Societies; 19 more men had joined by 1913.

Left to themselves, these unions felt neither obliged nor compelled to risk the popular discomfiture of extending the boundaries of their organisations to include non-municipal general labour. Their resources were limited and they confined themselves to the modest and rigidly achievable goal of selective recruitment. By tradition, general labour in the capital had lost hope of finding the main impetus and thrust for unionisation at a local level. More importantly, such a struggle required strong financial backing to fight the protracted strikes which were the only way to win, for a general workers' union, as much as a toe-hold in Dublin.

A labourers' union could only attract members if it won recognition from the various employer associations—a concession the latter were not prepared to concede if at all available. If recognition was granted without a struggle, then there was every indication that such a trade union was very much an employers' poodle and workmen were not likely to show enthusiasm for such a force. Consequently, it would remain small in number as did the United Labourers' Union which William Martin Murphy claimed to have had a hand in founding.[3]

'New Unionism' in Britain

As in business, what was required to get a fledgling general workers' union off the ground was an abundance of risk capital. In Dublin, where combination amongst the 'unskilled' unvariably intimated incipient rebellion to a committee of over-sensitive employers, the outcome was almost inevitably a protracted strike marked by bitterness on both sides. Without strong financial backing the men risked crushing and humiliating defeat following industrial action.

Yet if a new union could not strike a militant posture in its first months in existence, then it ran the risk of total failure. Nobody wished to join an organisation which failed to make dramatic strides towards achieving marked improvement in the wages and conditions of its members. Without a steady flow of subscriptions a new union could hardly make ends meet and, thus, was in no position to lead a strike. Here lay the classic dilemma of many local organisations: without members a union could not become solvent yet men would not join a combination unless it afforded some protection, which it could not do without money, to fight a protracted strike. This vicious circle worked entirely to the employers' advantage; they could rest sure in the knowledge that the threat from trade unionism was only spasmodic at worst. After the full fury of the early days of a strike had been beaten off by a resolute and united employer front, the workers were a spent force, left with little alternative but to seek peace at any price, their last state being usually worse than the first. Workers were aware of the harsh reality of their position, and many employers did not hesitate to exploit the situation and turn it to their own advantage.

The first real breakthrough for the general workers came in the late 1880s with the advent of the labour movement known as 'new unionism'. Tyneside was always a strong trade union centre with its large numbers of miners and metal workers, and it is not surprising that it was there the first new-style union was set up. Edward Pease, a Fabian socialist from London, founded the National Federation of Labour there in 1886, and the following year a young man called Joseph Havelock Wilson began the difficult task of organising the seamen. By 1889, Pease's union and Wilson's National Amalgamated Sailors' and Firemen's union each had a membership fluctuating between 20,000 and 40,000.[4] Other prominent unions set up at the time were: the General Railway Workers' Union (1889); the National Amalgamated Coalporters' Union (1890); the Navvies, Bricklayers' Labourers, and General Labourers' Union (1890); Mersey Quay and Railway Carters' Union (1887) and the Leeds Amalgamated Association of Builders' Labourers (1889).[5]

All these new organisations shared new characteristics distinguishing them from the craft and amalgamated societies. The old unions were essentially voluntary associations organised on a sectional or vocational basis; members were charged a high weekly subscription fee and in return were guaranteed friendly society benefits; strikes were eschewed and were to be avoided as something inherently evil; leadership was centralised and all spontaneity and over-demonstrative actions by rank and file members was strongly discouraged by the imposition of heavy fines on offenders.

In contrast, the new unions catered largely for the general and poorer paid workers, charging low entrance fees and subscriptions. Where the craft and amalgamated unions emphasised friendly society benefits, the new organisations concentrated on vigorous industrial action and aggressive strike tactics to win members and concessions from employers. Arbitration and conciliation was as much eschewed by the new, as strikes were by the older men. In the 1880s industrial action became the touchstone for success.

Furthermore, the hitherto acceptable voluntary principle in trade unionism was now ruled to be anathema. Where workers had, in the past, remained outside trade societies out of selfishness and benefited from hard-won union concessions nevertheless, the new unionism insisted upon the closed-shop system. Most importantly, the men of the late 80s used militant action as a fulcrum to force progressive social legislation onto the statute books. Not content with the ameliorative gains won in individual disputes through protracted and tedious negotiations, the new leaders sought less fickle and more lasting victories. Thus, when they struck for an immediate objective their long-term strategy was to amend the law, 'therefore a natural alliance sprang up between politically quite immature men seeking to organise certain "weak" groups of workers . . . and the revolutionary socialists of the 1880s, who supplied, or converted, the leaders of most, but not all, general unions'.[6]

Perhaps two of the most successful 'new' unions were Ben Tillett's Dock, Wharf, Riverside and General Workers' Union (1889) and Will Thorne's National Union of Gasworkers and General Labourers which was set up in the same year.[7] Moreover, the leadership and activities of the two unions exemplify the characteristics and mood of these vital years in labour history. In 1889, Thorne was a young illiterate Birmingham-born Irishman, employed at the Beckton gasworks at East Ham. Eight years earlier a wealthy radical named Henry Mayers Hyndman had established the Social Democratic Federation, a left wing organisation influenced by the teaching of Karl Marx which hoped to gain immediate social reform and set in train a movement aiming at the reorganisation of society along more egalitarian lines.[8] Thorne was a staunch member of the federation.

Within four months of Thorne's decision to set up a union he had no less than 20,000 men on the books, a meteoric rise due in no small part to the role played in the recruiting campaign by Karl Marx's daughter, Eleanor, and immigrant and second generation Irishmen like Mike Canty (general secretary), William Ward and Peter Curran.[9] As soon as Thorne felt strong enough he served a demand on gasworks to bring in the three-shift day to replace the two-shift (12 hours) system. The show of strength worked and one of the largest concerns, the South Metropolitan Gas Company complied with the union's demand immediately. Other companies followed. The victory had far-reaching repercussions in labour circles and the lesson learned from the gasworkers' struggle was not lost on other sections of workers.

A then relatively unknown socialist, Ben Tillett, had formed the Tea-Coopers and General Labourers' Union amongst men working on the East India dock in London in 1887. Buoyed by the success of the gasworkers, Tillett presented a demand for a minimum wage of 6d an hour for dockers, the abolition of sub-contracting and of piecework, a minimum hiring of four hours and overtime payments. In pursuance of these claims a dockers' strike took place in the warm summer of 1889. After a five-week struggle, the weight of public opinion was fully behind the men, due in large part to the justice of their case and also to a cleverly-engineered campaign of monster meetings, marches and public debates which were organised by a coterie of talented socialists. Amongst the more prominent were Tom Mann, John Burns, Hyndman and William Morris. With Cardinal Manning acting as mediator, most of the men's demands were soon met and another major victory of the 'new unions' was recorded following swiftly on the success of the gasworkers.[10]

It was then Thorne's turn to press forward the initiative. The employers in many towns in the south of England had met the gasworkers' demand for an eight-hour day but a number of industrial centres in the midlands put up a stiffer resistance. Leeds witnessed one of the fiercest and most bitter struggles. Thorne showed the movement's disregard for what he would have described as sectionally-motivated law by ordering an attack on a group of blacklegs who where working under police protection. Stones, bottles, bricks and every available missile were aimed upon the 'free labour' force by irate strikers. Much to the disgust of the more orthodox trade unionists, Thorne showed no remorse for conducting such an attack.[11] He added insult to injury by claiming that he would do the same thing again if the occasion and the necessity arose. The older men did not like the whiff of grapeshot or the tocsin of class war, but when it came to conducting industrial action, Thorne, Tillett and Mann did not believe in fighting with kid gloves. Their tactics were as rough and as robust as the men they were attempting to unionise. It is a wonder sometimes that they were so restrained in their actions, given the provocation they often had to face from both employers and police, yet the success experienced by these unions up to 1890 was quite considerable. Tillett's union spread to many ports especially in the south and along the east coast of England. In the north-west and Scotland, the National Union of Dock Labourers (NUDL) was set up in 1889 with its headquarters in Liverpool. James Sexton, one of the first members, was the son of a tenant farmer who emigrated from Avoca, Co. Wicklow in the 1870s. His mother was also of Irish descent and Sexton claimed that his grandfather was a Fenian. In 1893 Sexton took over as general secretary of the union, although two other Irishmen from the North probably contributed far more than Sexton in the early days towards the organisation of the NUDL. They were a printer named Richard McGhee, who was a friend of Michael Davitt, and a commercial traveller called Edward McHugh.[12] With such a large number of Irishmen involved in the formation of the new unions, it is not surprising that in the early days of their expansion they should turn their attention across the channel.

The Coalporters' Strike, 1890

Out of all the new unions which sprang so vigorously to life from 1887 onwards, the gasworkers' organisation seems to have been the only one to make any appreciable impact in Ireland, and in Dublin in particular. Havelock Wilson's Sailors' and Firemen's Union managed to gain a foothold in the capital, although its influence was never very widespread nor its foundations very secure.[13] Neither Tillett's Dock, Wharf, Riverside and General Labourers' union nor the NUDL seems to have bothered very much with Dublin in the early days.

Will Thorne, unlike his more radical colleagues, did not neglect to pay due attention to the Irish worker. He was a frequent visitor to the country from 1889 onwards and spoke at meetings throughout the south and south-east in an effort to organise men into a union. Thorne wrote:

> We were opening branches in Ireland at this time where, in many respects, the workers were in advance of their fellows in England. They had a federation of agricultural labourers, general workers and skilled artisans. This form of organisation was very strong in the south and when a strike took place, employers were unable to secure 'blacklegs' or free labour as they were sometimes called.[14]

The organisation to which Thorne referred so warmly was probably the Land and Labour League, set up in the 1880s by the left-wing of the nationalist party in an attempt to forge an alliance between town workers on the one hand and farm labourers and tenant farmers on the other. One of the founders, Cork MP, D. D. Sheehan, was obviously much better informed than Thorne about Irish Labour affairs and much more realistic in his appraisal of the federation's overall performance when he said that the Labour League was confined to Munster and never really affected an alliance between the workers in the town and country.[15] Thorne may well have been impressed by the novelty of the idea but could not have seen the federation operate in any concrete situation to have held such ill-informed views.

On one of his many visits, Thorne was reminded sharply that he was not in England when, to his astonishment, he discovered members of the RIC at meetings, taking notes of all he said. In Dublin, the DMP were equally vigilant. However, the watchful eye of the police did not seem to deter men from joining the union. In his efforts, Thorne was assisted greatly by a number of very able lieutenants such as Peter Curran, who was of Irish extraction and knew his audience well.[16] Moreover, in Dublin itself, there lived a number of talented and militant labour supporters who welcomed the opportunity of outside assistance to form a general labourers' trade union. Amongst these was Jim Connor, author of the 'Red Flag', who at one stage organised the coalporters. Maurice Canty was another activist who became district organiser for Thorne and later founded the corporation workers' union when the gas-workers' union collapsed.

The district secretary of the gasworkers' union was a Dublin printer named Adolphus Shields.[17] A committed socialist, it was a tribute to his powers of persuasion and organisation that he was able to set up, at one stage, a society for left-wing newspaper men, and officials of Dublin Castle.[18] But in 1890, Shields, accompanied by Canty and Connors, was deeply immersed in trade union affairs to the virtual exclusion of political activities. P. T. Daly, a Dublin

Typographical Provident Society member at the time, also contributed to the venture.

By May 1890, the gasworkers' union had 2,000 men on the books at its offices in Sandwith Street, making it the biggest trade organisation in the city. The largest number of recruits came from the dockside yards owned by some 154 coal merchants. These were employed as draymen, bellmen, winchers, bankmen and at filling, wheeling, weighing and loading. Some earned as little as 14s per week while it was difficult for anyone to earn over £1 per week. However, an employers' estimate placed the wages of draymen at between 25s and £2 per week. But this really refers to potential rather than average earnings. Most labourers were potentially capable of bringing home fat wage packets after working an 80-hour week in high season. But in a situation where men were recruited on a daily basis, subject to changeable weather conditions and for perhaps only a four-hour stretch, then to be replaced by a fresh man, annual earnings were often depressed far below the poverty line.

This sudden surge of union activity was sufficient to send shock waves throughout the coal trade in the city and employers determined to face the 'threat' in various ways. Some employers were fearful but did not feel sufficiently strong to take on the union; a larger section adopted a 'wait and see' policy; others agreed to hang fire until an opportunity arose to confront the union. The Coal Merchants' Association was in ferment. However one of the larger employers disagreed with trade unionism 'on principle'. On 23 May McCormick, according to the *Irish Times*, discovered that non-union workers in his yard 'were being pestered by two of the union men (on his staff) to join the society (and) those two men also made themselves disagreeable to the men in other ways'. Both were dismissed on the spot.

The union's account of the event differed sharply from the official press view. It was thought that as soon as McCormick discovered that two of his staff were recruiting men for the union they were discharged without ceremony. That, said the union, constituted victimisation of shop stewards and a strike was declared. McCormick was not a man to give up easily, and swiftly set about protecting his business by recruiting over 100 workers from Mayo and purchasing three large dwellings for the purpose of housing the 'Immigrants'.[19] While he was making such elaborate preparations to beat the union, McCormick was helped to fulfil all orders by his colleagues in the association, who delivered coal throughout the city for him. At the height of the dispute, 40 laden drays left his yard under police protection with the Mayo men driving. McCormick felt sure of victory: when told by the men of their intention to strike, he replied confidently: 'Very well, when you have pawned your clothes, you will return to work.'

Events took a turn for the worse when it was discovered by the men that merchants uninvolved in the dispute were delivering coal for McCormick. On one such run a drayman called at a house with a few bags of fuel only to be told by the occupant that since he was not from McCormick's then he had no right to deliver there. Reluctantly, the harassed driver produced the tell-tale docket revealing that, while he was working for another firm, he was being contracted to fulfil McCormick's orders. Once the cat was out of the bag and the gasworkers' union had managed to wring a confession out of the merchants' association declaring that it 'was customary for other firms to help out and that a few tons of coal had been delivered for him (McCormick) in the early days of the dispute',[20] there was little option but to take punitive action against the other employers. By 2 July, the only coal yard open in the city belonged to McCormick. All the major firms were closed down. There were 2,000 union men on strike and this figure does not include all those indirectly affected. Industry began to feel the force of the strike as coal deliveries dwindled and factory stocks began to run down.

Meanwhile, the union organisers devised a strategy to stimulate morale and maximise the crippling effects of their action on the commercial life of the city. They decided to stop the delivery of coal by bringing out as many men as possible. Men assembled regularly, from 4 a.m. on the quays, and at dawn a procession would wind down past the coalyards urging, persuading and intimidating men on their way to work to join them. On 2 July, some 150 men set out. When they returned their ranks had swollen to over 300.

Feelings ran high on these daily recruiting sorties (perhaps 'press gang' would be a more apt term). On one occasion as the coalporters marched past McCormick's offices on the quays, some women by-standers sang: 'We'll hang John McCormick on a sour apple tree . . .'[21] When the strike spread to depots of Kingstown, the city coalporters marched out in the driving rain to show solidarity with their colleagues. After the eight-mile march they were met by local coalporters who had engaged the services of the Kill-o'-the-Grange fife band for the event.

After a joint meeting the men returned home to the city and on the way a group encountered a McCormick delivery van driven by Thomas McHale, one of the 'imported' Mayomen. His horse was taken by some women marchers while the men set on him. The timely arrival of the police saved McHale and led to the arrest of some of the marchers.

Not all such incidents ended peacefully. Despite warnings from union leaders not to risk jail for trouncing a 'scab', men continued to attack delivery wagons and intimidate men on the way to work. On one occasion delivery horses were stabbed, and men were often beaten up in quiet back streets where police were afraid to venture. The penalties for such offences were quite severe, particularly when justice was administered by Judge Swifte, who was later to play a major role in the Larkin trials. On one occasion two labourers, Dennis Dunne and Thomas Colgan, came before him on assault charges. The plaintiff, James Wilson, told the court that he was a new lad at McCormick's yard and that while on his way to work, he had been followed and tripped by Dunne while Colgan 'kicked his hat'. He did not wish to press charges, but the justice said that assault had been committed and each received 14 days hard labour. (He would not take into account that both were drunk at the time of the offence). In another assault case arising out of the strike, Michael Walsh was sentenced to two months hard labour. Yet such severe sentences handed down to men without any previous convictions seemed to have little or no effect in deterring others from committing similar offences. As the strike progressed the level of violence rose and the number of assault incidents increased.

The main thrust of the union plan was alarming the city's non-labouring classes. Shields, Canty and Daly set about carrying the battle into the employers' camp. Instead of confining the strike to its source—McCormick's yard—other employers who had implicated themselves by surreptitiously delivering coal for a beleaguered colleague were also penalised by the union. This constituted a 'dismaying departure from traditional industrial practices', according to the *Irish Times*. As if that was not enough, the coalporters went a step further. At an open-air meeting in Phoenix Park, it was decided:

> That we the workers of Dublin hereby promise to cease work in any firm or establishment of business in Dublin or elsewhere on the delivery of any coal from Messrs McCormick.[22]

The sympathetic strike was put into use perhaps for the first time in the city, a tactic described by the chairman of the Board of Trade, George Askwith, in 1913 as:

> ... a refusal on the part of men who may have no complaint against their own conditions of employment to continue work because in the ordinary course of their work they came in contact with goods in some way connected with firms whose employees have been locked out or are on strike.[23]

The power of the 'secondary boycott' was soon discovered. About 20 labourers in Messrs Walter Brown and Co., Hanover St, walked out when coal was delivered by 'scabs' from McCormicks and work stopped in Bewleys and Drapers for the same reason. Later the men returned to Brown's mill on condition that no coal would be accepted from firms in dispute with the union. Labourers in the other two businesses returned when management gave the same undertaking and, as a sign of goodwill, each donated £2 to pay for the men's union subscription.

The leader writer in the *Irish Times* was incensed by the union's high-handed action:

> There is not a theory of strike upon which such conduct can be excused. The spirit of a fair strike is that which desires to limit it and to end it as soon as possible ... What we see here is a disposition to extend it to the utmost and render it impossible of settlement until all parties are worn down by privation and annoyance. The propagation of such difficulites is no function of a workmen's union.[24]

At the suggestion by the workmen to broaden the dispute and enlist the support of cross-channel unions in their cause, if McCormick did not send away his 'imported labour' and take on the old hands again, the leader writer appeared to be as bewildered as he was angry. He could not believe that anyone would seriously suggest involving sailors and firemen and the Amalgamated Society of Railway Servants in a coalporters dispute:

> It is a form of trade unionism which far transgresses any liberty of combination which law or natural right can allow to those who have their labour to dispose of and have no more. Freedom of labour is a principle which must have legislative and trading respect paid to it.[25]

The 'new unionism' was no respecter of tradition. As the merchants sought to replace the striking and locked out workers, the coalporters pushed their campaign a stage further. Since the delivery of coal had been made almost impossible within the city, it was decided to cut off the supply at source. Two colliers, the *Ensign* and the *Curlew*, were prevented from discharging their cargoes in Dublin and both sailed for Belfast. But there, as Maurice Canty told a meeting, the Orangemen stood by Dublin labourers and blocked the ships.[26]

The union was strengthened financially by gifts of large subscriptions from politicians and local unions. Michael Davitt sent a cheque for £3 'with my best wishes for the success of the coalporters' stand in defence of their organisation'. The Amalgamated Society of Tailors gave £30; the Bakers £30; London Council of the Labourers' union £50; gasworks labourers £13; the local dockers' union £2; £10 from the bottlemakers' society, and the builders' labourers £10.

The Coal Merchants' Association, representing the larger business concerns, stood firm and resolved to see the dispute through to the bitter end. However, some of the smaller merchants faced bankruptcy if the dispute was not ended rapidly. Three of the smaller employers were so desperate that they attended a meeting of the union in Sandwith Street. Mr Pudlow, who was only a coal merchant 'in a small way', determined to pay his men whether they returned or not, as did Mr McDonald, who agreed that the men were justified in going on strike. However, the men refused to return to work.

On 6 July, at a meeting in the Phoenix Park, the coalporters debated a peace which provided strong opposition from Maurice Canty. A motion urged a return to work on receipt of signed guarantees from the merchants not to support McCormick either 'directly or indirectly', and the controversial motion was passed with a slender majority. However, the peace feeler was rejected by the Merchants' Association 'as contrary to all usages of recognised ordinary trade principles'. Nonetheless, eight non-association merchants went to the union rooms to sign the guarantee on 9 July. The same day the men returned to work and bellmen queued to get coal supplies.

Behind the scenes, Fr W. C. Magill had been acting as a go-between and unofficial peace-maker. He had gained the confidence and respect of both union and association. Archbishop Walsh also offered to invervene if both sides thought it would be helpful. Fr Magill's peace mission suddenly began to pay off and there was no longer any need for the Archbishop to involve himself in the dispute. While the Merchant's Association rejected the coalporters' formula for a resumption of work on 9 July, it had made some conciliating noises; a composite resolution was adopted protesting that the 'merchants have never interfered with unions, nor have they any intention of so doing'. This implied a criticism of, and a break with, McCormick who was opposed to trade unions on principle.

A return to work was proposed on the basis that all future disputes would go to arbitration, one nominee coming from the merchants, one from the men and an umpire to be mutually chosen. After first rejecting the proposals, the men then accepted them as a basis for discussion. At a meeting in the Dublin Steam Shipping Company, the coalporters finally agreed to return to work and accept the employers' resolution in good faith. The news was greeted with relief by the leader writer of the *Irish Times* on 11 July:

> The point that seems to be settled by the strike is that when a difference springs up in an establishment it should be kept strictly within its own bounds. It is madness for men outside to make the particular dispute, which may be capable of easy settlement, if not agreed their vital concern also, and proceed to punish their own masters and themselves and damage the public and make enemies of them, from a quixotic notion that they are to be expected to stand by their fellow-workers.

However, peace celebrations proved premature for the settlement terms were ambiguous and open to conflicting interpretation. Moreover, the coalporters were not interested in a return to work without victory. The achievements of the struggle were not really tangible, but the affair had been valuable in another way—it proved, beyond all doubt, the durability of union institutions while under attack and the resilience and fighting spirit of the members. Some trade union leaders were anxious to press home their advantage and re-enter the fray without delay for if some real concessions could be wrung from employers, it was felt, then the union would be able to double its membership at least. After all, there were 14,000 labourers in the city alone, not counting more specialist forms of general labour.

Within two weeks of returning to work the union submitted a memorandum to the merchants outlining a list of grievances and demanding a 5s (25%) increase in weekly wages. Maurice Canty claimed that the men had given six weeks' strike notice when they were only obliged to give two. The men were only given one minute's notice of the lockout that followed. On 31 August, the coalporters' strike notice expired, but before the strike became official the merchants agreed to pay off the men. As far as the union was concerned this constituted a lockout.

Angered by the merchants' precipitous action, the local union leadership was more resolute than ever to fight. At a meeting in Sandwith Street, Adolphus Shields claimed that an attempt was being made to smash the union and outlined a strategy to defeat the merchants. He wanted to play the employer at his own game. 'While capital could not do without labour, labour could do without capital,' he argued. Why not bring in coal ships to be unloaded and distributed by union men and go into competition with the big yards in the city for as long as the merchants remain intransigent, he asked. Three days later, union bellmen were already on the streets ensuring that coal supplies reached the poor. Others waited in readiness for the union ship to arrive so that the coal war could begin in earnest.

Another monster meeting was held in the Phoenix Park and delegates from most unions attended. Significantly, many labourers from Guinness's brewery turned up in solidarity. Again Shields appealed for the men to help crush the attempt being made to 'smash their combination'. Canty told the meeting that 15,000 trade unions in the city were united in one bond, and he included Guinness employees amongst them. The organiser of the Sailors' and Firemens' union, Mr Lee, gave the backing of his union and promised substantial support if necessary in the future. Once again dockers outside Dublin stood by their colleagues in the capital. The *Captain McClure*, a coalship which belonged to the General Steam Navigation Company, had made an unsuccessful bid to discharge its cargo in Dublin. It then sailed for Cork where the dockers also refused to handle the goods.[29] Meanwhile, the strikers were paid a mere £200 from the London office, and it was not possible to conduct a long campaign with such meagre support.

On 18 September, the coalporters capitulated and signed a weak agreement with 14 leading Dublin firms. Employers were allowed to employ anyone 'in accordance with requirements' while the workers could not refuse to deliver coal without a fortnight's notice. Thus the union had been finally forced to concede one of the main planks of the 'new union' movement's platform—opposition to free labour. Neither did the second clause uphold the coalporters' right to refuse delivery of merchandise to a yard in dispute with the union. One concession to labour was the employers' recognition of the right to a week's notice by his workers. Here, too, there was a significant qualification, for casual labour was not entitled to notice and it could be argued that practically all staff were casual in the coal trade. In the event of a dispute arising out of the application of the agreement, a committee of equal number of merchants and men was to be set up to discuss the matter.

The *Irish Times* of 14 September was as happy with the agreement as the men were displeased:

> We presume the points of the agreement are a fair compromise giving the men some advantage but maintaining, which is the important matter, the freedom of the employer in the control and management of their business . . . the attempt to restrain masters in their enterprise is fatal. There must be freedom for capital if there is to be good and steady wage for labour.

Disillusioned by the penny-pinching attitude of the British executive, the coalporters had good cause to feel that defeat had been snatched from the jaws of victory. When the strike was going well and Shields' plan to set up a workers-run coal firm was just getting off the ground, the news came that London was reluctant to back a protracted dispute. In fairness to Thorne, his union was under great financial pressure from other quarters at the time. The initial honeymoon period of indiscriminate recruitment had brought with it attendant responsibilities. Not all victories were won as easily as the South Metropolitan Gas Company affair in 1889. The employers had regrouped and gone on the counter-attack, and while the union was struggling to establish itself in some of the largest industrial centres in Britain, Dublin was relegated to a low position on the list of priorities. While the local coalporters and gasmen complained loudly of Thorne's parsimoniousness, they failed to realise that the Dublin branch was not self-supporting and a liability on the union's books. Consequently, it would be the first to go under in a time of crisis.

The gasworkers' union in Dublin limped on for a few more years. In 1891 about 250 coalporters went on strike for a 25% wage increase, and were joined by the canalmen, who sought a 15% rise. Dublin was not the only city in which Thorne had trouble, for there were no fewer than 24 other disputes going in England at the same time. Nevertheless, he came over with his secretary, Mike Canty, to deal with the strike and arrived to find the union books in chaos; most of the members were in arrears and, thus, were ineligible for strike pay.[30] He paid 50 men the first night and 150 the following evening, but trouble arose when men out of benefit, and those who had not been in the union six months, demanded equal treatment with fully paid-up members. Tempers were lost when a consensus urged payment for all without discrimination. Finally, when Thorne and Mike Canty were threatened with defenestration, they ran for the door and down the stone steps followed by angry porters, 'and did a flying spring for the hotel somewhere in Sackville Street'.[31] Later Thorne remarked: 'It was the fastest and one of the most exciting moments in my life as a trade union official.'[32] Naturally, the experience did little to endear cross-channel workers to him. Dublin coalporters, he confessed, 'were the worst set of men he ever had to deal with'. Thorne held local employers in equally low regard. They resented the presence of a British union. Besides, 'those employers were some of the roughest types of men' he had met up with in his travels as a negotiator.[33] In 1892, the two largest Irish branches, in Dublin and Belfast, were wound up. The union had run into difficulties in England, and was now concentrated in the London area. The number of full-time organisers was reduced to six to serve eleven divisions.[34]

The brief interlude of 'new unionism' was of profound importance for the development of general workers' unions in the city. It illustrated the latent radicalism of the coalporters and their willingness to participate in militant trade union activity. The sympathetic strike or secondary boycott idea was taken up spontaneously by the coalporters without any real direction from the union executive. Other groups of workers in the city shared a common desire to join a union but they did not get the opportunity. They had to wait a further fifteen years before the chance presented itself. Shields, Canty and Connors bequeathed to their trade union successors an example of what could be achieved with a little effort, finance and imagination. For a brief period the men had been given an experience of self-dignity and the power to affect changes in their abysmal working conditions. In the hiatus, lasting until 1907, the general workers of the city were abandoned in the main to fend for, and defend, themselves on a personal basis. When the task to unionise this sector was taken up once again, the new organisers may not have been aware of the fact but they were building on and benefiting from the example and tradition of 1890. In 1907, through the work of O'Lehane, of the drapers' assistants and other left-wing officials, the general workers could depend upon the full backing of the craft unions. All that Dublin lacked, to set the movement in train, was a talented, dedicated and somewhat ruthless organiser, working with the 'risk capital' and benediction of a solvent union.

James Larkin in Belfast

In January 1907, the National Union of Dock Labourers (NUDL) sent one of its ablest full-time officials to organise workers in the North. James Larkin was an obvious choice for such a difficult assignment: he was second-generation Irish and had developed a fine understanding of the divisive effect of sectarianism on the working class through his organising tours of Scotland and his trade union activities in Liverpool.

Larkin was born in Liverpool in 1876, the second eldest of an Irish couple from Killeavy, Co. Armagh. His father, James, died a young man in 1887 when Larkin was only eleven years old. Both he and his brother, Hugh, went to work to support their widowed mother and the three younger children. At different times, the young Larkin was employed as butcher's assistant, paper-hanger, French polisher and docker. Living and labouring in Liverpool's Irish diaspora, Larkin experienced the personal toll of growing up in the festering slums of industrial Britain.

After an accident at the docks, Larkin was unable to work for nearly six months. He spent his time reading by day and attending socialist and labour party meetings at night. Thus began his lifelong commitment to the labour movement. His conversion to trade unionism came much later. In 1898 he had helped establish a Liverpool branch of the Workers' Union of Britain and Ireland, founded in the same year by the militant, Tom Mann. The latter was a member of the Social Democratic Federation and an official of the Amalgamated Society of Engineers who felt compelled by the selective and sectional nature of his union to form a breakaway society which 'barred none and welcomed all',[35] It embraced all industries and grades of skill, including the very highest. The Workers' Union stood halfway between 'general' and 'industrial' unionism in concept and objectives. However, Larkin ceased to play any part in the running of the Liverpool branch of the union after it had been established. He devoted himself almost entirely to the political side of the labour movement claiming, according to James Sexton, 'that trade unionism was a played-out, economic fallacy.[36] But in the spring of 1905, he had occasion to revise his opinion. Larkin had been an inactive member of the NUDL since 1901. He worked as a stevedore and had merited the name 'the Rusher' among the men because of his zealous efforts to get a job done as swiftly as possible. According to the fatuous suggestion of Sexton, Larkin 'went so far as to claim that his driving methods at the docks were promoted by a sincere desire to demonstrate to his fellow workmen some of the evils of the capitalist system.[37]

Larkin decided that all stevedores in his dock area should belong to the union. Most of these men were members of the NUDL but had allowed their membership to lapse after promotion. Over 600 men struck in order to force their bosses to rejoin the union. Larkin led the struggle after 'blacklegs' were brought in to work the boats. The effort failed, but Larkin played a conspicuous role and was appointed temporary organiser of the NUDL. So successful was he in attracting new members that he was soon made a permanent official of the union.

In Scotland his recruiting drives met with great enthusiasm and he managed to cross the sectarian divide with little difficulty. The situation in Liverpool was somewhat the same as he was to find later in Belfast. There the Irish community was split between southern Catholic nationalists and northern Protestant unionists. The former were employed on the docks while the latter controlled the carting jobs.[38] As election agent in 1906 for the general secretary of the NUDL, James Sexton, Larkin exhibited his skills as an organiser of unparalleled ability. Sexton was a Catholic and a Labour Party candidate. His rival for the West Toxteth seat, R. P. Houston, owed his comfortable 4,000 majority in the last election to the Orange Order:

> But nothing could frighten Jim. He plunged recklessly into the fray where the fighting was most furious, organised gigantic processions against Chinese labour on the Rand, faced hostile mobs saturated with religious bigotry who were howling for our blood, and last, but by no means least, competed with our opponents in the risky game of impersonation then played at almost every election in Liverpool.[39]

The frenetic campaign, which at one stage involved dressing men like Chinese labourers and marching through Liverpool behind a glass-sided hearse containing a coffin draped with a Union Jack, paid off and Sexton cut Houston's majority by over 3,000 votes.

When Larkin arrived in Belfast he was once again thrown very much onto his own resources. He was a convinced socialist with a new found commitment to the trade union movement which he recognised as a means of effecting radical changes in the structure of society. And like many adult converts, he was more zealous about his mission than the lifelong adherents and more impatient with his trade union colleagues. As a Dublin employer was to comment to the Board of Trade negotiator, George Askwith, in 1913: 'I don't know how you can talk to that fellow Larkin . . . you can't argue with the prophet Isaiah.'[40]

Larkin set about his task in Belfast with great energy and determination. Soon the 'tall, thin man with long dark hair and blue-grey mobile eyes, . . . wearing a very heavy black and drooping moustache, a large black sombrero hat and a kind of black toga' was a familiar sight in the area of York Street—the heart of Belfast's dockland.[41] He had the appearance of an athlete and 'would pass unnoticed in an eleven of Australian cricketers', when he spoke, 'he had common English faults of speech and an Irish intonation'.[42] Within six months of his arrival, the city's employers and civil authorities had cause to become intimately acquainted with his beliefs and unorthodox methods. Where employers proved intransigent, he proved even more resolute in his efforts to gain basic rights for workers. By August, the city was in turmoil:

> Guards (were) at the railway stations, double sentries with loaded rifles at alternate lamp-posts of the Royal Avenue, a very few lorries, with constabulary sitting on the bales and soldiers on either side, proceeding to guarded, congested, but lifeless docks, and ten thousand soldiers in and about the city. There had been fights in the streets, charges of cavalry, the Riot Act read, shooting to disperse wrecking mobs, a few men and women killed and scores wounded, and the whole business of the city at a standstill.[43]

The trouble began in May when some NUDL members refused to work with non-union labour at York Dock. Larkin repudiated their action and the men agreed to return to work the following day only to find that their places had been filled by 'free labour' sent from Liverpool by the Shipping Federation. These men were part of a strike-breaking task force which had been set up by British shipping magnates earlier in the century to deal with the threat coming from the more professionally run new unions. Another source of supply for strike-hit companies was the National Free Labour Association. Founded in 1896 by the 'king of the blacklegs', William Collison, it had 9,278 registered members in 1911.[44] These men were prepared to travel and put up with the discomfort of living in barrack-like quarters over a business premises under threat of assault for the duration of a strike and, of course, for wages above the local rate. The fifty 'free labourers' sent by the Federation to Belfast forced the local authorities to draft 500 troops into the city to cordon off the dock area from the strikers.

A few carters struck in sympathy with the dockers and were soon joined by many of their colleagues who were taking the opportunity of the dockers' strike to press for a 5s a week increase, bringing their earnings up to 26s for 60 hours' work. A 2s offer was turned down, and the Master Carters' Association retaliated by threatening to lock out the rest of the their men. On 4 July, carters of sixty firms pre-empted this move by ceasing work.[45]

The situation on the docks was a little more complicated. There the conditions under which men worked were far below what British dockers had won in 1889. Dock labourers were very much at the mercy of stevedores who set arbitrary pay rates for unloading and often two gangs working under different bosses on the same boat would receive different rates. As in Dublin in 1890, some would be paid $3\frac{1}{2}$d a ton while others would get 4d. The stevedore often demanded 6d a ton from the companies and pocketed the balance after paying off the men. Larkin's demands were modest; freedom for workers to join the union; a wage increase that would give his men 'the full, round orb of the dockers' tanner, plus 3d overtime', and the sacking of all 'free labourers'. The coal merchants, hit by the dock strike and unable to get supplies, locked out their men over the weekend of 12 July. Furthermore, they issued a statement signed by eighteen firms upholding the employers' inalienable right to hire and fire whomsoever they chose. They rejected the union's claim to operate a closed-shop system, a demand which, incidentally, Larkin at no time made during the dispute. But the statement went further by adding that 'no person representing any union or combination will after this date be recognised by any of us'.[46] The coal merchants also threatened a general lockout of the entire trade if even the smallest section of men struck without giving three days' written notice of their intention and grievances.

The attitude of the coal merchants, though extreme, was not exceptional. All employers involved in the dispute shared the same sentiments; while many were not prepared to state their views so explicitly, the effect was the same. The chairman of the Belfast Shipping Company, Thomas Gallaher, and his colleagues would not meet Larkin 'under any circumstances'.[47] By mid-July there were 2,500 men out on the streets: some 500 were dockers, 1,000 were carters and the remainder coal labourers. The problem for the authorities was worsened when a section of the RIC took 'industrial action'. Policemen had been bitterly disappointed by the failure to implement the findings of a Royal Commission report on RIC grievances. On 24 July, after a series of demands had led to the suspension of a number of constables, an acting commissioner was knocked down by his subordinates during a rowdy meeting in a police barracks. Constable Barrett emerged as the leader of the dissidents. Larkin took advantage of the unrest to spring to the support of the police. Earlier in the strike, he had told workers repeatedly that no decent, self-respecting person would be found in the RIC. On 16 July, he was solicitous for their welfare:

> The police were working eighteen hours a day at present and were not getting one penny extra and, if they dared, many of them would also go on strike. He would like to know if the heads of the police force had made any application to the authorities for extra pay for the men.[48]

Most RIC members were not fooled by this sudden conversion of convenience. An unidentified constable in the *Belfast Telegraph* on 29 July defended the right of the police to make their protest but as for the strikers:

> We cannot forget also the abuse that was hurled on us from strike platforms during the early part of the strike, when we were told no decent man could wear our uniform, and we will get our grievances remedied without the aid of men whose motives for assisting us I, for one, am not sure of.

The constable left nobody in any doubt as to where his personal allegiances lay. Strikers and dissident policemen had little, if anything, in common:

> We will also, you may be sure, disabuse the minds of the rowdies of Belfast of the idea they seem to have got during the past few days that they can do as they like. We will do our duty loyally in the meantime and the rowdies will get their eyes opened if they imagine we will not keep an eye on them as usual.

Indeed, the unidentified constable was far more representative of the feelings of his fellow officers than the 'strike' leader, Barrett. The latter had refused to ride with a 'blackleg' carter and was suspended for his pains.[49] This proved a highly popular move against his colleagues who feared for their own personal safety rather than felt any overt sympathy with the strikers. Less than 200 RIC men were directly involved in the action and many of these came from Musgrave Street barracks. The majority of the force preferred to process their claims in a more orderly and peaceful manner as reflected their role as professional enforcers of the law.

By the end of July all overt friction inside the RIC ended with the transfer of the dissidents to country stations, but its effects on the direction of the strike were decisive. Over 7,000 troops were drafted into the city leading to fierce rioting on the Falls Road in which two people were shot dead and many seriously injured. At another level, Larkin's support for the police dissidents had helped crystalise sectarian differences amongst the beleaguered strikers. This had come about when the Catholic daily, the *Irish News*, had given full news coverage to the RIC 'revolt' and opened its letters' page to the dissidents. Sectarian feelings were running high in Belfast at the time and many Protestant employers inclined to the view that the strike was a nationalist plot supported by a group of 'fifth columnists' in the police force. Thus a Belfast employer, F. H. Crawford, wrote to a southern Unionist friend:

> What a blessing all the rioting took place in the Catholic quarter of the City. This branded the whole thing as a Nationalist movement. Larkin the leader is the grandson of Larkin the Manchester Martyr (?) . . . The whole strike was a big political plot to ruin Belfast trade. The Nationalists are sick of people pointing out to them the prosperity of Belfast and protestant Ulster, they want to ruin us and this is one move in that direction. The serious part of the business is that they have a lot of Protestants, who call themselves Independent orangemen, and a few demagogues who love to hear their own voice.[50]

Had Larkin steered clear of the RIC dispute, he most certainly would have been better positioned to deal with the patently preposterous claim that the strike was a 'nationalist-inspired plot'. But once he opted to identify strikers and police dissidents, he was escalating the dispute to a level over which he had no control. Moreover, the authorities were then forced to give credence to the wild assertions of some of the more extreme employers that Larkin was out to subvert the most fundamental institutions of the state and the troops were called in. Besides, the sensational press headlines brought the timid James Sexton to Belfast quite determined to settle the affair swiftly and with as little cost to the NUDL as possible. Meanwhile, Larkin was the subject of some ugly sectarian rumours. It was claimed, without foundation, that Catholics were receiving preferential treatment over their Protestant fellow workmates from the NUDL. Indeed, much of the credit given to Larkin for holding Protestant and Catholic workmen together in the early days of the strike has been somewhat exaggerated and misplaced, and not enough of the credit has gone to the Grand Master of the Independent Orange Order, Lindsay Crawford, who was the editor of the *Ulster Guardian.* This breakaway organisation was formed in 1903 by T. H. Sloan after he had been ejected from the main Orange Order, but the leadership of the new organisation soon passed into the hands of Crawford who tempered Sloan's sectarian outbursts and gradually reshaped the image of the IOO. By shrewd politicking, Crawford had a 3,000 word manifesto adopted by the society in 1905. It advocated unity between Catholics and Protestants to shape a new Ireland: the Catholic Church was castigated for its devious political role; and most explosively, it advocated a form of Home Rule on a basis of true nationalism.

There were some defections when delegates realised the nature of the document which they had endorsed, but by 1907 the IOO was quite strong with almost exclusive working-class support. Crawford gave his whole-hearted support to the strike in the columns of the *Ulster Guardian.* He spoke at labour rallies and the IOO made a collection for the strikers at the Field on 12 July. Numerically limited, the IOO had still sufficient influence to allay the hostilities of the Protestant workers towards their Catholic counterparts for a brief respite at the beginning of the strike. Larkin was also influential in this regard but without Crawford he would have been far less effective.

On 13 August, a new member of the Board of Trade, George Askwith, was sent from London to help his colleague, Isaach Mitchell, bring an end to the strike which had crippled Belfast for over two months. After a briefing session with the Permanent Under-Secretary of State, Sir Anthony MacDonnell, they set out to find Larkin:

> He was very surprised to see us, but after intimating that the British Government and all connected with it might go to hell, launched into long exhortations on the woes of the carters and dockers and denunciation of the bloodthirsty employers, collectively and individually. I said that all this might be true, though not having been an official for more than ten days, I could scarcely be responsible for the acts of the British Government and in fact wanted some help myself. Could he tell me what the carters wanted, and put it on paper? Unless he

desired to continue the strike till starvation stopped it, it might be useful to know the claim. For all I knew, the employers might be willing to grant their demands; but I had not yet seen those gentlemen. I knew that carters are always difficult in a dispute, because of the variety of grades, the strict relative position of grades, and the importance of conditions, such as overtime, distance, care of horses, etc. Mr Larkin could not tell exactly what the carters wanted, so it was suggested some of them should be got, and we would jointly try to find out. This idea interested him and it was done. We got chairs from somewhere, and sat down to work it out, sending for some lunch to consume as we worked. So great was Mr Larkin's zest on this new tack, and so angry did he get at the carters' differences of opinion and changing proposals, that he did most of the talking, with an occasional phrase from me, and gave them lectures which no employer would dare to utter.[51]

Armed with a set of proposals Askwith went to the employers. The following day a provisional agreement was drawn up and put to the men who were called to St Mary's Hall by a crier with a bell. The carters were offered a 5s per week increase but the closed-shop principle was not conceded. Larkin explained the proposals to the men. Beside him was Sexton, armed with two revolvers in case of disturbances. The din was so great from inside the crowded hall that the Lord Mayor and his aides 'seriously discussed whether I (Askwith) ought to be rescued'. After a hectic hour and a half the agreement was ratified. Extraordinary scenes followed. Askwith went to leave for the Town Hall for formal signing through a side door:

> The passage was full of women, shawls round their heads. 'What is it?' they cried in unison. 'It's all right,' I said. 'Your boys go back tomorrow morning' . . . Women suffer from strikes. Some of them knelt in the mud to pray, others seized my hands, some kissed me, and others clapped my back, shot me through into the Royal Avenue, up which I ran so fast, with two or three thousand shouting women, dockers, and carters after me, that I could not answer at first, from lack of breath, the eager inquiries in the Lord Mayor's parlour as to what had happened.[52]

But this really was a qualified victory. The coalporters had gone back to work in mid-July with some gains, yet there were 500 members of the NUDL employed on the docks who were left to the tender mercies of the shipping companies. The dockers drifted back to work with nothing to show for their long strike. Some were considerably worse off because the shipping companies would not re-employ them, having filled their places with new men during the dispute.

In an effort to combat the ecumenical NUDL an employer-backed sectarian union was formed. Called the Belfast Coal-porters' and Carters' Benefit Society, it catered exclusively for Protestant workers and was a source of bitter friction on the waterfront. Labour troubles in Belfast was far from over. At the Belfast Trades and Labour Council on 5 October, Larkin claimed that the dock strike was still on, as the Barrow, Heysham and Fleetwood Steamship Companies' labourers had not been reinstated.[53] On 26 October, an NUDL union official found out that two members of the new society were working on the *SS Princess*, a ship chartered by the firm of Wright Ltd, Queen's Quay. When the company refused to dismiss the two non-NUDL men Larkin's workers quit work. About a dozen members of the new society were employed to discharge the ship and it became apparent that the new society had recruited members in most dockside businesses, including the company of the city's leading coal merchant, John Kelly. Over 300 NUDL men ceased work there when Kelly refused to sack members of the new society.

There was more trouble the following month amongst the coalmen who claimed the employers had broken the July agreement, but the national executive of the NUDL, frightened by the 'wildcat' tactics of Larkin, were not prepared to back a prolonged dispute. Sexton arrived in Belfast and ordered the men back, giving them to understand that he had reached a compromise with the employers. There was bitter disappointment the following day when the coalporters discovered that on returning to work no agreement had been arrived at and they were powerless to combat the ensuing victimisation.

The morale of the men was shattered. A further blow was dealt to the union, as a non-sectarian force, by the re-emergence of the bigot Sloan as a popular force in working class areas. Lindsay Crawford's spell of popularity was very much an aberration but it happened to coincide quite fortuitously with Larkin's push for new members. Towards the end of 1907 the sectarian pattern of industrial affairs had re-asserted itself. Crawford clung tenaciously to his post as editor of the *Ulster Guardian* and continued to champion the workers' right to a living wage and improved working conditions, but he was doing his job against the background of heightening sectarianism. In June 1908 he was dismissed from his editorship, and two years later emigrated to Canada, leaving Belfast to pass through one of its most formative sectarian phases untempered by the moderation of the former grand master of the Independent Orange Order. Larkin, too, had experienced the double frustration of working in the particularly difficult surroundings of Belfast encumbered by the over-vigilant eye of an unsympathetic and diffident union executive. Impatient with his slow progress and disappointed by his many failures, Larkin grew restive and decided to look elsewhere for a more suitable place to locate the Irish headquarters of the NUDL.

Trouble in Newry

On 27 September, 1908, a branch of the NUDL was formed in the important port of Newry after a meeting in the town hall addressed by the Secretary of the Belfast branch of the union, Cllr Michael McKeown. Larkin proposed a motion condemning the Lord Mayor of Belfast, the Right Honourable Earl of Shaftesbury, for drafting troops into the city to intimidate the workers. The motion also extended sympathy with the relatives of the 'murdered girl, Margaret Lennon and youth, Charles McMullan', who were shot by troops during rioting on the Falls Road. The proceedings were quite emotional, and many local dockers joined the union afterwards. James Fearon, who had worked with Larkin as an organiser in Scotland, was made branch secretary for Newry and Dundalk. A docker and a life-long socialist, his speech was rough and his methods of recruiting men even rougher. Known locally as 'Round-the-Ring', probably because of his way of addressing meetings, he was quick to get results. Militancy and aggression were the keynotes of his campaign.

By November, the NUDL had enlisted sufficient members in Dundalk and Drogheda to blacklist three Belfast-owned colliers bound for Newry. There they lay for a number of days and were forced to leave the port undischarged. The action was directed against Belfast shipowners only in sympathy with the men who had come out against the employment of members of the sectarian Coalporters' and Carters' Benefit Society.

On 30 November, Larkin and Fearon held a recruiting meeting in Warrenpoint, six miles from Newry, where the merchants threatened to send Belfast ships in future. Two days later a crane driver was dismissed, probably because of his decision to join the union. The dockers halted work, and attempts were made to recruit sufficient local non-union labour, at a bounty of £1 per man in addition to the ordinary rate, in an effort to break the strike.

Once again the additional scope given under the 1906 Trades Disputes Act was put into operation by the workers. A strong picket was mounted in the dock area to discourage any of the local men from accepting the £1 bounty. Police reinforcements were rushed to Warrenpoint from the surrounding towns of Bangor, Comber, Donaghadee, Gilford, Newry, Newtownards and Rostrevor when it was learned that thirty-five 'blacklegs' recruited by the Shipping Federation in Belfast were being employed to carry on the work of the port.

Picket reinforcements were brought from Newry but the police were sufficiently strong to get through the noisy phalanx of strikers and begin work. 'Round-the-Ring' persisted in his right, under the 1906 Trades Disputes Act, to persuade the 'blacklegs' peacefully to halt work. After receiving permission from the police to go ahead, he succeeded in inducing a craneman and five others to join the strikers.

The imported workmen were slow and inefficient and were further hampered by the hamfisted efforts of a motor mechanic to operate the crane. Feelings ran so high against the free labour at Warrenpoint that food and accommodation was provided for them in a large shed on the docks. In Newry some local coal merchants were threatened with violence by several strikers. In this heated atmosphere the Newry gasworkers, most of whom had joined the union, contrary to its constituion, threatened to strike. Fearon urged that stokers should be given a 3s increase bringing them up to the English rate of 30s per week. He also sought rises in basic pay for assistant stokers who earned 23s; fitters received £1; lamplighters got 17s; and labourers were the worst off with 15s per week.[54]

The gasworkers did not strike, but the effects of the dock dispute began to hit local industry. Several mills put their workers on short-time because of the shortage of coal. Leading Newry coal merchants, F. Fisher and F. Ferris, warned that unless the men returned to work within 24 hours they would apply to the Shipping Federation for free labourers and request the military to send infantry to the town for the protection of their workers.

On 11 December a public meeting was scheduled to take place in Margaret Square to be addressed by James Larkin, but behind the scenes the Catholic Bishop of Dromore, Dr O'Neill, had been working to bring the dispute to a speedy end. Negotiations had reached a delicate stage and in an effort to avoid upsetting the progress already achieved by the wild statements usually made at a mass meeting, the rally was called off.

A draft agreement was presented to the men which they accepted with two reservations. Fearon objected to the clauses which upheld the absolute right of the employer to hire whoever he wished and obliged the men to discharge all boats unconditionally. On 12 December, a package deal embodying the two objectionable clauses was accepted by the men. However the agreement was not entirely one-sided and by no means an abject surrender to the employers. True, the men had compromised two fundamental principles but these were really unachievable in the industrial climate of Newry. In Dublin, gasworkers had been forced to make similar concessions in 1890, and all three sections of the Belfast workforce who struck in 1907—carters, coalporters and dockers—were obliged to do likewise.

On the positive side, the merchants agreed to employ 'at their own expense a responsible man who shall engage and have charge of the men without any interference whatever'.[55] This went a long way towards obviating the pernicious influence of the predatory stevedore who could exact and withhold pay from his gang. Men were also to be engaged 'regardless of their religion or political beliefs or whether they are trade unionists or non-trade unionists'. The inclusion of this religious and political stipulation was of particular concern to men seeking employment in Fisher's yard. In the past there had been charges levelled against him over his predilection for Protestant workers. In nationalist Newry where many of the larger employers were Unionist the political directive spoke for itself.

A conciliation board was to be set up comprising two representatives of the harbour board, two *bona-fide* labourers accustomed to work at steamers in the Newry basin, and two representatives of the employers. If the board could not agree at a time of dispute, the matter was to be handed to a mutually-agreed arbitrator and his word was to be final. There was to be no stoppage of work during this process.

The terms were to run for twelve months but within three days of signing some trade unionists struck without warning. A ship owned by the Newry Provincial Coal Company had discharged 300 tons of its 500 ton cargo at Warrenpoint during the dispute. When the collier arrived at Newry the dockers there refused to work on the ship unless they received payment for the entire original cargo of 500 tons. The employers retaliated by scrapping the agreement entirely. Three firms immediately reverted to the old practice by appointing stevedores instead of the 'independent person' preferred by the men and provided under the terms of the defunct pact. Nearly twenty of Newry's leading employers signed a notice which was posted in the town stating that 'no man connected with the union will receive employment' in their yards.[56]

The only defensible explanation for such high-handed and precipitous action by the men rested in the conviction that the agreement had been signed over the head of the branch secretary, James Fearon. The negotiators appear to have ignored the truculent and demanding 'Round-the-Ring', particularly in the latter stage of discussions. Fearon certainly felt this was the case. His views were not compatible with the moderate line taken by the Bishop, and no sooner had the terms of the agreement been made public than he denounced them as a 'sell-out'.

The men had cause to regret such tactless and thoughtless action. Strikers' families had suffered greatly throughout the dispute and as the struggle recommenced the hardship endured by the women and children increased. One school-attendance officer reported that many children were almost naked and were starving. The plight of the dockers' families was exacerbated when the Board of Guardians refused all outdoor relief to strikers or their dependents, on the grounds that their hardship was self-imposed, although they did offer a place in the workhouse to the needy. Many Newry families enjoyed a lean Christmas thanks to such 'public-spirited' generosity.

The union was desperately anxious to get itself out of an impossible situation and at the same time salvage what members and honour it could from the morass. Both Larkin and Fearon attended a meeting of the Dundalk Harbour Board on 23 December to discuss a possible solution with interested and influential parties. A deputation from the meeting saw the Newry employers and conveyed the wish of both men and Dundalk Board that solid conciliation machinery be set up to deal with future disputes.

The suggestion was noted but not acted upon. However, the dockers themselves were now no longer prepared to continue the fruitless struggle when victory was so hopelessly out of sight. They gradually returned to work on the assurance that they were no longer associated in any way with the union, though this was not so in a lot of cases. Others, however, broken physically and morally by the long struggle, were willing to sign a document relinquishing all ties with the NUDL in order to secure work. By January 1908 the strike was broken and the union branch was in disarray. Indiscipline and bad leadership had combined to snatch defeat from the jaws of victory.[57]

Dublin of 1890 and Belfast and Newry of 1907 had one telling feature in common: all three experiments in trade union organisation ended in relative failure. This was due, in no small part, to the equivocation and lack of determination on the part of British executives to go on the offensive and stand over the consequences whatever the cost to the unions might be in terms of personnel and cash reserves. Armed with the knowledge that the militancy of the local organisers did not properly reflect the staid and pragmatic policies of the union leadership, the employers had only to bide their time and ride out the initial wave of rank-and-file radicalism. The next step was to help exacerbate the differences between the union organiser in the field and the union bureaucrats in central office by cold-bloodedly escalating the dispute. Once the union faced a hefty strike-pay or lockout-pay bill, the voices of the moderates were soon heard to out-shout and outweigh the strident call of radicalism. Surrender, capitulation or peace at any price often resulted in leaving the men dejected, demoralised and thoroughly hostile towards the union organiser who had promised so much and delivered so little in the way of protection, concessions or freedom from victimisation which was the fate of most activists. However, this pattern of events was not so prevalent in England. The Irish employer had a built-in safeguard when dealing with British unions. Their main theatre of action was really across the channel and as a consequence they showed a marked reticence to fight pitched battles away from home. The real campaigns were fought in the larger industrial centres of Britain where the pickings were richest. Ireland was very much an after-thought for the new unions.

In the three disputes dealt with above, however, all had something more positive in common. That was the willingness of men to join and plan an active role in a union when knowledge of such involvement could mean dismissal on some trumped-up pretext. In many cases an organiser's task was less to stimulate interest in combination amongst workers than to control and discipline their latent radicalism. Social deprivation coupled with the gnawing humiliation of patronage-structured employment patterns could not by themselves drive men into revolt. Organisation was a prerequisite for a campaign against industrial absolutism. Larkin possessed the talents to motivate and combine men into a unified force. He had shown what could be achieved in Belfast, provided a little more caution was shown on his part and a little more courage and determination on the part of his employers, the NUDL. His colleague, James Fearon, had demonstrated what could be achieved in small ports like Newry and Dundalk provided tact was used to temper courage. In 1890, Dublin had shown a flicker of the true potential of local general worker trade unions. In the interim, a number of factors had combined to make the craft unions, if not militant, then a little more aggressive and less self-centred. What was required was a catalyst to blend the latent radicalism of the hitherto unorganised general worker and the new-found self-assertiveness of the 'old-unions'. The former Liverpool stevedore provided the impetus.

Larkin Looks to Dublin

Larkin first visited the Irish capital when the Belfast strike was at its height, seeking money to prolong the struggle for as long as possible. The dispute was costing the NUDL over £3,000 a week but even more cash was required if food and clothing was to be distributed to the men and their families. Larkin also used the opportunity of his visit to Dublin to recruit local men for the union. The emotion whipped up by the bitterness of the Belfast strike afforded an ideal chance to get things moving in the South. By the end of September, after a few more flying visits to Dublin, Larkin had more NUDL members in Dublin than in Belfast. On 22 December, a strike occurred at the Dublin gasworks where, as a news report put it:

> Mr Larkin, who figured in the Belfast strike, and Mr Greig of Newcastle, have been sowing the seeds of discontent and exciting the men to insist on their rights as to more wages and the recognition of the trade union.[58]

This was significant because it was in this area in 1890 that Thorne's union made large inroads. The coalporters of the city had also joined the gasworkers' union in great numbers. Once again, this section of the labour force formed the backbone of the scheme to unionise the general labourers of the city. In July 1908, the Dublin Coal Merchants' Association was adopting its traditional attitude towards the unions—one of non-recognition and non-co-operation:

> It appears that the employers decline to have any dealings with the trade bodies to which the labourers belong, and when any complaint as to the

treatment of the men or as to conditions of work arise, they will only hold communication with the persons directly concerned.[59]

The men also claimed that the employers 'had shown of late a great preference for non-union men'. Trouble broke out when the merchants claimed they received a printed circular stating that from 20 July their employees would not work with non-union labour 'unless the latter wore the recognised badge of the society'. Larkin denied that he had ever issued such a directive. He did, however, instruct his men to conform to Rule One of the NUDL which ordered every union member to wear a society badge.[60]

Larkin flatly denied that he was trying to establish a 'closed-shop'. What he was attempting to do was to set up a union: the employers had combined to protect their interests and if it was legitimate for the merchants to combine then there was also nothing to prevent their employees doing likewise. On a theoretical level Larkin supported the principle of the closed-shop, but it would have been foolhardy of him to attempt to win the war with one battle. He realised that 100% union membership was an objective to work towards through years of negotiations and hard work, although he would not hesitate to use the threat of the 'closed-shop' to cudgel the employers into granting major concessions to his union. It was purely a question of tactics and Larkin was a practical man, untrammelled by the straitjacket of revolutionary dogmatism.

About 400 men were paid off on 10 July while other workers claimed that when they went to collect their wages they were told to either hand in their badges or face dismissal. The City of Dublin Steam Packet Company and Tedcastle and McCormick were among the principal offenders. The managing director of the former company, Edward Watson, said the whole question at dispute was one of free labour, to which the employers maintained they had a perfect right when they willing to pay the market wages. He had no objection to the union but the directive from the NUDL practically amounted to a declaration of war. He added that he did not feel that there was any necessity to import labour as there were plenty of unemployed in the city willing to work.

Posters had been put up in all the coal yards affected warning that 'men . . . continuing membership of the NUDL will not be allowed to resume work on Monday'. Larkin retaliated by placing a picket on sheds and posting notices all over the city appealing to men not to take the place of sacked strikers:

Unemployed men keep away from the harbour of Dublin. Don't scab on
your fellow countrymen who are locked out by the employers. Don't
Carey. Defer accepting employment. Call at 10, Beresford Place.[61]

But this did not prevent men taking jobs. Watson reported to the
annual meeting of shareholders in November that new workers were
engaged and housed and fed on the premises, while efficient
protection was afforded by the commissioner of police, and the
sailing of the company's steamers were not interrupted. Before the
affair really got out of hand, the Under Secretary of State, Sir James
Dougherty, and I. H. Mitchell of the Board of Trade intervened. It
was arranged at a meeting in Dublin Castle that the notices on both
sides should be withdrawn and the *status quo* maintained, pending
a further conference to be held on 18 July.

On Sunday, 12 July, a 'victory' meeting was held at the Customs
House. Larkin, who was obviously pleased with the progress, was
the picture of conciliation. He told the meeting that the Belfast
strike had brought more work to the men and better wages. They
wanted no strike in Dublin and they were prepared to arbitrate on
fair terms.

Some of the sitting MPs for Dublin were not so easily mollified.
William Field, who also spoke at the meeting, urged the men to be
loyal to the executive but warned that 'they should not throw down
their arms'. Nothing was won without agitation, he continued, for
'agitation was the life of freedom and the right arm of progress'. The
Lord Mayor drove in his carriage to the meeting and received a
rapturous reception. 'It's easy to gull the workers,' William O'Brien
wrote sarcastically in his diary.[62]

James Sexton arrived from Liverpool a week later in time for the
peace talks. The men had returned to work without major incident,
and the way was clear to resolve all outstanding problems. The
conference opened on 18 July in the Chief Secretary's office
presided over by Lord MacDonnell; Sir James Dougherty and Isaach
Mitchell were again present, in addition to representatives of the
parties involved. Sexton was anxious to set up permanent conciliation machinery to prevent any costly recurrence of the affair.

Rapid progress was reported but it was agreed finally to 'allow the
truce which is now in operation to remain in force until 30 July when
a final meeting will be held in London'.[63] It was Sexton, not Larkin,
who negotiated the final deal for the union and this was strongly
reflected in the terms, which were wholly unfavourable to the local
men. Practically every point demanded by the employers was

conceded without qualification or compromise. In essence, the union's role was to be more circumscribed than before. Questions affecting individuals only were to be settled by the individual and the firm concerned; the freedom of the employers as to the persons whom they could employ was admitted and no distinction as to work (including the delivery or reception of cargo) between union and non-union men was to be made either by employers or employed.

Another clause forbade men to wear distinguishing badges or buttons during work although this was contrary to Rule One of the NUDL. Clause Four was far more constricting: questions affecting general conditions of employment hours, rates of wages, etc. were to be communicated in writing by the men directly affected to the firm or firms concerned. Under this stipulation, Larkin was powerless to serve a general wage claim on a trade or even petition as a trade union official for the men he represented.[64]

Under the agreement, if the firm did not see fit to grant the claim from the shop floor, the men, through the general secretary of the National Union of Dock Labourers, could then make further representations to management, who would undertake to give further consideration to the matter. Thus Larkin's power as local organiser was effectively eclipsed. Sexton had successfully muzzled one of his worst trade union enemies, or so he thought.

A clause in the agreement made provision for a final court of appeal which would come into play if the general secretary failed to find a settlement. This conciliation board was to consist of a representative of the employers, a representative of the employed and an umpire. The neutral chairman was to be mutually agreed upon, or failing agreement, to be appointed by the Board of Trade.[65]

Taking into account the explosive nature of general labour affairs in Ireland and the highly volatile character of its leading pro-tagonist, such cumbersome machinery set up under the agreement had hardly any chance of working efficiently or effectively. It was very short-sighted of the Board of Trade to expect to confine trade union involvement in disputes to a general secretary who was living hundreds of miles form the source of the trouble. It was a recipe for industrial disorder, but Larkin accepted the terms with outer equanimity. In private conversation with William O'Brien, he contended—'It was the best settlement that any union had got in the past ten years'.[66] After discussing the matter further, 'he practically admitted that they (the union executive) were not prepared to fight and had accepted the best terms they could get'.[67] Larkin felt disinclined to betray his real feelings to O'Brien: he was national organiser of a union which had treated him rather badly, but he still retained a modicum of loyalty, despite the machinations of Sexton, to the NUDL. Privately, he was fully aware of what the agreement presaged though he was still prepared to try and work within the constricting structures of the union.

When Sexton returned to Dublin to explain the agreement to the men at a meeting in the trades hall, Larkin took the chair, but sat sullenly through the proceedings without uttering a word. As expected, the agreement was accepted by the meeting.[68] It was very much a pyrrhic victory and nobody was more aware of this than Larkin. Perhaps it was because the agreement itself was so preposterously unworkable that he acquiesced at all.

Larkin's conflict with Sexton began to take on a new significance. He was spending more time than ever in Ireland where he was gradually getting a greater understanding of local affairs. By regularly attending the Dublin Trades Council, he was in a better position to comment upon and influence local labour affairs. He familiarised himself with alacrity with the running of the corporation. At a council meeting in July, he spoke on the contentious issue of 'direct labour'. It had been the practice of the corporation to sign contracts for municipal contracts and services with private individuals. Besides encouraging 'graft', this system also hit the trade unions because many of the men who were given the jobs recruited the cheapest labour possible. Organised labour is never cheap labour so the unions felt that they had legitimate grounds for complaint. In an effort to mute such criticism, the corporation had introduced certain regulations to control this practice. However, Larkin contended that the terms were too vague and impracticable. At a later meeting the corporation was once again under fire from Larkin for not employing union labour in coal contracts. Again showing a meticulous eye for detail, he made the serious charge that two-pound loaves were often as much as six to eight ounces underweight. He was not content just to condemn these abuses but urged that action be taken at a number of levels. Larkin was more vocal than ever on the issue of old age pensions being discussed in the Commons. He also had a motion passed supporting 'the action of the British Labour Party in their Right to Work Bill and condemning the government for its apathy'. The council agreed to set up a committee to work with any *bona fide* labour organisation that would assert the national right to work. On his initiative, deputations were sent to public bodies because the Fair Wages Resolution was not being carried out 'and there were men who opposed trade unionism'.[69]

Hardly a week passed without Larkin making some contribution to the DTC debate which also involved some practical course of action. Gradually, as his importance in local labour circles grew, he began to spend almost all his time in the city. He had married in 1903 and was the father of two sons, James and Denis. His family saw very little of him during the hectic year of 1907 and he found even less time to get home in the first six months of 1908. As Irish union affairs were likely to absorb his full-time attention for quite some time, he moved his family from Liverpool to Dublin.

Under Larkin's guidance, the NUDL established branches in Derry, Belfast, Newry, Dundalk and Drogheda. In July 1908 Larkin, acting under specific instructions from Sexton, set about organising the port of Cork.[70] James Fearon, dejected by the Newry debacle, was sent to deal with the day-to-day running of what promised to be a very troublesome new branch. The standard abuses, found in every unorganised port in Ireland, were very much in evidence in the Cork docks. On 9 November, the union felt strong enough to move against the shipping companies. Over 100 men suddenly stopped work on the City of Cork Steam Packet Company's docks and the strike began to spread. Larkin arrived two days later and agreed to submit the union's claim for higher wages to arbitration. The agreement reached in the following month was not all unfavourable to the men. Their gains were considerable.[71]

In Dublin, Larkin had headed a seven-man Right-to-Work committee and organised outdoor protest rallies amongst the unemployed,[72] yet the success of this novel group was qualified. In his efforts to discipline Dublin workers, he also used the temperance movement. A lifelong teetotaller himself, he was very much aware of what excessive drinking could do to a man and his family. For example, in 1912, 3,615 people were drunk when arrested as against 2,968 in 1911. The charges of drunkenness in 1912 numbered 2,345 (1,542 males and 803 women). This figure is exclusive of 1,087 people (517 men and 570 women) who were charged with being drunk and disorderly, while 96 others were convicted for drunkenness combined with some other offence.[73] Every trade union had its own problems with alcoholic members. Stiff fines were imposed on anyone coming to a meeting 'with drink taken', but this did not solve the problem nor did it even prevent men turning up at weekly meetings more in condition to fight than to contribute to proceedings. The problem was particularly acute among dockers who were often paid in public houses by stevedores who often insisted upon their cut in liquid form. However, it did not need a stevedore to lead the average docker into intemperate temptation. The irregularity of the hours worked by dockers often forced him to spend long hours in the public house where he either sheltered in bad weather or waited for work. Larkin tried to stamp out intemperance and was not very choosy about the methods used. Men were dragooned into taking the pledge. For his efforts, Larkin was named principal speaker at a big 'pioneer' rally organised by Fr Aloysious, OFM Cap. in August, 1908. Some 700 dockers marched through the city to the meeting place, where Larkin told them that while a man might have the right to get drunk, he had not the freedom to pauperise his family. His enthusiasm was infectious and it was not lost on the audience. But Larkin was already taking more practical steps to combat what he would describe as 'wage slavery' in the city.

Revolt of the Carters

Of all the unorganised groups of general workers in the city, the carters, carriers and draymen were possibly the most vulnerable to exploitation. In 1901 there were roughly 2,000 men so employed in the city and by 1911 the figure had risen by another 1,000. According to Larkin, some men were earning as little as 9d a day and the employers were using the excuse of tough competition between firms to reduce the pay rates still further. Most carters in the city, who did as much work in a day as any carter in Manchester or Liverpool, would earn no more than one pound while the cross-channel rate was 28s. In one firm the men had sometimes to work 112 hours a week and they would be expected to do more if the horse did not need rest, he claimed. Exaggerated Larkin's claims may well have been, but they also had a strong basis in truth. Statutory regulations governing the length of a working week in the trade did not exist. Nor did rules exist governing the loading and unloading of merchandise. Helpers seldom travelled with a driver. Individual employers were therefore left to do what they saw fit and the outcome was rarely in the interest of employees.

Larkin sent a letter to the merchants in April requesting a meeting between union and management to discuss a list of grievances and seek an increase in wages for the men. However, the master carters, like their colleagues in the coal trade, did not feel compelled to truck with combinations, and Larkin's request went unheeded. More specific increases were sought in a circular sent on 30 September and again four weeks later. Tempters ran high among the men when no acknowledgement was received to the third letter. On 16 November, Larkin was in Derry when he received a telegram to return to Dublin because over 150 carters belonging to four firms had struck without notice. The following day there were over 300 out on the streets. Pickets were mounted on recalcitrant firms. The most serious of a number of violent incidents involved a dray belonging to Cullen and Allen Ltd. Strikers surrounded the driver as he was travelling along the quays, unyoked the horse, and pushed the cart with its load into the Liffey.

That night, Larkin made an ambivalent speech which did little to cool tempers. 'The bulk of the employers were Freemasons who recognised "the grip",' he told strikers. The NUDL was not prepared to have a stoppage of work, but what he wanted was an opportunity to meet management 'face to face'. He regretted the outbreak of the strike and the injury to policemen, did not want to quarrel with the DMP and deplored the throwing of carts into the Liffey. Such action would not help their cause. Strikers should subjugate their tempers and work by moral persuasion. However, he warned that there would have been no stoppage of carts if the employers had treated with the union in the first place. Unless the master carters met the men fairly soon now, 'they would meet their Fontenoy', he said to cheers.[74]

The master carters had their own ideas of how to deal with the problem. A deputation saw the police commissioner at Dublin Castle where it was agreed to draft 200 reinforcements into the city. The employers were determined not to submit to what they interpreted to be blackmail and intimidation.

The strikers were more disciplined the following day. Four drays carrying bananas were surrounded on the quays by a crowd who, according to the *Irish Times*, adopted all the verbal practices which nowadays come under the designation 'peaceful picketing'. The men hooted, groaned and remonstrated with the drivers to no avail and the carts were finally left to go on their way. In another incident at Moss Street, near Butt Bridge, strikers and sympathisers unyoked a carter's horse, but when it was discovered that the cart did not belong to any firm in dispute, it was promptly replaced between the shafts and the driver went on his way.

In yet another incident William O'Brien tells of a union member, and a sympathiser with the strikers, who was ordered to do some carting work for his employer. Not wishing to run into trouble and be faced with the possibility of a beating, he sent word to Larkin to send a picket to hold him up somewhere near Butt Bridge. Everything went according to plan; picketers intercepted the cart and toppled it over spilling the contents across the road. Some zealots, unaware of the driver's union status caught him and were about to deposit him in the Liffey when somebody intervened to save him from an unwanted winter swim.[75]

It was impossible to contain the dispute. On 18 November, trouble spread to the Grand Canal Company. Nineteen 'bulkers' quit work and were soon followed by the crews of a few barges. The general manager of the company, George Tough, said that 600 might be out of work if the men did not return immediately. Two days later, fifty were out in Dublin while twenty were laid off at Shannon and eighty lock-keepers were placed on half-wages.[76]

Larkin supported the action of the canalmen in their drive for more pay. Earlier, he had warned the men that there would be no compromise this time. Referring to the coalporters' agreement of July, he said that they had been 'humbugged' then but things would be different this time. Lord McDonnell had actually gone down on his knees and implored him to consent to settlement for the sake of the women and children.[77] But there was too much at stake in the dispute to take the easy way out, he said.

If courage was any substitute for money, Larkin could have won almost any dispute, but as far as the NUDL was concerned, Larkin was a voice crying in the wilderness, without even locusts and wild honey to feed the strikers on. The Liverpool executive washed its hands of the dispute, and one source claims that when Larkin requested aid from his union executive, Sexton answered with a postcard bearing the simple message: 'stew in your own juice'.[78]

Larkin brought his plight to the attention of the DTC. At a council meeting on 23 November, he explained the difference of opinion he had had with his general secretary over the dispute. The local branch had given them full permission to conduct affairs, and the chairman, Michael O'Lehane, supported his stand and appealed on his behalf to all unions for financial support so that the employers' efforts to starve men into submission could be routed.[79] The unions responded quite willingly to the plea. Meanwhile, a joint appeal was sponsored by the Independent Labour Party and the Irish Socialist Party for strike funds 'to free the down-trodden workers of Ireland . . . from the thraldom of capitalism'.

The Board of Trade official, Isaach Mitchell, had returned to Dublin on 19 November and immediately held separate talks with employers and men at Dublin Castle. That night Larkin did not miss the opportunity to inform both employers and government officials of the mood of the men. If anything, he exaggerated his own militancy for effect. At Beresford Place, he reportedly told a large gathering of workers that:

> The employer should recognise the right of the men to combine and the men would then recognise the employer's right to combine and they could treat together on those terms. But they were not going to accept any condition laid down. He regretted physical violence in connection with the strike but if any class should be injured it should be the class who had been degrading and despoiling the workers, and if some one of the employer class were to get a crack behind the ear, he would not very much mind.[80]

Throughout the dispute, Larkin adopted a moderate and conciliatory tone in comparison to his more extreme speeches, went out of his way to avoid violence on the picket lines. Yet on the eve of vital talks at Dublin Castle, he chose to unleash an attack on the employers, the board of trade and the government. This may have appeared quite tactless but it worked and the following day he ordered his men back to work pending talks later in the week. He had won round one. He had got management to the conference table, although the dispute was far from over.

Arthur Griffith and his 'Green Hungarian Band'

Larkin was never the most popular man in Dublin. He had many natural enemies amongst the employers of the city, and his coterie of detractors were in no sense confined to that category. There were few to rival in intensity the dislike the printer-turned-journalist, Arthur Griffith, had for the man he described as 'a strike-organiser from England'.[81] The reasons for Griffith's animosity are difficult to discern. On a philosophical basis, Sinn Fein was anxious to sever all possible links with Britain. Cross-channel unions, which practically controlled large sections of organised labour in Dublin, were anathema to Griffith and his followers. Micheal O Flannagain, writing in 1906, set out the SF argument in clear form:

> Unquestionably the aim of our movement is to build up a nation from within, and in this task our principal hope lies in the Irish artisan, but if he continues to have his councils swayed by the dictates of an Executive having London, Liverpool or Manchester for its headquarters, the possibility of establishing even a healthy industrial atmosphere in Ireland is indeed remote. Ireland at the present time seems to be a sort of happy hunting ground for English trade union organisers, who come over to preach of the glories of amalgamation and its consequent benefits.[82]

O Flannagain argued that all British unions were really interested in was the cash to be creamed off in subscriptions. As far as they were concerned Irish organisational matters were 'purely commercial transactions'. Strikes were supported, he added, 'solely with the idea of diverting industry into English channels'. And that was not all: 'strikes in Ireland engineered in England have done more to supplant native artisans than any cause I know'. In essence, O Flannigain, felt that British unions were taking out vast sums in subscription fees but they were also engineering strikes to divert Irish trade abroad and then replacing sacked Irish workers with opportunistic British colleagues. The fact that the points were unsustainable did little to deter them enjoying widespread popularity. O Flannagain was not so much presenting a closely reasoned argument founded on fact, as pandering to popular prejudice by reiterating a number of artibrary emotionalisms, albeit in good faith.

Griffith's own thinking followed very much along the same line, but there was a more abrasive strain in the SF leader's arguments which gave them a more bitter and vindictive edge, best described as a virulent form of anglophobia perilously approaching racialism. One incident in 1908 will illustrate this point. On 21 December the editor of *The Peasant*, W. P. Ryan, gave an open lecture in the Central Branch offices of Sinn Fein entitled 'Has Sinn Fein a Serious Social Policy?'[83] Arthur Griffith was in the chair and his temper was not helped by the less than flattering tone of the lecturer who argued trenchantly that SF was really 'a mixture of melodrama and moonshine'. William O'Brien made the following entry in his diary after the meeting:

> Griffith, who was in the chair, showed considerable hostility to speakers and refused to allow Edwards (ILP) to speak on grounds first that he

was an Englishman and later because he represented an English organisation. One Sinn Feiner said Edwards was of that nation that murdered Parnell . . . speaker replied by saying that he knew of many English organisations that had grasp of Irish situation.[85]

In the first edition of the *Irish Nation*, the editor commented on the incident:

> Mr Edwards is a long time in Ireland, is married to an Irishwoman, has more advanced ideas about Irish Nationality than half the people of Ireland, and has protested, we believe, by voice and pen and vote against British government of Ireland and of Britain for that matter. Besides objecting to the British system of government here, do SF leaders expect us to be discourteous to thoughtful, educated and sympathetic Englishmen?[86]

Edwards also defended himself in the same edition. He referred to a previous meeting where Griffith had given a lecture advocating a protectionist economic policy. Again he had been challenged by Edwards who vigorously opposed any tariff system.[87] The questioner was once again reminded of his English origins as if that was a substitute for an answer, but Edwards dealt specifically with the latest incident. 'Never in all my life have I seen an Irishman excluded from a bout of dialectics in England', he taunted.[88] Edwards own construction of the events in his letter are interesting on a number of counts:

> Firstly, he (Griffith) declared that I was an official of English Labour Party (in disguise I suppose and therefore sailing under false colours) and then when corrected on this point and so driven from his subterfuge, the poor man seems to have lost his head, crying out that I belonged to the nation which murdered Parnell. 'Well, if it was not you that did it, it was your nation, said the wolf.[89]

Here Edwards, unlike O'Brien, states that it was Griffith himself who compounded his earlier remarks by exhuming Parnell for the occasion. This verifies even further the view that much of Griffith's thought was conceived in hatred for all things British, and his condemnation of Larkin can now be seen in a new light. Not only was the 'strike organiser' a divisive force sowing the seeds of class consciousness before national commitment; he also was an Englishman working ultimately in the interests of Whitehall.[90] Writing about the carters strike, Griffith said:

> At the behest of an English labour union a number of Irishmen were brought out on strike, with the possible effect of paralysing half the trade of the city, and inflicting compulsory idleness on thousands of the artisans of Dublin whose interests the trades council was instituted to

safeguard . . . It must not again be possible for any foreign labour union to call a strike in Dublin, or in any part of Ireland . . . The sooner the men who were brought out on strike last week by an English organiser erect themselves into an Irish labour union, as the corporation workmen have done, and affiliate themselves directly with the trades council, the better. English trade unionism has no interest in this country except England's interest, and the events of last week have fully opened the eyes of a good many Irish trade unionists to its sinister aspect.[91]

Neither Sexton nor Mitchell of the Board of Trade could possibly agree with Griffith on this point; neither the NUDL nor Westminster was drawing any benefit whatsoever from the dispute in Dublin: Sexton was facing a revolt of very serious magnitude inside his union, Larkin had proved ungovernable, and Dublin Castle was confronted by a highly combustible security problem. Yet Griffith was right about one thing—the need for a new locally controlled general workers' union—but for the wrong reasons.

The Carters Strike Back

Peace talks had proceeded rather haltingly for a number of days until 26 November, 1908, when the Grand Canal Company withdrew. The next day the master carters locked out their men after some of their employees had refused to deliver to the Grand Canal Company. At Beresford Place that night Larkin claimed that the employers had torn up the treaty and had intended to do so a week before. They would fight big carters first and then the small ones and O'Lehane, who was in the chair, said that every fair-minded man in the city would support the struggle. When P. T. Daly, who was a member of SF, tried to speak, the crowd refused to give him a hearing. Hecklers asked whether it was SF policy to attack the workers, but Larkin intervened and said that Daly was the only Dublin worker who travelled to Belfast to give support to the carters in 1907.[92]

Once again Larkin had to find the strike money for 2,000 men, and was in no humour to be mollified. The incidents of street violence grew rapidly. Carts driven by clerks were attacked, and the Lifeboat Association's annual procession had to be abandoned because the men learned that the organisers had hired some 'tainted' wagons. Larkin said he had heard that trams were being used to carry parcels, and if that was the case then people should boycott the cars. Some of the men took more direct action. Tram tracks were lifted at Clontarf. The outskirts of the city sent police reinforcements to the centre for guard and escort duty. Larkin took advantage of this and set about out-flanking and over-extending the beleagured security forces. Furthermore, he instructed the men to mount all-night pickets because some firms were working late to avoid harassment. If the strike went on much longer he had plans to put union carts on the road in competition with the employers, as Adolphus Shields had also threatened in the coal dispute of 1890.

In the courts, strikers were receiving stiff sentences for minor misdemeanours. Justice Swifte gave one man 12 months for technical assault on a policeman. Instead of acting as a deterrent, the publicity surrounding such sentences often provoked further violence as retaliation against what Larkin termed 'class-motivated' justice. Larkin taunted the authorities at public meetings. 'Let them now get the British army out as they did in Belfast,' he delared, and hoped the day would arrive when these men would have to face a citizen army.[93] He was not the only one to have lost faith in the ideal of a neutral and impartial police force. Cllr Sheehan (SF) also speaking in Beresford Place, talked of the 'tame snakes in the crowd'. He advised every man to come to meetings armed with sticks to protect himself from police brutality.

Behind the scenes, moves were afoot to end the dispute. Archbishop Walsh offered his services as a mediator. The idea was taken up by William Partridge at a public meeting and he urged that the two Archbishops and the Lord Mayor should mediate together. Larkin was all too willing to get a chance to go to the conference table; it was what he had sought throughout the dispute. But after a few days of desultory talks the master carters retired from the proceedings and the carters and canalmen were once again on the street. They were joined the same day by 400 maltsters from 20 firms who were also striking for more money. The latter received sixteen to eighteen shillings per week and one shilling was withheld and returned at the end of the year if employees had not transgressed company rules. The maltsters worked a seven-day week with no regular meal breaks, and were at the kilns constantly, working in temperatures ranging from 60 to 212 degrees. One firm, Carter and Son, wrote to the papers claiming that the men's description of their working conditions was misleading. This company paid 18s per week plus one shilling per week bonus at the end of the season, and they operated a 'spell shift system', where men worked three 'spells' in twenty-four hours. They were free for one and a half hours from 9 a.m., from 1 p.m. to 7 p.m. and from 8.30 p.m. to 5 a.m. This scheme, which gave a man very little time to be with his family, was hardly anything to feel proud about. Larkin wanted eventual parity with the maltsters in Guinness's, who received 23s per week. He served a claim for one pound per week; hours were to begin at 6 a.m. on Monday and end at 3 p.m. on Friday; overtime at rate of 6d per hour and time-and-a-half from 12 midnight on Saturday to 12 a.m. on Sunday.

Dublin Distillers granted an increase of 4s per week immediately but other firms were more reticent and decided to sit tight. There were 3,000 men on the street. The Shipping Federation was offering to send over 1,000 carters and 100 were already at a port in England waiting for the word to travel. A few days later it was reported that steamers were in readiness to send in dockers from Scotland and England. The Chamber of Commerce sent a deputation to the Lord Lieutenant requesting military protection. Christmas was one of the busiest times of the year for city traders and it was feared that the strike could destroy the profits of a whole year. Some even faced bankruptcy.

A third truce was arranged on 21 December and the men agreed to allow their claim to go to arbitration. There was a general return to work throughout the city the following day. Larkin felt assured of justice for his members 'for if there was any honest man in Ireland belonging to the capitalist class it was Sir James Dougherty'.[94] He was to revise his opinion when the findings were published in February.[95]

If Larkin's success is measured in terms of concrete concessions and dramatic wage increases, these six months spent in Dublin were a failure. Little was achieved at that level. However, it would be to misunderstand the former Liverpool stevedore's tactics if our judgement rested there. He was really fighting a different battle but, of necessity, he was operating on two fronts. The more important struggle superseded any campaign for better conditions, etc.; Larkin was attempting to achieve what most British unions had won by the end of the nineteenth century—recognition of a man's right to combine and engage in collective bargaining. Were this principle conceded, no one knew better than the employers that it would open the floodgates for all sorts of demands and concessions which they would be in no position to refuse. Larkin knew this, too, and pressed on relentlessly to achieve his goal. The employers were just as relentless and determined to frustrate the workers in their demand. The ingredient of fear added a certain ruthless air to their 'backwoodsman-like' posturing. The majority of employers were prepared to make a last-ditch stand, if necessary, to defeat the sudden rush of trade unionism in the city.

However, Larkin's achievement was really quite remarkable when it is considered that he carried on a protracted strike, punctured by truces, without any support from the NUDL. He had to rely almost entirely on local money to fill his war chest. Neither did he make any effort to control the dispute or prevent new members signing on who had just come out on strike. At its height there were 3,000 men relying on him for support. He did not provide very well for them, but they were prepared to endure the hardship of a lock-out for a principle.

Despite this the whole affair looked like ending in personal tragedy for Larkin. As his popularity soared in Dublin among the strikers his erstwhile colleagues on the dockers' executive in Liverpool were deciding how to sack him. The quarrel between Larkin and Sexton had developed into an open feud and neither tried any longer to conceal the mutual contempt they felt for each other. On 28 November, the executive passed a resolution 'strongly condemning' Larkin for 'acting contrary to instructions'. His fate was sealed when Sexton was authorised to suspend him 'in the case of a similar breach' of union discipline.[96]

In a letter to Larkin, dated 7 December, the general secretary exercised his mandate. Sexton also reiterated that the union was 'not in any way responsible for the late disputes in Cork and the one now in progress in Dublin'.[97] But this stricture only provoked Larkin to further indiscretions. Regardless of all warnings, he continued to ignore utterly the explicit instructions of his executive. He really had no alternative if he was not to destroy his year's work as an organiser. Sexton was in no mood to understand problems unique to Dublin and Larkin was sacked from his four-pound-a-week job. As a result, the movement to unionise the city's general workers was seriously threatened. The men had found a capable leader but the leader had lost the backing of his organisation.

6 The Founding of the ITGWU

If Larkin had lost his job he had not lost his will to fight. On 22 December, he told the weekly meeting of the trades council that 'the genesis of a great movement had been started in Ireland' and he intended to stay in the city for the rest of his life 'to see what he could do to organise men of his own class—the bottomdogs—as they were sometimes called'.[1] He was obviously confused at this stage, for the pace of events had overtaken him and rushed him into a situation where available courses of action were too rigidly defined. He was at a crossroads and all the signposts were blurred: either he could patch up the quarrel with the NUDL, join another English general workers' union or he could 'go it alone'. At a meeting in Beresford Place, at the beginning of December, he outlined his dilemma:

> He had always believed in the solidarity of labour the world over but it might be that the best way to bring Irish workers into line with the workers of the world was to organise them on Irish lines first. He couldn't say yet whether he would put his hand to the plough—but if he did he would not turn back. In any case he meant to organise the port and docks boardmen, the tramway men and the shop porters in the immediate future.[2]

Larkin did not even consider returning to the fold of the NUDL. Neither was he too happy with the idea of founding a national union. This course was immediately repugnant to his internationalism. Moreover, working-class solidarity transcended the devisive forces of nationalism which were working to segregate and weaken the workers of the British Isles. Such thoughts certainly exercised the mind of Larkin and made his choice all the more difficult. Yet when he turned to the last avenue of escape he realised that it was even less attractive than the other two paths. No rival British union would be prepared to risk triggering off a bitter 'poaching' war throughout their territory with the NUDL by adopting the outcast Larkin and the truculent, troublesome dissidents of Dublin. Repugnant as the 'nationalist' path was to Larkin, it was really the only viable way out of his dilemma. But there were still more compelling practical reasons why he should channel his energies in that direction for to do otherwise would be to swim against the tide of popular feeling and risk total failure. This was underlined by the experience of the Workers' Union in Dublin.

Tom Mann's union was an attractive proposition for any working man. It cost one shilling to join and weekly subscriptions were three pence halfpenny. In return, members received lockout or strike pay of 12s 6d a week; accident benefit of 10s for two weeks; a grant of £20 for total disablement; victimisation money was given for 54 days at 1s 6d a day; and legal assistance was available free. Funeral benefits were also paid to dependents; £9 for a member who had joined under twenty-five and £4 at death of a wife. A further 3d per week entitled a member to 10s for 10 weeks from the Sick Fund. By 1908, after only ten years in existence, the Workers' Union had over seventy branches and nine of them were in Ireland. There were no fewer than five branches in Belfast, and others in Derry, Dungannon, Lisburn and Limerick. The national organiser was a Dublin cabinet maker, Joseph Harris, who had moved to Belfast to find work. However, he was anxious to start a branch in his native city and on 28 February, 1908, a preliminary meeting was held in the Trades Hall, Capel Street.[3]

Harris spoke to O'Brien after the meeting and urged him to join to give encouragement to others; and O'Brien was one of the few people to take the meeting seriously enough to join up. A few days later, at a meeting in the ILP rooms in Beresford Place, he took the chair and it was decided to hold a public meeting to organise workers in Jacobs' biscuit factory. By this time O'Brien was secretary of the Dublin branch and had been elected Workers' Union delegate to the DTC, but recruits were not flocking to the union and O'Brien was disappointed when some socialists turned down his request to join. One of his colleagues said despairingly that there was 'no hope of building up a socialist movement in the present state of the country',[4] and O'Brien himself urged the socialist party to define its attitude towards trade unionism. At a later meeting, after some bitterness amongst members at which one man resigned, the group recommended that members take an active part in the trade union movement. This 'would result in a wider dissemination of our objectives and principles and would also have a strengthening effect on our propaganda generally'.[5] The resolution further recommended that 'those ineligible for ordinary unions should join the Workers' Union'.[6] But despite the backing of the diminutive socialist party and the support of the ILP the outlook for Mann's organisation was bleak. All hopes were pinned on a mass meeting at which Larkin was engaged to speak, posters were printed and distributed, and every effort made to encourage a large turnout, but to no avail. Further efforts to get the union off the ground met with even less success. The workers of Dublin seemed to have no interest in joining one of the most effective unions in Britain, and Harris was dispirited. Everywhere he went in the country he ran up against the same problem—nobody really wanted to join an English union. The only way to combat this view, Harris explained to O'Brien, was to capitulate before it and form an autonomous, national union.[7]

O'Brien favoured the idea and immediately set about sounding out opinion amongst his trade union colleagues. At first, all the signs pointed to success and O'Brien's enthusiasm for the scheme grew. On 6 May, the practicality of founding a national workers' union for Ireland was raised at a meeting with P. T. Daly, Harris and J. Smith of the United Labourers. Harris read the proposed union's platform and it was adopted by all present. Daly and Harris were then appointed to make a formal approach to the United Labourers' Union suggesting possible amalgamation with the proposed national union. However, O'Brien was anxious that preparations for the launching be carefully planned and requested Harris to stop Daly putting the platform in the newspapers at the time. Speed was the worst enemy of progress, thought O'Brien.

His caution proved justified. On 24 May, at a meeting to lay down plans for the new union, an opinion was expressed that Harris 'was not playing fair in attempting to found a rival union'. It was the view of those present that 'the Workers' Union branch should be kept on whether a national union was founded or not'.[8] Already O'Brien's interest in the proposed union was on the wane. As he began to realise the magnitude of the task facing him and the dissention and obvious lack of interest amongst his colleagues, he immediately sought a way out from his commitment to the idea. Harris travelled to Dublin and met O'Brien on 30 May, and at a special meeting of the Workers' Union it was agreed to make a fresh effort to build up Tom Mann's organisation in Dublin.

On O'Brien's advice, Harris agreed to drop the idea of setting up a national union. Every effort was once again thrown into building up the Workers' Union, but the results were consistently poor. For example, a meeting at Tallaght on 21 June, addressed by Harris, failed to get any members. 'Looks like fiasco', O'Brien wrote in his diary. Fortunes changed in July when about 20 of the staff of the North Dublin Union formed a branch, thanks probably to the canvassing of O'Brien who was employed there as a tailor. Soon afterwards another branch with 29 members was opened in Rathcoole. Disaster struck when William Murphy of the brush-makers' union, resigned because 'work was only being done in a half-hearted fashion and that it was next to impossible to get (Harris) to do anything'.[9] Amid 'signs of a storm Harris came from Belfast, and at an executive meeting O'Brien argued that the ILP offices were not the best place to hold assemblies as the Labour party identified with socialism. He added that an attack on the ILP was imminent as a socialist pamphlet had been sold by its members outside a Catholic Church. However, it was decided that the union should be included in the attack. Shortly afterwards, O'Brien resigned from a union he thought was doomed, and was succeeded on the trades council by Darcy, another socialist party member. But the union was too far in decline for even Darcy to bring about any sort of revival. On 3 October, O'Brien audited the book of the union and found that there were only twenty-two fully paid-up members in Dublin. The workers' union remained in existence, only to drop its role as unifier after a while, and become instead an instrument of division and discord. Larkin was not unfriendly to Harris at any time, but as a member of an English-based union, the former did not support this desultory move to form a national union. 'I might accept the view that there was a case for an Irish Socialist Party but I would never agree to divide the workers on the industrial field,' he once told O'Brien, yet by the end of December 1908, he had cause to change his mind. The idea of establishing a national movement had not failed in May; it had not been tried. But once the NUDL had so ignominiously deserted the carters the local groundswell of emotion against English-based unions manifested itself more strongly than ever before. Some left-wing Sinn Feiners, like the ubiquitous P. T. Daly, saw their opportunity to channel popular feeling in a constructive national direction. The weight of trade union opinion was clearly in favour of industrial 'self determination'. The 'home rule' policy of the amalgamateds and the new unions had given the local men neither the scope nor support they were seeking to press for tight combinations of workers capable of concerted industrial action. After some reflection and conversation with leading, local trade unionists it was clear to Larkin that all signposts pointed towards the 'national union' path. His own personal following was so strong in the city that he felt sure he could take the local NUDL men with him into the new organisation. All he had to do really was overcome his natural revulsion to the idea, put his pride in his pocket, and get on with the job.

The new scheme was launched on 29 December. A private meeting was held with delegates representing carters, dockers and other trades in Dublin, Belfast, Dundalk, Cork and Waterford present. The new union, to be called the ITGWU, was to cater for those engaged in the distributive trades, and it was to adopt 'exactly that attitude of friendly co-operation towards the English unions that they extend to the new unions of Germany or France'.[12] But it would not merge itself in any English union, 'as too many Irish unions have done'. The whole venture had a very stong nationalist flavour. And the first edition of the *Irish Nation* 'hoped that this example of independence would be followed by the workers throughout Ireland'.[13]

There followed large defections from the NUDL in most ports. It was particularly badly hit in Dublin where all the top personnel joined the ITGWU. The men simply changed offices and substituted one headed notepaper for another. John O'Neill ran Dublin Number One Branch, helped by Thomas Foran who was union president. No national executive was formed until after 1914 and the task of looking after the affairs of the whole union fell directly on Number One Branch. Another was started a short time later, with its headquarters at Emmet Hall, Inchicore, and catered largely for the railway workers.

Larkin, as general secretary, was not the easiest man to work with. He was a supremely disorganised person who never tried to conceal his contempt and loathing for the busy bureaucrat. His spirit was administratively uncontainable and not even a battalion of bureaucrats could untangle the list of untended correspondence, unpaid bills, etc. left in his wake. His inside pocket was his filing cabinet, and his spontaneity had its drawbacks. In his efforts to get on with the practical work of setting up the union insufficient thought was given to the general labour philosophy underlying the 'new departure'. In Dublin and in the south generally, the ITGWU was a positive step forward, but in the north the same organisation was viewed as a secessionist body at best and a nationalist aberration at worst. Larkin's only declaration of intent was a preface to the union rule book, written in 1909, but rather than allay the suspicions of anti-nationalist trade unionists, its confused message had the opposite effect. Indeed, part of its message was not out of keeping with SF thinking:

> Trade unionism in Ireland has arrived at a certain stage of growth when this question confronts us—What is to be our next step in fostering its future development? Are we going to continue the policy of grafting ourselves on the English Trades Union movement, losing our own identity as a nation, in the great world of organised labour? We say, emphatically, no. Ireland has politically reached her manhood.[14]

No loyalist worker in the North could possibly join a union which was so explicitly nationalist in outlook. While this was really a false emphasis, it was an emphasis that Larkin did little to correct, and later paid for his mistake on the floor of congress.

The ITGWU platform went on to warn that Irish society was changing rapidly, and that 'the capitalist class in Ireland was being reinforced by the influx of foreign capitalists, with their soulless, sordid, money-grubbing propensities'. It continued in curiously biblical language:

> It behoves the Irish workers to realise the power of the employing class, who are not only well organised industrially but practically monopolise the political power in this country as they do in all other countries at present.[15]

Larkin warned also against the outmoded structure of sectionally motivated unions, both for skilled and general labourer alike:

> The Irish Transport and General Workers' Union offer to you a medium whereby you may combine with your fellows to adjust wages, regulate hours and conditions of labour, wherever and whenever possible and desirable by negotiation, arbitration and if the conditions demand it, by withholding (*sic*) our labour until amelioration is granted. Further, we demand political recognition for the enforcement of our demands. Our immediate programme being legal eight hours' day provision of work for all unemployed, and pensions for all workers at 60 years of age. Compulsory Arbitration Courts, adult suffrage, nationalisation of canals, railways and all means of transport. The land of Ireland for the people of Ireland. Our ultimate ideal, the realisation of an Industrial Commonwealth.[16]

And that was by no means all:

> By the advocacy of such principles and carrying out of such a policy, we believe we shall be ultimately enabled to obliterate poverty, and help to

realise the glorious time spoken of and sung by the Thinkers, Prophets and the Poets, when all children, all women and all men shall work and rejoice in the deeds of their hand, and thereby become entitled to the fulness of the earth and the abundance thereof.[17]

Larkin was a poor administrator, confused in his thinking about the ITGWU and at times positively chiliastic in his vision of trade union power. He was not blameworthy for founding an Irish-based trade union, but he was not cognizant of the dangers of such a course of action, and must therefore share the blame for not sugaring the pill of a national organisation for northern Protestant working men.

Another fundamental mistake was made in not giving sufficient thought to the structure of the new union. The first rule book was drawn simply by plagiarizing rules from other societies. A Cork delegate, John Murray, describes how this came about:

> They went to business on Sunday evening in the Transport Hall in Beresford Place. Mr Larkin took the chair, and there were present Mr Green, witness and Mr Fearon, and from nine to twelve more. The rule books of other unions were produced, and Mr Larkin read them, and each rule that would suit the new rule book they were going to form would be marked off, and it would be sanctioned by the meeting for the transport union.[18]

The final product bore a great resemblance to the Workers' Union rule book. It was strikingly unoriginal in content. It was hardly likely that anyone could ever call the transport union anarcho-syndicalist. But apart from the industrial struggle, Larkin and his transport union colleagues were leading members of the new organisation into a trade union minefield.

Predictably, the first to attack the new union was Arthur Griffith. With an inconsistency that stood SF policy on its head, the retired printer sympathised with the NUDL over the 'wildcat' activities of Irishmen who took a decision to strike 'without the sanction of the executive of the union to which the men were affiliated'.[19] Up to this, one would have thought that disobedient and independent-minded actions by Irishmen, be it against British trade unions or other foreign institutions, was laudible in the eyes of Griffith and Sinn Fein, but not any longer. Griffith had sided with Sexton despite his national origins and the origins of his organisation. The SF attack on the transport union was really part of a vendetta between Griffith and Larkin—and it was not all one-sided. The latter could give as good as he got. In one speech, he told an appreciative crowd that Griffith was in the pay of the master carters. And the verbal brickbats continued to fly. O'Brien made a pertinent entry in his diary: 'A. G. keenly feels Larkin's trenchant criticism and as a consequence has badly lost his temper.'[20] Emotion certainly dominated Griffith when he wrote:

> The English union of dock labourers having repudiated the strike organiser, that person is now seeking an opening for himself as organiser of an Irish transport workers' union to be run in opposition to the society in whose name he has hitherto carried out his strikes. We wish well and will give all our assistance to any genuine Irish organisation of transport workers but to assure the public that it is genuine the first essential of such a body is that those connected with it are not suspended or dismissed officials of the English union which they formerly lauded as the one and only union to which Irishmen should belong.[21]

Griffith's attacks on Larkin were as unrelenting in this matter as his logic was impaired. Others who were not Sinn Fein activists supported Griffith although they would never join his organisation. Furthermore, he opened the columns of his paper to those who wished to discredit the 'strike organiser'. Patrick J. MacIntyre was one of the most prominent critics. As an official of the Workers' Union, he had run foul of Larkin while trying to recruit men for his union in competition with the ITGWU. But the differences between the two men ran even deeper, for while both were members of the ILP in Dublin they had little else in common except a limitless capacity to heap scorn on an enemy.

In early 1907 there were few unions bothering to organise the Irish general workers. Two years later there were three major unions in the field and no love was lost between the officials. Larkin's row with Sexton made co-operation between the NUDL and the transport union impossible. Liberty Hall's relations with the Workers' Union was, if anything, even less harmonious. As many moderate trade unionists had feared, the foundation of the transport union had signalled the outbreak of an inter-union war characterised by bitterness and bloodshed.

In Dublin the transport union swept aside all opposition but it was a different story in Belfast where the Workers' Union had a strong hold. Life was particularly difficult for all general unions in the northern capital since the labour struggle in 1907. A free labourers' bureau had been opened by the stevedores and ITGWU members were boycotted and not given work. In Dundalk and Newry the transport union had partial success in rekindling the spirit, which once drove the now defunct NUDL branch, amongst the disheartened local men.

Some of the most bitter inter-union fighting took place in Cork where all three organisations fought for control. Liberty Hall managed to carry many local NUDL men into the transport union. The methods employed by Fearon to achieve this were rough. Many Cork dockers were simply handed a transport union card when they went to pay their subscriptions at the Liverpool union's offices. Bullying, threatening and boycotting of recalcitrants was not uncommon, nor were the techniques of persuasion used by James Fearon (Round-the-Ring) and his colleagues in Cork uncommon or excessive. The rough and tumble of the docks necessitated a strong physical approach.

Events took a serious turn for the transport union in February 1909. The parliamentary committee of congress, of which Larkin was a member, received a routine complaint from the Belfast organiser of the ITGWU, Michael McKeown, requesting that a sub-committee be appointed to look into the claim that 'members of the NUDL union are at present blacklegging on the members of the former union'.[22]

In less troubled times, the composition of the committee with a high representation of amalgamated union representatives might have favoured Larkin, but he could not have had a worse tribunal to deal with the problems arising out of 'secession'. The temper of the delegates was not helped by the fact that the committee was neither approached nor consulted about the setting up of the breakaway ITGWU. The majority felt snubbed at not being asked to intervene at an early stage in the dispute to try and bring about a reconciliation which would have vitiated the need for another organisation. Perhaps some delegates felt that if Larkin was not wholly responsible for the break with the NUDL he certainly had not gone out of his way to avoid the rupture. Sexton's theory that he had actually planned and orchestrated the rift may not have been far from their minds. To complicate matters, Larkin had few real friends on the committee. It was his first year on the body. Furthermore, of the nine delegates four were from the the north and they regarded the transport union as a betrayal of the international character of the labour movement and a capitulation to Sinn Fein sectionalism. The two Dublin delegates were hostile to Larkin for personal reasons, and only Stephen Dineen from Limerick could be relied upon for support.

The McKeown complaint was trivial in itself but was sufficient, in the prevailing climate, to refuse an invitation to the ITGWU to attend the congress in Limerick pending settlement of the Belfast dispute. Worse was still to follow. Larkin was a member of the parliamentary committee as a representative of the NUDL. Sexton did not miss his chance and wrote to the committee on 1 March:

> At our executive meeting on Friday a resolution was adopted to the effect that 'we, on behalf of the union, protest against Mr James Larkin voicing the opinions or representing in any way the Dock Labourers' and Transport Workers of the UK or any part of it, as he was originally elected on your parliamentary committee as the representative of our union but has since broken away and formed an opposition union in Ireland.[23]

Sexton did not neglect to point out that, according to the ruling of the joint board of the British Trade Union Congress, 'any so-called new trades union started with the object of catering for any class of workers for which industry an organisation had before existed, shall not be recognised'. The ruling was commended to the committee for its consideration, and after deliberation Larkin was expelled from the committee.

William O'Brien was allowed to attend by the Dublin Branch of the AST although he had to pay his own expenses. He was met at the railway station by Larkin who 'told (him) he had been expelled from EC on motion of E. W. Stewart on previous day'.[24] By a narrow majority, the Standing Orders Committee recommended that the transport union's affiliation be accepted without delay, although it was later agreed that the matter be taken up in the discussion on the report of the parliamentary committee, provided Larkin's name would appear on the ballot paper for the committee were the transport union admitted.

When the parliamentary committee report finally came up for discussion, P. T. Daly moved an amendment deleting all references to the dock labourers. It was a queer instance of impartiality, he argued, but there were two separate organisations of bakers represented without an objection from anyone while when there were two organisations of dockers, one was excluded. The Dublin brushmaker, William Murphy, seconded the amendment, urging that there was no necessity for Irishmen to be subscribing to English funds. Greig defended the committee's decision, claiming that a great deal more importance was attached to this discussion than it was worth. Their action was in support of no person but of trade unionism, 'and if congress was going to say that Larkin and his section could break away from the amalgamated union, then it was goodbye to trade unionism'.

E. W. Stewart embroiled affairs by saying that Larkin, who had gone to Belfast as the 'henceman' of Sexton, came to Dublin and 'fell into the arms of Mr P. T. Daly and some socialists and Sinn Feiners'. The initial division between Larkin and Sexton had only taken place on some personal grounds but now 'there was a question of deliberately dividing trade unionism in the interests of a political party':

> Mr Daly and his political faction were attempting to smash the combination of trade unionism in Ireland and if they succeeded in capturing congress they would eventually do so. It was now the feeling of the labour movement that every step should be taken to prevent the multiplication of organisations affecting the same trade or industry.[25]

The most articulate spokesman for the committee was the Derry tailor, James McCarron. If congress recognised the transport union, he argued, what guarantee had they that the organisation would not split up into further factions in either Dublin or Cork and then step in and demand recognition. As trade unionists they did not oppose the formation of an Irish union but they should not allow the principles of combination to be disregarded. He could not perceive a more vital moment for the labour movement in this country. The decision of the congress might mean the wiping out of their committee and trade unionism, but the members had a duty to discharge and they would not shirk it, he exaggerated. The principle of trade unionism should not give way to the question of nationality. They should not think of themselves as either Saxon or Irishman. They were all brothers, no matter which might be the colour of their skin and no matter at what altar they worshipped.

But it was useless for McCarron, one of the more progressive men in congress, to try and gloss over the feelings of delegates. Nationalism was a force just as loyalism was and had to be recognised as such. Men occupying the middle ground of strict labour politics were becoming fewer. Finally, as the meeting became rowdier and more difficult to manage, O'Brien, who seemed to feel immediately at home in his new surroundings, moved to suspend standing orders and allow Larkin to speak in his own defence. Several delegates protested loudly when the motion was ruled out of order. At this point Larkin, who was sitting in the gallery with the other barred ITGWU delegates, stood up and began to speak. This move, noted O'Brien, created terrible scenes; when the vote was finally taken the parliamentary committee's report was carried unamended by 49 votes to 39. Later it was agreed to appoint a seven-man committee of inquiry to look into the cause and development of the dispute which led to the formation of the transport union. Larkin's followers had done particularly well in the elections for the nine seats on the parlimentary committee. O'Lehane was voted in; Rochford of the hairdressers' union was also elected and one or two others formed the panel who were capable of being won over, as O'Brien noted with dismay in his diary.

The balance of power in Congress was so narrow that the admission of the ITGWU would swing the voting in favour of the South. Larkin and his followers had lost narrowly in Limerick, but had no reason to feel dejected. O'Brien set about working out the chances of the ITGWU getting a favourable hearing from the committee.[26] No sooner had Larkin fought off the first attack from congress than he discovered that this was really the signal for a full-scale offensive against him. On 10 June, O'Brien was told by Larkin that 'there is a strike of his men on in Cork and that Egan and Lynch have brought down Harris to play the game against him (L)'.[27] This was only the beginning.

The Cork stevedores had every reason to feel unhappy about the presence of the transport union in the port. Under the new conditions the men themselves bargained with the shipowners as to the price of discharge. The middleman or stevedore was virtually redundant as a result. All the money paid by the firm was now divided amongst the men by one of themselves, generally a trade union official. The disquiet of the stevedores was shared by some of the shipping companies, and finally it was decided to form a rival union which would recognise the former practice. Harris of the workers' union was invited to the city and a meeting was held in the office of one, O'Rourke, a stevedore. The transport union men regarded the new union as bogus.[28]

Harris felt perfectly justified in moving into what the transport union now considered to be their territory. On 10 June, the day Larkin had spoken to O'Brien, some coalporters objected to working with eight Workers' Union men. Over 140 dockers quit work at the Cork Steam Packet Company line, and some ITGWU goods porters on the Great Southern and Western Railway came out in sympathy. As the strike spread, Harris immediately set about arranging with the shipping company to have members of his union replace the striking transport men. Some 130 men had been sent by the Shipping Federation to help the Cork employers through the strike. A further 100 railwaymen struck when the goods porters were dismissed, and the carters followed them out soon after.

As extra police poured into the city all efforts to bring the employers to the conference table proved unsuccessful. The Cork Employers Federation agreed to dismiss immediately any employee who should 'wilfully disobey any lawful order out of sympathy with any strike or trade dispute', fill the vacancy left with local labour or from any available source; and that no member of the Federation would employ any men so discharged. The Federation had thousands of pounds behind it, but according to a correspondent for the *Irish Nation,* the men had made 'a deplorable blunder', because they had come out without any money whatever.[29] Consequently, the employers prolonged the dispute deliberately, refusing all offers of mediation. The Federation appeared to want to stamp out general worker unions in the city altogether. By 26 July, the strike was broken, but public opinion was not fully on the side of the masters. The punishment was far in excess of the 'crime'. W. P. Ryan editorialised that the Cork employers were not 'practical Christians':

> Whatever the faults and vices of the unfortunate dock labourers they are indeed mild when compared with the unchristian and selfish action of these persons who pretend to have a monopoly of intelligence and culture.[30]

The strike had one beneficial effect however: the Workers' Union was everywhere held in disgrace. On 5 July, the DTC suspended the Harris union after MacIntyre had failed to turn up before the committee to answer certain changes brought by the transport union. Even the mention of the name led to fierce recriminations in the trades hall. Paradoxically, it was the left-wing members of the council who had done most to get it off the ground initially and many of the older members were not slow to use the chance to score some debating points over their rivals.

Harris and the workers' union were the least of Larkin's worries. On 18 August he was arrested while on his way home to Auburn Street on a warrant issued in Cork alleging conspiracy to fraud. The same day James Fearon was also held by police along with two other labourers, Denis Sullivan and Daniel Coveney.[31] The next day Larkin was brought to Cork where he was formally charged. The magisterial enquiries into the particulars of the case were protracted from 24 August until 21 September. Basically, the case was brought out of spite and revenge by some of Larkin's many union enemies and with the tacit consent and approval of the Cork employers. F. W. Wynne who was the Cork Employers' Federation solicitor appeared for the prosecution. During the three-week hearing every effort was made to demonstrate that a properly constituted branch of the NUDL never existed in Cork. Once this was satisfactorily proven the prosecution could draw the damaging conclusion that Larkin had defrauded the dockers by taking subscriptions for a non-existent branch and making promises of benefits which could not be delivered.

Key witness for the prosecution was James Sexton who came to Cork as he did to Dublin later in the year—clutching the butt of a revolver. Carrying his 'very life in his hands', he told the inquiry that although he had sent Larkin to Cork no branch had ever been established. He never received a weekly statement from Fearon, not so much 'as the stroke of a pen'.[32] Further examination revealed that an executive meeting must ratify a new branch and no such meeting had taken place until January, 1909. Consequently, the prosecution case was proven.

From a trade union point of view, however, the inquiry before the trial worked very much to Larkin's advantage. This can be gauged by the changing mood of the DTC. On 23 August, Daly moved the suspension of standing orders to discuss Larkin's arrest, only to be told by Rochford (Hairdressers, in the chair) to carry on with normal business.[33] But by 31 August indifference had turned to disgust with Sexton and the judiciary, and open support for Larkin. Daly again proposed a motion of solidarity with Larkin and he was supported by one George Leahy, a powerful man on the council and no friend of Larkin. Not everybody could be expected to overcome their enmity for 'Big Jim': 'I suggest,' said another delegate, 'that in order to get Mr Stewart's support, the resolution should be altered to read "that Larkin should be hanged".'[34]

Larkin was returned for trial to the winter assizes in Cork and again granted bail. O'Brien met him in Dublin and found him 'quite confident of winning in conspiracy trial'.[35] He had every reason to feel more confident when the venue was shifted to Dublin at his request, but he was also underestimating the prosecution. He faced no fewer than twenty-four charges ranging from criminal conspiracy to deception and misappropriation of funds. Hearing the trial in Cork or Dublin really made very little difference. He was hated equally in both commercial centres.

At least in the capital he was able to take care of union affairs. Fortunately, the trial was postponed until July so Larkin was able to devote his time to preparing for congress and the battle to have the ITGWU accepted as a *bona fide* union. Larkin went to the congress in Dundalk in a dual capacity. He led the transport union delegation and was also representing the DTC; he had to be admitted this time. Stewart, as secretary of the parliamentary committee, tried to frustrate this tactic, and instructed the DTC to have a substitute ready because he could not issue credentials to a man whose union was barred from congress. On O'Lehane's proposal, a letter was sent to Stewart informing him that the two delegates chosen by the council would be sent.[36]

Congress opened in Dundalk on 16 May on an acrimonious note. Vice-president, Miss Mary Galway, on taking the chair, said the first duty of delegates was to pass a vote of condolence with Queen Alexandra in her bereavement. O'Brien was on his feet immediately protesting that the sympathy of Irish workers had much better be extended to the victims of the recent colliery disaster of Whitehaven. The Galway motion was carried and after other preliminaries congress settled down to deal with the ITGWU question. McCarron was in the chair for the debate. Stewart, a bitter critic of Larkin, read the sub-committee report on the cause and development of the dispute between the two unions. The committee was obviously deeply divided and this was reflected in its findings.

After two days and further long depositions from the disputants, the committee found that 'no real justification existed for the secession, based on the complaint, as to illegal action or improper treatment on the part of the national union'. However, the committee also recommended, although it was outside their terms of reference, that:

> As it is accepted on all sides that there is no objection to the formation and existence of an Irish union, we are of opinion that the Irish Transport workers' union is a *bona fide* labour union, and entitled to recognition in the trade union movement.[37]

Maurice Canty was first to his feet to support the transport union. His experience of English organisation was that they would take all, and when Irish branches were 'in a hole' would leave them there (applause). O'Lehane rejected Stewart's amendment to postpone a decision pending the outcome of the Larkin trial, and said they must presume the innocence of fellow trade unionists until they were found guilty. There were nearly 3,000 workers in the union and were they to be denied representation because of one man? The man in question had been assailed by capitalists, and were they as trade unionists to join in a vendetta against him, asked O'Lehane. He thought that any action to exclude Larkin was reprehensible in the extreme.

Joseph Clarke (Amalgamated Soc. of Carpenters, Dublin) supported O'Lehane. Another Dublin delegate, 'who differed with Larkin', wanted him admitted, at least as a DTC delegate. Harris countered by asking how congress could possibly admit a union which had seceded from its parent body without justification. This was only the thin edge of the wedge of nationalism, he argued, because the aspirations of the men supporting it were to oppose all amalgamateds. Harris lost all credibility when William Murphy told the congress how the previous speaker once tried to start an Irish union and published an outline of the scheme in the papers. Moreover, Murphy added, he was present when Harris offered his services to Larkin to complete the very union which he now so bitterly complained of as an enemy to trade unionism. Harris stood disgraced but others, particularly northern delegates, kept up the fight. McCarron refused to act as an impartial chairman. There was no man in Ireland who had done more service to the employers than Mr Larkin, he shouted. He would never support a man who went round creating strikes, taking out men without any support and leaving the poor people wandering about.

The Stewart amendment was lost by 38 votes to 22 and a Belfast delegate then proposed that the transport union be excluded from congress for at least two years. Willie Walker of Belfast, opposing the amendment, said the chairman was unwittingly building Larkin up to be a martyr. They were making him loom large because of their opposition and if they only let him alone Larkin would soon find his own level. He moved a further technical amendment, which was carried by 42 votes to 10, and the amended resolution was then put and carried, although the chairman refused to admit the transport union men until after lunch. Larkin rushed onto the floor and asked why he should be debarred. There were sitting in congress 'notorious blacklegs' and enemies of trade unionism, he said amid a chorus of boos. Finally, the ITGWU delegates were allowed to take their seats. Larkin 'thanked the dels. and almost broke down in speaking',[38] apologising for his hasty action a few moments earlier. The remarks made by individuals he was prepared to pass over, but he intended to deal with them at another time. He did not belong to any party—Sinn Fein, Unionist, or United Irish League. In no country could a person point a finger of scorn at Jim Larkin. It was a moment of personal triumph for the general secretary of the ITGWU although the cost of the victory on the Irish trade union movement and the labour movement was high. The transport union had been born in a welter of bitter recrimination, had caused personal hatreds amongst union activists, and had exacerbated the differences between unionists and nationalists. Numerically, the trade union movement was stronger after the transport union had joined the ranks, but feelings of political sectionism ran higher than ever. Congress was ill-equipped to withstand one of the most serious challenges to the solidarity of labour in Ireland brought about by the Home Rule struggle.

Larkin's trial was really a formality. When the hearing opened his initial confidence about the outcome gave way to pessimism. O'Brien, who always kept his ear close to the ground, heard that 'Larkin says he will be convicted by the County Dublin jury and that he thinks he would be as safe if tried in Cork'.[39] Sexton travelled from Liverpool and repeated his damaging evidence. The defence had really no evidence to counter the charges of wilful fraud and misappropriation of funds. No account books were produced. Later, O'Brien was told that Daly said the reason the transport union did not show the books was because 'they knew that if they did L(arkin) would have got 12 years instead of 12 months'.[40] The defence laboured on, resting its case on Larkin's fine, moral character, but the jury was not impressed.

On 17 June 1910, the jury found Larkin guilty and strongly recommended his co-defendant, Coveney, to the consideration of the court. Justice Boyd sentenced Larkin to 12 months, with hard labour. He then turned to Coveney but Larkin interjected:

> Mr Coveney is an ordinary workingman in Cork—Don't give him an hour. The man never received one penny of this money. Though things are put before the jury in a different position, Mr Coveney has had no hand, act or part in it, and to sentence this man would be a travesty of justice. He has a wife in Cork. I ask you to allow him to depart. Like myself he has never been in jail.[41]

The justice paid tribute to the generosity of Larkin in taking all the blame and released Coveney. O'Brien recorded the reaction to the news in his diary: 'Larkin found guilty . . . Terrible shock to everyone. The judge had seemed to be very favourable all day.

Universal sympathy with Larkin.'[42] The *Freeman's Journal* later summed up popular liberal feeling over the outcome of the trial: '... although technically he had broken the law he had been guilty of no moral turpitude, and that the sentence was altogether disproportionate to the offence'.[43] Larkin's popularity had reached its zenith and the men were more loyal to him than ever before. The ITGWU supported him fully:

> That we the members of the above union, in common assembly, desire to place on record our appreciation of the services rendered our union and the cause of labour generally by our respected organiser, James Larkin. And we do humbly pledge our explicit confidence in his sterling honesty and integrity of character.[44]

On 20 June, the DTC endorsed the stand taken by the transport union on the jailing of their general secretary:

> That we firmly believe in his honesty and integrity of character and protest in the strongest manner against the unwarrantable sentence which has been passed on him ... We do hereby pledge ourselves to use every means in our power to have his sentence revoked and that a memorial be presented to the Lord Lieutenant for consideration of his sentence with a view to its remission.[45]

Support also came across the channel. *Justice* demanded that Larkin's sentence should be suspended pending the outcome of a judicial inquiry. The *Clarion* also voiced its condemnation. The Industrial Workers of Liverpool 'entered their emphatic protest against the savage sentence' passed on such 'meagre evidence'.[46]

On 2 July an application was made for a new trial and on 29 July it was refused. This was the signal for an all-out campaign to have Larkin released. A memorial was distributed and sent to the Lord Lieutenant. The clamour was so loud that Aberdeen could hardly afford not to listen. O'Brien visited Larkin in Mountjoy, and found him 'in good spirits but looked worn out and haggard. Says if he gets out God help Sexton'.[47] But Liberty Hall could not cope without Larkin. The transport union was 'sinking fast', according to Daly.[48]

Larkin was released on 1 October and received a hero's welcome from the trade union movement. After a torchlight procession through the streets he addressed a rally at Beresford Place, where he attacked the prison system although he assured the crowd that he had been treated quite well. The following day he spoke at another monster meeting on the same theme. Gifted with the sense of the dramatic, he produced a small box from his pocket and proceeded to tell an attentive crowd that it contained half an ounce of flour and a quarter of it consisted of weevils, worms, grubs and maggots on which the prisoners of Mountjoy were fed. His spell in jail had done little to impair his talents as a mass orator. He was master of the public platform and it was in this area he relied to maintain his hold over the workers. On one occasion, William O'Brien recounts how Larkin suddenly stopped in the middle of a speech and said he wanted to send a telegram. He 'wrote the wire while the crowd looked on, the bulk of them fascinated as if he was performing some miracle'.[49]

After his release he seemed more relaxed, more ebullient and more vitriolic than ever before. He was at once martyr and messiah riding the crest of an emotional wave of revulsion against his 'unjust' imprisonment. It was felt that he had been sent to Mountjoy, not because of the crime, but to propitiate the employer class who wanted him out of the way. W. P. Ryan felt that Larkin had been punished 'for Sinn Fein principles in the social order':

> Many thousands of us workers, employers and the rest have been more surely in prison since mid-summer than he—not within stone walls but within the worse prison of apathy, prejudice, self-interest and more.[50]

Ryan read the popular guilt complex over the treatment and criticism of Larkin quite well, yet the transport union general secretary's *vox populi* canonisation process established a highly dangerous precedent. Larkin was being placed on a lofty pedestal putting him outside the mundane realm of criticism and normal accountability. For the moment this was lost sight of in the welter of excitement that followed his dramatic release from Mountjoy. He was invested with a new sense of urgency, an impatience and determination to get things done quickly. Larkin's 'unjust ordeal', predicted Ryan, 'will give a new spirit and momentum to his mission'.[51] He was proved right.

A Shift to the Left: The Politics of the Dublin Trades Council

Larkin was an indefatigable campaigner. On the industrial front no issue ever escaped his attention or the lash of his aspish tongue. At the beginning of 1910 the DTC was grappling with the problem of coming to terms with labour exchanges. Under the Unemployed Workman Act (1905) exchanges had been formed alongside municipal schemes for absorbing the unemployed, and the London exchange had enjoyed most success. After four years of experimentation an Act extended the scheme throughout the country. Britain was divided into ten divisions, over each of which there was a divisional officer, with so many exchanges of first, second, or third class, according to the number of cities in the division. Ideally, those exchanges had managers, and sub-offices existed in minor towns, while there were waiting rooms in the smaller towns. They formed a network with a central clearing house in London.

Ireland formed a division by itself with Dublin as the centre. First class exchanges were scheduled for Belfast and Dublin. Third class centres were to be set up in Derry, Limerick and Waterford, while Cork was to get a second class exchange. In country areas post offices were to act as sub-centres. Employers and workmen would fill in forms detailing their needs and these would be forwarded to first class exchanges where they would be sorted and co-ordinated. They were to deal with all classes of. labour, except domestic servants.

On the drawing board, the scheme exhibited all the precision of the German model on which it was based. But it had one major defect as far as Ireland was concerned. It would not work. It was based on the principle that what was appropriate for England was equally effective across the channel. The Board of Trade was of the impression that the major cause of unemployment in Dublin and other urban centres was due to the flow of emigrants from the country. Put popularly, the philosophy supported the commonly-held view that but for the 'culchie' there would be plenty of work in the cities and towns for the indigenous population. Industrialisation, not redistribution of the work force, was the key to the labour problem. Consequently, labour exchanges were of very little direct assistance to an under-developed, agrarian economy. What Dublin needed was factories to give employment, not labour exchanges to register and catalogue the chronically workless masses.

Every effort was made to sell the idea to the workers. Askwith explained the hopes and aims of the institution to trade unions in Belfast, Dublin, Cork and Waterford.[52] But there was a basic hostility to the idea based on the suspicion that the exchanges would turn into agencies for the simplified recruitment of free labour. Tom McPartlin (Amalg. Society of Carpenters and Joiners) was usually very balanced in his views, but on the question of exchanges he was adamant. He opposed the idea from the outset:

He felt they were merely to provide jobs for the wastrels left over from the South African war. Labour exchanges would nullify everything the trades council had done for the past 20 years. These exchanges would put the scab on an equal footing with the ordinary worker without requiring the scab to pay for the upkeep of his trade organisation.[53]

The issue united the conservative George Leahy and the left-wing William Murphy. The former said the exchanges could only damage organised labour while the latter said he was instinctively distrustful of employers' Acts. Murphy claimed that what was required was not an Act to enable surplus population to be transferred from one district to another; what was really wanted was a better division of wealth to meet the problem.[54]

Major Fuge, who was director of exchanges for Ireland, came before the council to explain the project and answer questions, but he was by no means addressing the converted. Larkin was not over-enthusiastic about the idea: his main complaint centred around the appointment of people 'who knew nothing about labour in this country' to run the exchanges.[55] After Fuge had gone out of his way to allay the suspicions, the misconceptions and fears of his audience regarding free labour, strike breaking, union rates and working hours, he was cornered by Larkin. With disarming frankness, the transport union general secretary asked him if he thought it right to appoint an almost total stranger to the industrial conditions of Ireland to supervise exchanges. Fuge replied rather testily that as for his own credentials, he was an Irishman, hinting at Larkin's Liverpudlian origins perhaps. Not to be out-witted, Larkin countered that he was not speaking of an Irishman, Creole or Hottentot. He was speaking of a gentleman who had been engaged in a country where Hottentot and low class labour was the rule, coming to Ireland to work the exchanges.

At the next council meeting, however, Larkin argued that trade unionists should give qualified approval to the scheme but reserve their final opinion until the Act was seen in operation. He also thought that trade unionists should be represented on both the advisory committee and the administration board. Despite bitter opposition, he carried the council on a resolution of qualified acceptance of the project.

At this stage Larkin and his followers were gaining the upper hand on the council. Two years previously, he could not have hoped to get such a motion passed. The council executive was far from being 'Larkinite' but an unwritten alliance had grown up between the progressive nationalists like O'Lehane and Daly and the socialist delegates represented by O'Brien and William Murphy.

Between them they formed a majority on the executive and it was not difficult for the tail to wag the dog. The united Irish League had been ousted from its position of dominance by an 'unholy alliance'. In 1909 P. T. Daly headed the poll for the executive with 45 votes, followed by John Farren and Tom McPartlin with 40 votes; Larkin was third with 37; William O'Brien and William Murphy were also elected.

The next year the executive and council were clearly in the hands of the progressive wing with Larkin, McPartlin, O'Lehane, O'Brien, Daly and William Murphy all returned. In 1911, Thomas Murphy was made president and William O'Brien replaced John Simmons, who retired temporarily from the post as secretary of the council because of ill-health. During the next three years the Larkinites further strengthened their hold over the council.[56]

However, Larkin did not exactly convert people to his own image and likeness. The reason for his popularity was partially due to his ability to adapt and sail with the prevailing political wind. When he came to Dublin to settle in 1908, he was a comparative neophyte in the trade union movement. During most of his earlier life he had put more faith in politics as a fulcrum for social change. He had spent his time listening to Social Democratic Federation lecturers in Liverpool, imbibing 'ambiguous' philosophy and working for the Independent Labour Party. Even as a busy trade union organiser he still retained a firm connection with the ILP. He was really a trade unionist by accident, a politician by vocation and a socialist by conviction. He did not so much draw his inspiration from the writings of Marx as from marxist thinkers, pamphleteers, street orators and his personal experience of the 'class struggle'. There was one other influence which shaped the direction of his thought and that was Christianity. Raised in Liverpool's Irish ghetto, ritualistic Catholicism as he saw it practised there repulsed the young Larkin. Yet, he saw behind the facade a philosophy which offered both an explanation and a remedy for social injustice. Marxist categories, Larkin thought, amplified and best expressed the radical essence of the Christian message. His marriage of secular and sacred thought was that of an eclectic rather than a scientific synthesis. Publically, Larkin declared himself an avowed Marxist but in no sense was he a purist.[57] For example, at a Socialist Party of Ireland meeting, he said that the principle of socialism was not class hatred, it was brotherhood:

> Perhaps he might be thought to have more reason than most to hate the capitalist class, yet he did not, and had known humane employers who

had recognised the evils of the system. But they were powerless individually to remedy it. As for denunciation of the Catholic Truth Society that socialism was anti-Catholic, etc., speaking as a Catholic, he advised working men not to be deceived by it. It was part of the old Tory Catholic wheeze. There was the Catholic Socialist Society in England and there were as good Catholics in it as Mr Belloc . . .[58]

Larkin really cast himself in the role of a secular Savonarola. His socialism was neither a science nor a sociology: it was a cry of pain.

In Dublin he soon became dissatisfied with the ineffectual efforts of the revived ILP branch to effect radical political change. In the growing nationalist atmosphere of the capital, it was really an English organisation with no indigenous roots. Although it had attracted a number of prominent men, mainly from the amalgamated unions, it lacked any popular following. William O'Brien rarely tried to conceal his contempt for the ILP; many of its members, he thought, were a crowd of rowdies. At an SPI meeting in 1909, some ILP 'roughs' attended, including 'Lynch the boxer', with the intention of 'kicking up a row'. O'Brien heard 'some terrible stories about the ILP', or the 'thimble riggers of Francis St', as he preferred to describe them. Evidently, someone had suggested a social as a means of raising funds and Lynch had suggested a ten-round boxing match. 'What an outrage on the socialist movement. If some of our opponents get this "twill be horrible",' O'Brien wrote in his diary in disgust.[59] But the North Dublin Union master tailor had little to fear. The respectability of the socialist movement was not threatened, and on 17 June, he made the following entry:

> Hear ILP have left High St and gone to room in York St. Looks like break up. What an ending to all their projects. When they started they were to do the devil and all.

Larkin was not slow to realise that the ILP was tottering and had no political future in Dublin. In May 1909, he advocated the formation of an Irish Labour Party while addressing the Drumcondra branch of Sinn Fein. The proposed party would have as one of its main planks the lay control of education. Larkin had no faith in the Nationalist Party and had left its leader, John Redmond, in little doubt about his opinion when he saw him as a member of ITUC parliamentary committee in February, 1909. The transport union general secretary said flatly that the Irish party was not a labour party. But he urged Redmond to insist on the nationalisation of canals and railways and also to get their own shipping and run it under the

Irish flag. Redmond clung to the traditional line:

> When I entered the House of Commons there was no labour party, but
> for my part I have always claimed and I think, truthfully claimed, that in
> that state of affairs the work of the Labour Party was done by the Irish
> Parliamentary Party.[60]

Larkin was not convinced. He saw the necessity to form an
independent Irish labour party which would participate at local and
national level. Most of the problems created by municipal bodies
employing and encouraging non-union labour could be resolved if
there was a strong labour representation on the boards. Many trade
unionists, however, wanted to go further than Larkin. Daly and
O'Lehane wanted to organise labour on an entirely national basis in
federation with the workers of other countries. The idea was hotly
contested and defeated by congress in 1909. The following year
Larkin proposed the founding of an Irish Labour Party and he was
seconded by O'Lehane. The former said it was nonsense to talk of
internationalism in Ireland until they had made men first realise
their responsibility to their own nation. Larkin was showing a new
side to his character. He was a nationalist besides being a Catholic
Marxist.

James Connolly Returns from America

The left-wing lobby for a political party received a great fillip with
the return of James Connolly to Ireland on 26 July, 1910, when
Larkin was in jail. Both men shared a mutual respect for each other
which at times, in the course of the next few years, was often put
under great strain. Connolly differed in almost every aspect with
Larkin. He was small of stature, cautious, reflective and almost
academic in his approach to problems, be they of a practical or
theoretical nature. He was a Marxist and an atheist, while Larkin
was a practising Catholic with little time for theorising. Writing to J.
C. Mathreson in 1908, the former admitted:

> For myself tho I have usually posed as a Catholic, I have not gone to my
> duty for 15 years, and have not the slightest tincture of faith left. I only
> assume the Catholic pose in order to quiz the raw freethinkers whose
> ridiculous dogmatism did and does annoy me as much as the dogmatism
> of the orthodox. In fact I respect the good Catholic more than the
> average free thinker.[61]

Connolly was out of touch with political affairs in Dublin after
his seven-year absence. Writing in the *Irish Nation* from New York

in 1909, he had suggested trying to establish a rapproachement between Sinn Fein and socialism.[62] But for all his political naivety he was excited about the transport union project. Much of his propaganda work from 1908 had been devoted to examining the idea of industrial unionism, and his conclusions were summed up in the pamphlets *Socialism Made Easy* and *The Axe to the Root.* The goal of the movement was the establishment of a Workers' Republic, organised along syndicalist lines.[63] Social democracy, Connolly argued, 'must proceed from the bottom upward, whereas capitalist political society is organised from above downwards'. This was to be done in the following way:

> . . . Under a Socialist Democratic form of society the administration of affairs will be in the hands of representatives of the various industries of the nation; that the workers in the shops and factories will organise themselves into unions, each union comprising all the workers at a given industry; that said union will democratically control that workshop life of its own industry, electing all foremen, etc., and regulating the routine of labour in that industry in subordination to the needs of society in general, to that of its allied trades, and to the department of industry to which it belongs; that representatives elected from these various departments of industry will meet and form the industrial administration or national government of the country.[64]

Such a plan envisaged the withering away of the craft unions and the substitution of vertically organised syndicates belonging to one big union. Connolly was as much out of touch with Irish industrial affairs as he was with national political developments if he thought that the ITGWU had the potential, or its officers had either the wish or intention to move towards anarcho-syndicalist institutions.

Connolly's first few months in the country were marred by confusion and recrimination. His pamphlet, *Labour, Nationality and Religion,* which answered Fr Robert Kane's lenten pastoral attack on socialism, had just been published and had caused an unfavourable reaction in trade union circles. One trades council member said Connolly had a cheek to attempt to reply to Dr Kane.[65] There was further DTC opposition voiced over Connolly's proposed lecture tour. George Leahy used it as an opportunity to denounce socialism vigorously.[66] A motion, proposed by O'Brien, seeking the council's endorsement of a number of Connolly's Dublin lectures, was defeated. But the elderly secretary, John Simmons, surprised everyboy by saying that he intended to attend every talk given by Connolly and he was prepared to chair a meeting if asked.

When the meeting took place Simmons was in the chair, declaring afterwards that 'if the lecture was socialism then he was a socialist'. 'Prominent trades council men all absent,' noted O'Brien. A public meeting was later held at Beresford Place to enable Connolly to answer Fr Kane but it ended in disaster:

> Brady of SF spoke on request and nearly broke up meeting. Said Kane was blind as a bat and did not write his own sermons. Brady would have been mobbed. Most unfortunate incident that occurred in our propaganda for years.[67]

Connolly wanted to remain in Ireland and bring his family back from America but he was not prepared to do so without a firm guarantee of a job. O'Brien and other members of the SPI thought that he would make the ideal national organiser but were doubtful of being able to raise the annual fee demanded by Connolly. An appeal was launched to get that money, but did not meet with much success. Connolly was adamant; he wanted a guaranteed wage to keep his wife and family, a legitimate request as a parent which led some of the SPI to question his commitment as a socialist. One T.K. told O'Brien that Connolly had become the professional propagandist and did not believe in making sacrifices while he did not hesitate to demand austerity from the members.[68]

However, the dilemma was soon resolved by requesting Larkin to make Connolly the Belfast organiser of the ITGWU even though the latter was somewhat reluctant to take the post if offered it. Writing to O'Brien on 20 September, 1910, he said:

> As for Larkin's job, I fancy that Jim will have enough to do to pull his forces together without bearing the responsibility of my sins. I was glad that I was able to initiate the move that led to his release but don't want to demand a price for it.[69]

A month later he explained his hesitancy more clearly:

> Personally, I would not dream of allowing Jim Larkin to push me upon the payroll of his union and thus make me the target for all the malcontents and reactionaries who hate him but fear his influence, and so would wreak their petty spite upon the paid official thus forced upon them from abroad. Nay, nay, William, that job would be far more valueless than any guarantee from socialist sources.[70]

Connolly was obviously more interested in directing socialist propaganda and organisation. However, he took the job and accepted Larkin, whom he described as 'an overgrown schoolboy', as his boss. He threw himself into the arduous task which faced him in Belfast but he still felt that it was not the proper work for him. His dedication to the transport union was not helped by two factors: his political beliefs and the strained relations with Larkin.

Politically, Connolly was a republican and a separatist. As organiser of an Irish-based union, his strident nationalism did little to advance the interests of the ITGWU. Before he returned from America, he made his position quite clear:

> If I were asked upon their (ILP) platform (in Belfast) what my views are . . . I would state frankly that I am a separatist, and do not believe that the English government has any right in Ireland, never had any right, and never can have any right. I can imagine the mess that would make of an ILP meeting in Belfast.[71]

Although Connolly may not have realised it, his political views, expressed in so vigorous and forthright a fashion, did much to impede the growth of the transport union. But the real drawback was the national structure of the ITGWU, and Larkin did not help matters either:

> To make matters worse, I confess to you (O'Brien) in confidence that I don't think I can stand Larkin as boss much longer. He is singularly unbearable. He is forever snarling at me and drawing comparisons between what he accomplished in Belfast in 1907, and what I have done, conveniently ignoring the fact that he was then the secretary of an *English* organisation and that as soon as he started an *Irish* one, his union fell to pieces and he had to leave the members to their jobs.[72]

Connolly, who rarely indulged in personal recriminations, was unbridled in his criticism. Larkin, he added,

> is consumed with jealously and hatred of anyone who will not cringe to him and beslaver him all over. He tried to bully me out of the monies due to our branch for administration benefit of the Insurance Act, and it was this that brought me to Dublin last week. He did not succeed, and had to pay £37.0.0 which was due to my staff in wages. I told him that if he was Larkin twenty times over he could not bully me.[73]

Yet despite their many differences both Larkin and Connolly shared a common ideal; both wanted to strengthen the political wing of the labour movement. Their aim was achieved two years later in 1912 when the ITUC, meeting in Clonmel and presided over by Michael O'Lehane, agreed to found the Irish Labour Party. By that time it was too late to reverse the order of events. The industrial struggle had taken precedence over the political road to socialism.

The Transport Union Comes of Age

After getting off to a very shaky start, the ITGWU began to find its feet from the time Larkin was released from jail. It is difficult to be accurate about the number of members actually in the union prior to 1913. From a public platform it was not uncommon for Larkin to claim that there were 15,000 in his organisation. In reality, his union had less than a third of that figure. In the absence of records, annual affiliation fees paid to congress provide the best, although not the most reliable, gauge. In 1911, Liberty Hall paid for 5,000 members, enough to give them the strongest delegation at congress.[74] It is not at all unlikely that extra money was paid in order to ensure the presence of a few extra delegates at congress to strengthen Larkin's hand in some of the more crucial votes. If the membership figures were deliberately falsified for this purpose, then it seems possible that the ITGWU was as low as 3,000 at the beginning of that year. But Larkin was about to step up his propaganda work. As editor of *The Harp* in 1910, he had shown his ability as a journalist. Unfortunately for the Dublin labour movement *The Harp*, along with its predecessor, *The Dublin Trade and Labour Journal* of 1909 died because of production difficulties and the weakness of content. In 1911, Larkin was determined to launch a successful paper for workers.

The labour movement in the city could expect little sympathy from local dailies. The *Daily Express* was ultra-Unionist as was its sister paper the *Evening Herald*. The *Irish Times* was also Unionist although less partisan than the *Express*. Nevertheless reportage was heavily biased and its editorial columns gave unqualified support to the employers. The *Irish Independent,* although nationalist in outlook, shared the suspicion of the *Express* for organised labour. The *Freeman's Journal* and its sister paper, the *Evening Telegraph,* were most sympathetic to the trade unions, but their support could not be depended upon.

The first number of the *Irish Worker and People's Advocate,* edited by Larkin, appeared on 27 May, 1911. It was a weekly and cost one penny. By June, 26,000 copies were being sold; the following month, 66,000 were being printed and bought; in September, 94,994 copies of the *Irish Worker* were being sold in the city according to union sources.[75]

The *Irish Worker* was not out of keeping with the prevailing trends among the 'minority' journalists in the city. In common with

Sinn Fein, the *Leader* and even the *Irish Rosary,* Larkin's paper was abusive, tendentious and made light of character assassination. But the *Irish Worker* went a stage further. It was vitriolic, scurrilous and many of the issues were 'a libel a line'. Nobody or no organisation was safe from the hatred of Larkin's pen. In the first issue, which proved markedly restrained by comparison with later numbers, Larkin's front page editorial outlined 'Our Platform and Principles'. The various definitions of freedom, imputed to the numerous nationalist factions, were dismissed contemptuously by the author:

> The word Freedom to the All-for-William (O'Brien) League means a joining of hands with that party of sycophants, privilege-mongers, place-hunters, nation-levellers, blood-suckers, and carrion-crow that go to form the Unionist party in this country . . . And what do the Ardilauns, Dunravens, Moores and Campbells mean by Freedom?— that they, the privileged minority, shall continue to monopolise all places of profit and interests that we, the common Irishry, as they call us, will continue in the future as in the past to allow them and the fell brood who have battened on us and our people for the last 800 years to keep 'adoing it' as the Cockney says. Freedom to exploit; Freedom to degrade, to insult, to ridicule the Nation which feeds and clothes them, and which too long has given them shelter. The day is coming fast when those vampires will find that this right-little-tight-little island, is too circumscribed for such creatures, who mean by Freedom liberty to foul the nest in which they were too tenderly reared.[76]

Arthur Griffith, with his 'imported economies and imported capitalists' was also denounced in ringing tones. The Nationalist party which, Larkin claimed, had opposed every bit of ameliorative social legislation being applied to Ireland, was honest about where it stood even if it was reactionary. It had no interest in the material welfare of the Irish worker, according to Larkin.

But politicians and employers were not the only people to be held up to obloquy as oppressors of the poor. The partially-justified prejudice of the Dublin poor towards the DMP was given substance. Some police were 'skulking bullies' lounging 'against the street corners of our city'. Larkin even charged that in order to get promotion in the DMP one had to be a time-server or 'kick off with the right foot'. He also suggested that if a policeman changed his opinions and, still better, 'his creed to suit the parties in power not only in the police but in many other government offices', it would be conducive to advancement.[77] The city's 3,000 publicans were attacked with equal ferocity as were Freemasons and recalcitrant trade unionists. There were even regrettable examples of anti-Semitism, pandering to local prejudice. The overall tone of the paper was intemperate and inflammatory. It pursued a policy of pouring oil on troubled waters.

But the *Irish Worker,* despite its many shortcomings, filled a void. It exposed scandals of 'sweating' and boy labour in the factories of the city, taught the workers their rights through a legal column and engendered in many a sense of hope against the crushing prospect of lifelong poverty. It did not undermine the authority of the state, as opponents claimed, but it did accelerate the deteriorating respect that the common people held for discredited institutions which turned a blind eye on municipal corruption and Rachmanism. Larkin and his paper did not produce an original Labour philosophy. Together they released a force among the workers which had been suppressed for years by factionalism and sheer poverty. This confused and palpitating sense of grievance and unrequited appeals for redress became known pejoratively as 'Larkinism'.

Strike Fever in Dublin

Trade union unrest in the city extended far beyond the bounds of 'Larkinism', and many employers continued to show a great reluctance to deal with even the longest-established, *bona-fide* unions. A typical example of the latter presented itself in the case of the brushmakers employed by Varians of Talbot Street. In November 1909, a dispute arose after an effort was made to cut the wages of the seventy employees and seven apprentices. William Murphy, who was shop steward for the British-based union, was warned that unless the men acquiesced they faced dismissal. Varians were Quakers and their factory was run on near-Calvanistic lines where it was demonstrated that if anyone was pre-destined for salvation and its attendant benefits in this world, it was certainly not the workers. Murphy, knowing the authoritarian views of his employer, did not treat the warning lightly but nevertheless decided that strike action was the only course open to the men. Feelings were intensified against Varian when the men discovered that he had been trying to recruit brushmakers in Oldham and Liverpool even before the strike began.[78] At a meeting of the DTC, Murphy referred to his employer's reputation as a philanthropist; he said the brushmakers had to pay themselves for the upkeep of the factory choir and its annual outings. Another speaker added that the real nature of Varian was revealed in his effort to reduce his workers' wages by 30% while, at the same time, he imported brushes in order to break the strike.

By February, Varian was using 'blackleg' labour recruited principally in Belfast, and housed on the premises. All efforts by the union to submit the case to arbitration were turned down and as the strike dragged on, without any hope of settlement in sight, a novel attempt was made to set up a rival business, to be called the Dublin Brushmaker's Manufacturing Company Ltd. The Lord Mayor, Nannetti, Fred Kelly, Lorcan Sherlock, Briscoe and others were behind the scheme; it was intended to float a company with a share capital of £10,000,[79] and trade unions were encouraged to buy a quantity of shares at 2s each. The venture never really got off the drawing board, the strike lasted nearly eight months and ended in total disaster for the men. In August some of the 'blacklegs' considered that conditions were so bad in Varians that they risked going to the trades hall in Capel Street to look for assistance to get home, claiming that Varian was literally paying them whatever he wished.[80]

By August the strike was broken; O'Brien wrote in his diary:

> I hear that about a dozen of the strikers from Varian have gone back to work there. They went to Varian and he (got) them to submit a list of names which they did. He then selected a number of those who had not taken any part in the strike and got them to sign agreement that they would not belong to any trade union and that they would work on his terms. This they agreed to and the society sanctioned going in on their terms.[81]

The brushmakers' union in the city was shattered. Many men remained out of work and were forced to seek jobs outside their trade, and as far as the employers were concerned it was just like old times.

On 14 June, however, a threatened strike by seamen and firemen began at Southampton. Two days later, Goole followed their example and, on the twentieth, Hull was paralysed by the strike. The men had discovered a national programme and were determined to press their claims in spite of ruinous effects their action might have on the coronation ceremony. In Dublin the transport union helped out their striking seamen colleagues by implementing a selective sympathetic strike. On 26 June, 350 dockers struck for higher wages. The following day, Manchester dockers ceased work and were joined by the carters on 3 July.

In the midst of the labour unrest the new king, George V, visited Dublin and was given a rapturous reception by all classes. Workers turned out in their thousands to see the new monarch. As he went in procession through the city: 'Slumland too was passed through; and the very humble classes in our city evidenced their cead mile failte with no uncertain sound.'[82]

Touched by this reception, the king gave £1,000 to the poor of the city and added, when leaving: 'We can only say that our best wishes will be ever for the increased prosperity of and the contentment and happiness of the Irish people'. But there was neither happiness nor contentment in some quarters of the city. On 14 July, the carters and fillers in J. J. Carroll's had gone out in sympathy with the seamen and firemen. This was seen as a breach of the 1908 agreement and the men were ordered back to work on threat of a lockout of the entire trade.

On 16 July, all the leading coal merchants paid off their men; about 800 were affected by the decision. However, some of the smaller firms remained working because they did not wish to risk a confrontation with the union. More significantly, they realised that by 'scabbing' on their fellow employers they could extend their own businesses by poaching customers from the others. Three firms who did not employ union labour were not affected. A further 130 men were on the street when a fertiliser plant on Sir John Rogerson's Quay was hit by a strike. On 20 July, the Customs House docks were paralysed when the men went out without any warning.

As carts travelled under police escort through the city they were subject to attack. Objects were dropped from tenement windows onto the drays; bricks and bottles were thrown at the drivers and some carts were overturned and their contents pilfered and strewn across the road. An effigy of one of the coal merchants was burned in Shaw Street by some strikers. Meanwhile evictions were imminent due to non-payment of rent. Yet the majority of the strikers remained calm. Each day, they dressed in their 'Sunday best' and trooped to Beresford Place:

> With scrupulously clean faces and hands and attired in their best apparel they are hardly recognisable as the men who throughout the year drive through the city shining in what the Americans call 'carbon powder'. The coal porters and seamen are fraternising, and over foaming tankards, they discuss their hard fate and sigh for the period when the tyranny of capital will be completely abolished.[83]

On 5s a week strike pay, the number of 'foaming tankards' of stout or porter available to men who had to support large families was few and far between. Larkin was anxious to bring the strike to a speedy conclusion but his hands were tied by the prolongation of the dispute in England. Askwith was battling to hammer out a settlement by means of arbitration rather than by the usual method of coercion. Finally, the shipping federation caved in and recognised the seamen's union and agreed to an increase in wages, a great victory for Wilson and Mann. In Dublin, Larkin shared the fruits of victory. After refusing Sir James Dougherty's request to open discussions with the employers on the basis of the 1908 agreement, the union was invited back a second time when they met two representatives of the employers, Mr McCormick and Mr Watson.

> We went there (Dublin Castle) as the accredited representatives of the organisation of the workers, namely, the Transport Union, the Dockers' Union of Liverpool, the Carters' Union of Liverpool and Firemen's Union of Great Britain and Ireland. We spoke in their name. We told them we came as the representatives of these unions, accredited to discuss the matter with the employers.[84]

For a man like McCormick to sit at the same table as Larkin was a great triumph for the latter. It meant that of the ITGWU had gained implicit recognition, at least from some of the most powerful employers in the city. The wage concessions made to the seamen were substantial: they were put on the Glasgow rate of 32s 6d per week. At a meeting in Beresford Place, Larkin was happy with the outcome. He told his audience that he had no respect for the King or His Excellency as such, 'but as a man I say the Earl of Aberdeen is very sympathetic . . . and well disposed towards the working class'. Sir James Dougherty who had received 'a good training' had done more than any other person to settle the dispute and he deserved thanks 'for acting a man's part'. Larkin knew that the victory was far from decisive for other firms had stood aside and refused to be privy to a deal with the rebellious transport union. But before Larkin could decide on an independent course of action, industrial unrest in England began once again to dictate the pattern of the struggle in Dublin. The Transport Workers' Federation brought the dockers of London out on strike on 8 August. Ancillary trades soon followed their example and the port was brought to a standstill. On Tower Hill, where the strike committee had established its headquarters, meetings were held nightly. On one occasion, Ben Tillett cried out: 'O God, strike Lord Davenport dead.' The latter was the chairman of the London Dock's Board and was, according to the pen of cartoonist, Will Dyson, the personification of the uncaring 'fat capitalist'.

By the end of August the docks strike had been settled and the men had increased the 6d per hour rate, won in 1889, by two pence. The railwaymen were even more militant. On 5 August thousands of union carters, employed by the North Eastern Railway came out at Liverpool for higher wages and shorter hours, and were soon joined by other railway men. Sectarian rioting broke out in the city between the Catholic and Protestant Irish and the Lord Mayor wrote for military assistance from the Home Office. Winston Churchill, Home Secretary at the time, quickly complied with the request. Troops were poured into the city but without effect. Rioting was so bad by 14 August that the local shipowners decided to lock out all men engaged in cargo work. On 18 August, troops opened fire on strikers at Llanelly, in Carmarthenshire, killing two men and wounding another. The Amalgamated Society of Railway Servants called a general strike the same day. In Dublin an ASRS emergency meeting was assured that the society had half a million pounds in fighting funds while ASLEF had £183,000. Some 2,000 men answered the call, and all the lines were badly hit except the Great Eastern. Most of the workers of the latter company belonged to the breakaway Irish Railway Workers' Union which refused to bring their men out. It had been organised by J. S. Kelly and M. McCabe earlier in the year. Both men were conservative and bitterly anti-Larkin. The GNR line was not so badly hit either because the train drivers did not belong to ASLEF but to the breakaway Dublin Locomotive Engine Drivers' and Firemen's Trade Union. Outside Dublin, there was really only trouble in Derry and Limerick, while Belfast refused to take part in the strike. Between shunters, permanent-way men, porters, checkers, signal men and engine drivers, there were at least 2,000 out in Dublin alone.

Great dissatisfaction existed among the railway workers. Porters were paid 14s per 7-day week; engine cleaners received 8s; and platform porters were given 15s. Sean O'Casey, a regular contributor to the *Irish Worker,* worked at one time for GNR, and claimed that the gate-keeper at Sutton received 9s per week while the two married men who looked after the level crossings of Kilbarrack and the Claremont Hotel, also on the Howth line, received little more; moreover, each was supplied with a house 'less healthy and picturesque than the caves inhabited by pre-historic man'.[85] However, employers and *The Irish Times* did not feel that these were low wages:

> So far as the confused and foolish strike in Ireland had any *raison d'etre* its cause was the question of recognition for the unions. In recent years the companies have been able to combine generous treatment of their men with reasonable dividends to their shareholders. The bulk of the Irish railwaymen are now well paid. The Irish public cannot allow them to make further unlimited demands on the strength of the government's promised legislation.[86]

The Master Carters, timber merchants and coal merchants locked out their men. To add to the confusion, the newsboys struck for more money, and the delivery and sale of papers was prevented by mob violence. Some shops were looted and plate glass windows were smashed. Police who made an arrest had to take their charge through the streets concealed in an ambulance wagon. Standish O'Grady wrote to the papers requesting the government to halt the export of Irish foodstuffs to prevent a black market in essential commodities. The following day the railway strike was called off and the men returned to work after agreement had been reached in London.

In Dublin the trouble was far from being resolved. The men had returned to work without any trouble but a great deal of resentment was caused when the companies began to reward the 'loyal' workers, who had ignored the strike tocsin. Company directors published their thanks in the papers and gave the 'loyalists' on extra week's wages. Members of the public were also thanked for offering to run the trains. But Dublin had hardly time to draw its breath in relief when a strike broke out in Jacob's biscuit factory. Nearly 4,000 workers were involved, most of them women and girls. One worker said she was paid 6s 6d per week. Pending discussions with the transport union there was a general return to work. A week later Jacob agreed to pay workers for the time out. On the question of wages, 'we are quite aware that the cost of living has a tendency to rise' and an increase of 2s was granted, with 1s given to girls and boys under twenty-one. Recognition of the ITGWU was not granted however and in making the concessions, Mr Jacob warned 'we are making a great personal sacrifice, beyond which we cannot go under any circumstances'. He added that heavy export costs had forced the company to consider setting up a subsidiary plant in England but so far they had refrained from doing so because 'we felt our employment was so much needed in our city'. If conditions did not improve in the immediate future the company would have no alternative but to close down the entire factory. Finally, he appealed to reason, and urged: 'we spend our lives in your midst and are at any time prepared . . . to hear, and if possible, put right any grievances brought to our notice'.

On 6 September, the timber merchants explained to the press that they were not responsible for the trouble in the trade. Because of the rail strike they were forced to lock out some 500 men on 21 August. But when an effort was made to get the men back to work with payment for the day lost, the workers refused. Their union demanded 2s a week increase, and on 13 September, T. and C. Martin's let 40 cabinetmakers go. At East Wall national school, the children struck in protest against the 8s 6d which had to be paid for books in fifth class, and also demanded a shorter school day. On a more serious note, two porters at a Great Southern and Western railway yard refused to handle goods from a timber firm which was in dispute with Liberty Hall. A walk-out followed and the men refused to return until the company agreed not to handle 'tainted' goods.

The *Irish Times* suspected a deeper significance behind the move. The intention of Liberty Hall was to form a union which could paralyse the whole trade of the country, if its demand was not accepted without question. Were this allowed to develop the 'employers would be faced with an intolerable tyranny and they would rather close their works than submit to it'.[87]

The Irish organiser of the ASRS, Nathaniel Rimmer, announced that the mood of his men was militant and that he had been given a free hand to deal with this case as he best thought fit. The strike spread rapidly and a general strike was threatened. The general secretary of the Railway Clerks' association, Mr Walden, also instructed his 1,500 Irish members not to handle 'tainted' goods.

Rommer claimed that the strike was a well-planned fight between capital and labour. As police reinforcements were again rushed into the city and troops were sent to guard railway stations, the *Irish Times* said that this new union policy was not merely one of socialism but anarchy. And if the railway men were not conscious socialists, argued the leader column, then they were merely using the timber strike as a speedy conclusion to their own grievances. The paper was right but for the wrong reason. The dominant motivation behind the ASRS in Dublin was not socialism but the residue of resentment left over after the August dispute, coupled with a number of grievances, not the least being low wages.

The executive of the ASRS moved to Dublin to deal with the strike and was completely ignored by the employers. The strikers suffered a severe setback when the train drivers belonging to ASLEF refused to come out in sympathy, and the London executive of the ASRS proved far less militant than the fiery Mr Rimmer. It refused to call a general strike which would encompass the whole of the British Isles and decided to limit its action to Ireland alone, much to the disappointment of the Dublin members. By 21 September, there were 5,642 men on strike. The line most affected was the Great Southern and Western Railway with 5,000 men out. The Dublin Locomotive Engine Drivers and Firemen remained at work on GNR lines. When Rimmer attempted to address one of their meetings he was barred from even entering the room and told that Irishmen were tired of being dictated to by English 'bummers' and that he was free to return home and conduct strikes if he so wished.

This attitude was not held generally by organised labour in the city. They supported the transport men and the ASRS and subscriptions were sent to the strike committee, but despite the good-will of the trade unionists and the general militancy of the men, the railway workers were really 'beaten to the ropes' by 28 September. The men returned to work after a complete surrender at the conference table. Men were to be taken back, according to Sir William Goulding, on condition that they undertook to handle all traffic, obeyed all commands and tendered an expression of regret for having gone on strike without notice to the company. However, this did not necessarily mean that they were to be taken back immediately. The 'loyal' men who had been recruited during the strike were to be kept on and the compliant old hands could reapply. Much the same procedure was adopted by the timber, coal and general merchants. As a result, the ITGWU now stood in very bad odour in the city.

Lockouts in Wexford

A branch of the transport union was founded in Wexford on 10 July, 1911 after a meeting which had aroused great enthusiasm in the town, though some local employers were less happy about having a militant workers' organisation in the area. A month later, the ITGWU had made sufficient ground to constitute a potential threat to the businessmen of Wexford. One of the biggest employers in the town, Philip Pierce, decided on a 'wildcat' lockout. Without receiving any demands from his employees, the iron foundry owner put them on a week's notice and divided the £70 thrift fund among them.

Doyle and Co. of the Selskar ironworks followed Pierce's example. William Doyle admitted that the men had not presented any complaint but they had joined the ITGWU and 'it was necessary for employers to know with whom they were dealing in a situation like the present'.[88] A third firm took the same 'pre-emptive' action leaving, in all, 700 men on the street and some 2,000 others affected if dependants are included. P. T. Daly was dispatched post haste by Liberty Hall to deal with the dispute.

The strike followed much the same pattern as anywhere else. The employers had forced the issue with their 'over-kill' attitude towards the transport union. The rank and file workers had been pushed into taking a militant posture by the reaction of Pierce and his colleagues and were determined not to return to their jobs until they had wrung full union recognition from the employers. The only outcome of such deadlock was violence.

Two foremen were assaulted by a crowd of strikers and Pierce's motorcar was stoned. In retaliation Pierce decided to shut down and ordered builders to brick up the entrance to the factory. He planned to move the business to Paris where the firm already had a depot while Doyle intended to shift to Belfast. The employers seemed wounded by the 'disloyalty' of the men. One employer, Thompson, said his firm had been open for 43 years and he had not only treated the men fairly, but indulgently. Some of his men were with the firm over 20 years and a man who was employed in 1868 had only died recently, yet his men had to choose between the firm and the ITGWU.

This clash of principles led to serious rioting in the town: a young striker, Michael O'Leary, was killed by a policeman's baton and the transport union decided to escalate the dispute affecting five large firms in Wexford itself. The coal quay labourers in Enniscorthy struck for an extra 2s per week, and trouble also spread to New Ross. Larkin visited the 'battle front' and told the Wexford strikers that the question of wages was always a matter which could be put to conciliation, but recognition was not negotiable.

The strikers were getting from 3s 6d to 10s per week from the union. Daly boasted that he could support his men for twelve months without a penny of Irish money (using British finance) but it would be charged that English industry was taking advantage of Irish unrest. The strike dragged on for nearly six months with neither side wishing to give way. In January, 1912, Daly was deported from Wexford and his place taken by Connolly who saw the need to sue for peace. In September, a letter to the *Irish Times* had suggested that the men form their own independent union. Connolly, whether he was aware of the anonymous letter-writer's idea, took this course of action, and the Irish Foundry Workers' Union was established. It was little more than a front for the ITGWU and the two bodies merged two years later.

The strike was only partially successful, but at least the employers had to recognise the principle of combination, and it was a significant step forward. The Wexford strike was important for a further development. Coinciding with the railway strikes, the timber lockout and the trouble on the docks was a growth in hostility towards the transport union. The *Irish Times*, an accurate mirror of moderate employer opinion, considered Pierce perfectly right and justified in the position he had adopted over the Wexford dispute; the transport union was liable through its practice of the secondary boycott to call out men in support of other members in unrelated and independent disputes. The paper went a step further in its diagnosis of the ITGWU; Larkin's union was not any ordinary combination of workers forced into using unorthodox methods under duress. It had freely elected to take the path of trade union unorthodoxy because it was motivated by syndicalist doctrines. The *Irish Times* reflected the growing irritation of the employers:

> We are getting into a position in which the fight between capital and labour will have to be fought out to the bitter end. If this is the case, most people would rather have the contest now, and get it over. Anything is better than these constant strikes and threats of strikes, which dislocate business in all directions and an infinity of harm . . . the strikers must be taught that they are not omnipotent.[89]

The lives, property and trade of the people had to be protected and 'if the forces of the crown were necessary for that purpose they should be employed without delay'. There was hardly an employer in the city who did not echo those sentiments even if the *Freeman's Journal* demurred from the use of the military.

Counter-offensive: Employers and their 'One Big Union'

The rapid growth of the transport union seems to have taken the employers by complete surprise. They had been caught badly off guard by Larkin's guerrilla tactics. However by July 1911, they had taken stock of the situation and realised how inadequate their own associations were to defend the commercial interests of the city against a militant combination which represented workers in every sector of the transport industry. Indeed, the employers suddenly found themselves in very much the same invidious position as the sectionally-motivated and individual, craft-centred unions. The master carters, and merchants, master drapers, etc. each had their own organisations which often acted in a divisive fashion particularly in a moment of stress.

The Dublin Chamber of Commerce did provide some liaison among employers, but it had a large membership and it was a cumbersome and difficult body to control. However, many of its leading members provided the nucleus of militants which planned to set up a federation of Dublin employers, modelled on the same lines as that set up in 1909 by their Cork colleagues. The Lee-side organisation, according to some Dublin employers, had been a singular success and Cork employers 'have experienced little or no troubles since the federation was founded'.[90]

During a carters' strike in June, Dublin manufacturers, merchants and other employers met to consider the dispute. The men had gone out without notice and then prevented other workers from returning 'by intimidation and violence'. The feeling of the 30 June meeting demanded action to deal with the trouble at source rather than just patch up the present dispute, and a provisional committee was nominated to organise the setting up of an employers' federation.[91] After several meetings the committee had enlisted the active support of prominent employers of labour and leaders of trade and commerce:

> It has been decided to form a company limited by guarantee to be called 'The Dublin Employers' Federation Limited'. The objects of the company to be mutual protection and indemnity of all employers of labour in Dublin who join the federation, and to promote freedom of contract between employers and employees.[92]

The idea received widespread financial support and within weeks it was operating effectively, co-ordinating the actions and activities of employers in the city to some effect. Yet no sooner had the federation got on its feet when Dublin was hit by a wave of strikes which paralysed trade and infuriated the impotent employers.

The two rail strikes sent some of the employers into paroxysms of rage. At a meeting of the combined associations of chambers of commerce of Great Britain in Dublin on 29 August, the president, Earl Brassey, launched an attack on the 1906 Trade Disputes Act which authorised peaceful picketing and relieved trade unions of the responsibility for their acts of 'intimidation, interference and violence'.[93] Many Dublin employers wanted the picketing clause repealed, and action from the authorities. A resolution was sent to Dublin Castle from the local chamber on 21 September:

> This council view with alarm the apathy hitherto displayed by the authorities (in the railway strike) and their apparent disregard to the safety of the people, and the suffering and distress which has resulted, and must increase if the law of the land and the rights of the people are permitted to be flouted by a comparatively small number of discontents.[94]

Alarm soon turned to panic when the troops were not called out to deal with the 'comparatively small number of discontents', and panic gave way to bitter resentment. On 3 November, one James Shanks proposed a censure motion against the Irish executive 'for conspicuously neglecting in a crisis of great gravity their obvious duty as defined by Mr Churchill'. The chamber could no longer regard the administration 'with respect or confidence'. Shanks felt sure that the hawkish Winston Churchill would have called out the military in the same circumstances. 'Peaceful picketers' had injured carters even when they went under police protection. On one occasion a man, 'occupying a highly responsible position in a well known Dublin concern' went to the station with his wagons and was 'seriously mauled' by picketers.[95] Indeed, he felt it might be necessary, because of the recent example of peaceful picketing and peaceful strikes, to coin a new word for 'peaceful'. Everyone had suffered: one had only to ask the parish clergy about the condition of workers' families. Even the cooking untensils had been pawned in an effort to buy food. The Executive were to blame, Shanks said, and he demanded firmer action. George Bennett also felt that the Executive had proved a traitor to its trust. They were not going to let the forces of disorder ride over them. However, Sir Horace Plunkett, an invited guest of the meeting, spoke forcefully against the motion. He was supported by the vice-president of the chamber and one of the elders of the council, William Martin Murphy. The action of those who proposed the censure motion was distinguished by altruism, he said, because they had not suffered in the strikes at all. Besides, they had absolutely no evidence to substantiate their assertions. In the past a gathering of three or four people or a crowd was called an unlawful assembly. The members of such a crowd could be arrested but now peaceful pickets were protected by law. He continued:

> The Government had given some protection, but the Government might have done more; but to suggest that the Government should have brought out an army to mow down peaceful pickets was neither possible nor thinkable. What was known in the early days as the massacre of Peterloo was not likely to be repeated in their time.[96]

This was not a well known side of Murphy's character; it was the voice of experience. He pointed out that the motion referred to Churchill, but that if they compared the result of his administration in England with the administration in Ireland during the same period the result would be favourable to the latter. There was no bloodshed in Ireland, no people shot down as in England and Wales, and there was no serious rioting. The motion was lost by a mere seven votes, Murphy getting thirty votes. Shanks lost, not because the delegates were moderate men, but because the motion was clumsily worded, and the Dublin Chamber of Commerce still favoured firmer action. It wanted to extirpate the ITGWU from the Irish body politic, root and branch.

The fulminations of Larkin against the evils of capitalism, and his cavalier approach to the intricacies of industrial relations, as demonstrated by his opportunism during the rail strike, struck terror into many employers. The owner of a large drapery store chain, P. O'Reilly, gave his diagnosis of the trouble:

> He sympathised with the workingman; no man in the community grudged him a living wage; every effort in the country had been in the direction of improving the workingman's condition—giving him better means of reading, better light, a better house and better sanitation. Every effort that had been made on the social side of life had been largely in the workingman's favour. And it was a melancholy fact, and a sorrowful one too, that notwithstanding all the efforts and inconveniences of society, of merchants, of trades people in this country, yet there was no reciprocal action from the workman, who was not the grateful being that they would wish him to be. The workman of this country had been brought under the influence of that continental socialistic plague, which had had its origins in Russia and had spread

into France and England. The grace of God was wanted more among the workingmen; the grace of God was not with them as it ought to be and they were permitting themselves to be made the tools of these foreign emissaries who preached doctrines of immorality and socialism in their midst.[97]

Edward H. Andrews was no less insistent. He had no objection to strikes in the normal sense of the word. It was, in his opinion, the last resort of the working man to ventilate his grievances provided the cause was grave enough and there was no other course open to him:

> A strike under such conditions would have the sympathy of many, but what do we find on the present occasion? Not a strike in the ordinary sense of the word, but the beginning of a social war—a revolution—a social war in the sense of setting class against class, a revolution in the fact that it is an endeavour to force the railway companies to do an illegal act, and therefore to break the law of the land. I fear the present move is the thin end of the wedge of socialism, now so rampant in other countries, and of which it seems we are to have a foretaste . . . How far the extravagances of the few and the almost universal love of pleasure of the many have tended to this condition of affairs I am not prepared to say. Remember, if the present condition is continued for a much longer time there will be an end to all law and order and private rights, as well as public duties, of the people, will be destroyed . . . A small party of agitators have thought well to make Ireland the cockpit for their experiments . . . The present is only the beginning of the trouble.[98]

William Crowe said he happened to be one of the band of timber merchants affected by the rail strike and listening to some of the remarks that had been made by previous speakers, he thought a good deal had been misunderstood as to the real situation. The railway strike was merely a coincidence—an attempt to carry out the methods of the organisation which had been at work for some time in the city. In his opinion, the settlement of the railway strike would not get rid of the evil that had brought it about. They had to go beyond the strike and try to get at the disease before they could preach peace on this subject. The organisation responsible for the plight of the economy, said William Crowe, was permeating the whole country like a plague and the present afforded an opportunity which might not occur again during their lifetime to get rid of the pestilence which had come into their land. If it got roots it would be difficult to get rid of it. Now they had a real chance of striking a blow for the liberty and commerce of the city and county.

As a remedy, the chamber proposed to set up an all-Ireland employer organisation which would advise its members on labour troubles and protect their interests in strike situations. James Mahony felt that such an organisation would be able to offer the best legal opinions to its members; enforce, by the legal process, contracts with workers; pressurise public carriers to fulfil their legal oligation and make such preparations as the GNR company had made 'by which the vacancies created by a strike may be effectively and promptly filled. Edward H. Andrews felt the time was right to form such an organisation:

> Gentlemen, the country and the press are at our back, all religious denominations are with us, we must not falter in our duty, nor stand at ease until full liberty is restored to us and this we cannot expect to see unless we are united throughout the length and breadth of this land, and united also with those who think with us in other countries.[99]

The motion was passed and circulars were sent to employers.

The provisional committee consisted of six members of the Dublin Chamber to be nominated by the council; seven members, one each from the chambers of Belfast, Cork, Waterford, Derry, Limerick, Newry and Drogheda; and seven others from smaller towns. Subsequently, a meeting convened by the Dublin Chamber was held in the city and the national employer association was put on a firm footing.

The year 1911 was punctuated by serious strikes, strikes which, paradoxically, were spearheaded by outside influences such as the ASRS. Yet Larkin was presented with the blame for all the trouble by many of the employers. He was an *agent provocateur* whose arrival in Ireland had reduced Belfast to a state of havoc, disrupted the placidity of Newry, forced the employers of Cork into revolt and driven the Dublin industrialists to the point of despair. If Larkin did not believe in the class war, then the employers of Dublin certainly did and they resolved to defeat the conspiratorial body which was masquerading as a trade union. What the employers neglected to remember was that it would have been impossible to agitate successfully without widespread grievance.

7 A Bloody Sunday

In January, 1912, Larkin turned his attention to local politics. He was determined to give Labour a strong voice in the City Hall. Twenty Corporation seats were up for re-election and after a bitter and acrimonious campaign at the hustings, the fledgling local labour representation committee took five seats. Despite the best efforts of the news media, and the *Irish Independent* in particular, to smear Larkin, he polled 1,500 votes as against 600 for his opponent, but he was given no time to prove his worth as a councillor. As a convicted criminal he had no right to sit in the corporation and his enemies were not slow to exploit this situation. When he was sued for his seat the court upheld that the pardon given by the Lord Lieutenant in 1910 was not a 'free pardon' and he was barred from the corporation for five years.[1]

It was an understandable move on the part of his opponents but it was as spiteful as it was shortsighted. Prevented from taking part in legitimate political activity, Larkin was again forced to channel his enormous energies into the trade union movement. The result was far more disastrous for many employers. By the middle of 1913 the ITGWU had 10,000 members, its own union headquarters and a sizeable bank account which ensured a willingness to strike with alacrity.

The employers' apologist, Arnold Wright, was not so prepared to give Larkin the credit for the growth of his union. He claimed that the National Insurance Act was the major recruiting agent for Larkin.[2] On the basis of available evidence, Wright's assertion cannot really be disproved. However, the effect of the Act on the numbers in cross-channel unions was minimal, with one or two possible exceptions,[3] and consequently, it is fair to postulate that the Act had very much the same effect in Ireland.

Between February 1912 and July 1913 the ITGWU spread beyond Dublin. A branch was opened in Sligo and within a short time had nearly 500 members.[4] Limerick followed, although it was in Dublin, where the ITGWU enjoyed most success, that Larkin proved his powers of leadership. In June 1912, he managed to convince the stevedores in the port to form their own association and by so doing undermine the power of the employers over both themselves and their work gangs.[5] Once this had been achieved Larkin's union had a stranglehold on the port.

The Irish Women Workers' Union

There was one other section of the work force which had been badly neglected for decades—the women workers. Unlike Belfast or Derry, Dublin had no industries which could absorb its huge female work force. As many as 15,000 worked as domestic servants, according to the census of 1911; the pay was generally poor and there was no restriction on the hours worked by maids. For example, on 1 December, 1906, the *Irish Times* carried the following advertisement for a 'domestic':

> Wanted for Stillorgan, young maid. Attendant for two young children aged six and five; must have good accent and appearance; good needlework and able to cut out; Protestant.

While no wage was cited, judging by other such notices the annual rate might have been about £18 per annum and £12 to £15 for general cooks. The benefits of such coveted posts were obvious. However badly treated a domestic servant was by her mistress, at least she was assured of frugal meals and shelter. In the 'sweating industries' the women were badly exploited. And really the same held good for female factory workers generally. In 1894, the average female wage in the box trade was 5s 3d weekly, while at match-making it was much lower. The general lack of employment opportunities in the city often forced women into what was called, in polite circles, the white slave trade. A garrison city such as Dublin ensured a regular clientele. About 5,000 troops were stationed there permanently and many disported themselves in the brothels of the Monto. Horse Show week also brought extra business to the trade.[6]

The plight of the woman worker often met with little sympathy from trade unionists. Generally, women were discounted as cheap labour who could often undercut trade union rates in a job and jeopardise the livelihoods of tradesmen. The book-binders complained constantly against this, yet they were not prepared to allow women to join their union or guarantee equal pay for equal work.[7] This feeling ran throughout the trades without an exception. Even the bespoke tailors who were often rivalled at their own craft by tailoresses were adamant about retaining a wage differential.

However, by 1911, women were playing a more prominent role in public life. Inghinidhe na hEireann, founded by Maud Gonne in 1903, were involved in social work, and were providing free school meals for 150 children at St Audeons, High Street. The Irish Women's Suffragette Society was led by Mrs Sheehy Skeffington, although it was not so socially orientated as Maud Gonne's organisation or the Women's National Health Association. Finally, the impetus for a women's trade union came from Liberty Hall. James Larkin's sister, Delia, came to Dublin in August 1911 and a month later the Irish Women's Workers' Union was set up. Delia Larkin was made general secretary and her brother became president. It was a sign of Larkin's personal conservatism that he refused to allow women to join the ITGWU and preferred rather to found an autonomous organisation.[8] By September 1913, there were less than 1,000 members in Dublin and considerably fewer in Belfast.

Industrial Unrest Spreads

Larkin had continued to build up the strength of his union during this period of comparative industrial calm. The antagonism of the employers towards the transport union abated somewhat as genuine efforts were made at reconciliation and the trade unions took part in talks to set up a Dublin reconciliation board. By July 1913, the chamber of commerce set about,

> organising a panel who shall have the duty of selecting the employers' representatives of the board, from the Dublin Building Trades' Employers' Association; Dublin Employers' Federation Limited; Dublin Coal Merchants' Association; Dublin Carriers' Association; the Dublin branch of the Shipping Federation; Timber Importers' Association; Master Tailors' Association; Drapers' Association; Brewers; Distillers; Master Bakers; Biscuit Makers; Master Printers; and the manufacturers of tobacco, chemical manure, laundries, wool and poplin.[9]

On 18 August, a general meeting of employers discussed the scheme and a panel of employers were nominated to sit on the board. But the trade unionists had grown disgruntled with the proposed scheme and, feeling that the board would give the employers too much of an advantage, talks were broken off. With the benefit of hindsight, the employers felt in 1914 that at that time it was plainly evident that 'there was a feeling of unrest among the general transport workers, and that a vast sea of insurrection and insubordination was accumulating'.[10]

The breakdown in these efforts to found a board proved a tragedy. Conciliation boards were working in England with some success by 1910. The real value of these 262 boards lay in their ability to prevent stoppages of work, rather than in their power to settle strikes or lockouts. Of the 7,508 cases settled by conciliation in the ten years between 1900 and 1910, only 104 were preceded by a stoppage.[11] Dublin employers, however, were left very much to their own devices. In the absence of any machinery to defuse industrial disputes at an early stage, even the most trival incident on the factory floor could trigger off a strike or a lockout, for as a rule, it is easier to prevent a dispute taking place than it is to settle one.

Employers, generally, believed in the 'prevention is better than cure' industrial relations philosophy but in most cases their understanding of labour unrest was simplistic; get rid of the trouble-makers and peace will be restored. The rising cost of living and the significant drop in real wages seem to have been conveniently swept to one side and by 1913 the economic factor could no longer be ignored by the city's employers if they wished to stay out of trouble.

The first six months of 1913 were punctuated with strikes by men demanding higher wages. In March, there was a dispute at Messrs Atkinson and Sons, silk and poplin manufacturers. About 110 members of the Silkweavers' Union were involved, some of whom had been with the firm for twenty and thirty years. But with Michael Mallin as general secretary they were determined to revise the log; payment was based on piecework and an intricate pay scale had been drawn up over the years which did not lend itself to easy review.[12] Mallin gained the support of the trades council and the backing of affiliated unions for the strike. He explained how Atkinson had tried to 'bribe' other men to take the place of strikers. Later twelve 'scabs' had been employed when the Dublin silk-weavers stood firm. Finally, Atkinson was forced to train girls to do the work. But the weavers had now bought their own looms and were about to set up a workers' co-operative, and with the threat of such competition from the best silkweavers in the city, Atkinson was forced to make a favourable settlement in June.[13]

There was also unrest in the building trade. Most of the craftsmen were seeking shorter hours and more pay to meet the rising cost of living. In May, the Master Builders' Association granted carpenters and plasterers an increase of one penny per hour and a reduction of four hours in the week, bringing the working week down to 50 hours.[14] However, there was one contentious clause in this pay deal: when the carpenters and plasterers signed the agreement they undertook to charge builders who were not members of the Master Builders' Association one penny per hour extra over the agreed rate. Presumably, in this way the employers hoped to force recalcitrant colleagues into their association while the craftsmen hoped to make some additional money.

The bricklayers would not agree to such a term when they were offered the same deal. They wanted a 50-hour week, from 7.30 until 5.30, with two meal breaks; a penny an hour increase in summer; three pence an hour increase in winter; and a shilling per day country money![15] They were not successful in pressing their claim and trouble followed.

The printers also added their voice to the chorus for higher wages, seeking an increase of four shillings per week. Despite the fact that the DTPS was the strongest and most disciplined craft union in the city it had not, at this stage, won less than the fifty-hour week for its members. Neither had it won a week's paid holiday although this was general in English cities at the time.[16]

There were many other areas of discontent among the craft unions and no less than thirty strikes took place in the first six months of the year. Foremost in the struggle for better pay and conditions for the general workers was Larkin and his colleagues at Liberty Hall. The City of Dublin Steam Packet company, which held the government mail contract, was hit by strike. Larkin was endeavouring to establish a closed shop but was always prepared to settle for less. On 26 May, the ITGWU signed an agreement with the City of Dublin Steam Packet company, and to avoid any trouble in the future the other five main shipping lines in the city also signed a pact with Liberty Hall. Larkin's achievement was significant. One of the largest employer associations in the city had recognised the transport union as a *bona fide* union. Secondly, the men had been given an increase in wages. But there was one major drawback; he had conceded the use of the sympathetic strike. The relevant terms of the agreement read:

> Any question as to the interpretation of this agreement, or any dispute arising between the men and their employers, to be submitted to the latter in writing. No stoppage of work to take place pending negotiations

regarding such matters. This agreement to be binding on all concerned and at least ONE MONTH'S NOTICE in writing from either side to be given of any intention to terminate.[17]

The most destructive tactic in Larkin's arsenal had been surrendered in the port area, where it was most likely to be effective.

The transport union next shifted its campaign to the outskirts of the city where the harshness and misery of the agricultural labourer's lot rivalled in intensity the worst experiences of his inner city colleague. If a labourer was lucky he would earn 17s a week all year round, but generally the work was seasonal. The employers were large farmers with strong business ties in the city.[18]

Recruiting was carried out by Larkin on Sundays with the help of the ITGWU (Fintan Lalor) pipe band. The majority of workers tended to live in, or near, the villages of Baldoyle, Kinsealy, Swords, Finglas and Lucan.[19] The success of Larkin's efforts can be gauged by the fact that the County Dublin Farmers were forced to form their own protective association, but the new organisation was impotent because of the approaching harvest. Larkin knew the employers' hands were tied and did not hesitate in threatening a strike if his demands were not met. An agreement was signed on 17 August, giving farm labourers increases of up to twenty per cent on their basic wage. The new conditions were far from satisfactory but at least they were an improvement, giving the labourer a contract for the first time in his life. The men agreed to work in winter from 7 a.m. to 6 p.m. with one meal hour; in summer the hours were from 6 a.m. to 6 p.m. with two meal hours; wages were increased from 17s to £1, while casual labour was paid at 4s a day and 5s a day for threshing up to 1 November.[20] For many it was a charter of freedom.

The farmers did not feel that they had entered the contract willingly and many awaited an opportunity to strike back when they were on a stronger footing. Larkin again averted his attentions to the industrial front where he was determined to 'infiltrate' two of the city's union blackspots—Guinness's brewery and the Dublin Tramway Company. For some time he had paid particular attention to the trams, while the *Irish Worker* had left its readers in little doubt as to who was considered by Liberty Hall to be the corner-stone of Dublin capitalism. It was Martin Murphy, described at one time or another by the *Irish Worker* as an industrial octopus; a tramway tyrant; an importer of swell cockney shopmen; a political and social Captain Mick McQuaid; a financial mountebank; a pure-souled financial contortionist; and a whited sepulchre.[21] The *Irish Independent* returned the abuse in kind, until a vendetta developed between Larkin and Murphy. Both were determined to triumph over each other no matter what the cost might be; but behind the rhetoric, had Larkin grounds for his opinion of Martin Murphy?

The Dublin United Tramway company, of which Murphy was director, had an authorised capital of £1.3 million in 70,000 ordinary and 60,000 preference shares of £10. The ordinary shares yielded six per cent, payable around February. In 1911 a bonus of one-half per cent was paid in addition to the usual six per cent.[22] The company was doing well but, Larkin argued, it was at the workers' expense.

The Dublin tram man was paid 21s 6d (conductors) and 28s (drivers), or about twenty-five per cent less than his colleagues in either Belfast or Liverpool earned.[23] According to an anonymous memorandum sent to Archbishop Walsh in 1913, the running of the company was conducted on authoritarian lines: 'discipline is too severe for an industrial concern, military in character. Promotion depends on favour and plasticity of employees' character rather than efficiency and seniority.'[24]

Beginners in the firm were known as 'sparemen' and they might have to wait for up to six years to get a permanent appointment. For the first year they had to turn up at work every day, including Sundays and holidays, and wait from 7 a.m. to 12 p.m. to see if they could fill in for a sick man or an absentee. Frequently, sparemen worked only three days and their pay was never much more than 9s a week. Heavy deductions were often taken from this meagre remuneration: 2s per week for twenty weeks as security for uniform; 6d for rule-book; 6d a week for sickness benefit; 3d per head levy in case of death; licence to conduct or drive, 2s 6d down and 1s annually for renewal. To gain admission to the service, they had to obtain a guarantee of £20 with character references to cover the previous five years. For the first six weeks, while learning the work, the men were paid nothing at all.

Conductors and drivers got one day off in ten. The working day varied from nine to seventeen hours and a man could be reported for leaning or sitting while running a car. The company rules commanded inspectors 'to guard their authority with their inferiors through firm, becoming conduct'. The inspector's word was final and if a passenger complained about the conduct of an employee, the 'inferior' faced instant dismissal. A conductor might lose a day's pay for omitting to collect a 1d fare; allowing a passenger to exceed the distance paid for; punching a ticket in the wrong space or on the line; talking to passengers; or if he was 2d short in a day's cash. Not surprisingly, about 200 conductors left annually or were dismissed.

Drivers also faced a similar labyrinth of rules and restrictions. For example, a driver could lose a day's pay if he arrived at Nelson's Pillar one minute before his time by the inspector's watch. In the parcels department the conditions of employment were equally harsh. Boys worked from 9 a.m. to 8 p.m. and at peak periods, up to 11 p.m. Wages were 7s a week flat rate of 3s a week basic and $^1/_4$d a parcel; in outlying depots the basic rate was 4s per week and $^1/_4$d a parcel or $^1/_2$d beyond three miles' radius of the depot. The messenger boy also had responsibility for the parcel.

The memorandum claimed that no union had ever been tolerated among the men. Every effort to form a tramway organisation 'has been frustrated by the company and the leaders either corrupted by promotion or dismissed on flimsy pretexts:

> The company on one occasion formally refused to listen to a deputation of their own men attending on behalf of their own union, Dublin Trammen from the Trades Hall, Capel St. Mr Murphy was in the chair, and he would accept no general statement of grievances, but only a statement of personal grievances from each member of the deputation. Union men are systematically tracked down and penalised; non-union men promoted by preference.Rule 7 (general instructions) makes informing a matter of duty and ordinary comradeship an offence. Reports (Rule 8) are to be made in writing to the traffic superintendent, yet all employees who have an oral message for the manager have the right of access to him at any time. Those rules bear a plausible interpretation; the men complain that the more sinister meaning conveyed above represents the truth, and that the judicial methods of Venice in the Middle Ages are still in force in the Dublin Tram Company of today.[25]

Although an emotional document, the substance of the allegations appears to be well founded. Certainly the trade union movement as a whole, and many of the tram men in particular, believed them to be true. There was sufficient unrest within the tramway company for Larkin to win new union members in the parcel section and in the transport area. The ITGWU had also 'infiltrated' the dispatch department of the *Independent*.

Murphy saw an ugly situation developing because of the progress being made by Larkin; he would not entertain the thought of negotiating with men from Liberty Hall under any circumstances. By taking such an intransigent position he was contributing to the conditions under which a strike was inevitable, and although he did not want this to happen, he was guilty of a form of self-fulfilling prophesy.

On 19 July, soon after midnight, Murphy addressed 700 of his tramway staff in the Mansion House:

> My friends—and I may truly call you my friends, because every employee of any undertaking that I am connected with I look upon as a friend (applause)—the position I hold tonight, and the occasion on which we have met, are rather unusual; in fact, I think they are without precedent. We cannot disguise from ourselves the fact that an attempt is being made by an organiser, outside the company, to seduce the men for the purpose of inducing them to go on strike. Well, I can tell you, when I ask you to come here to meet me tonight, I have not the least apprehension that there is even a remote possibility of such an event occurring. But I know there are hot-heads—young men, who have very little experience of the world—among you who might be seduced and who are endeavouring to seduce other people to go against what I may call their bread and butter.[26]

He told the men that the directors had no objection to the men forming a 'legitimate union'. He thought there was talent enough among the staff to undertake such a project without allying themselves to a 'disreputable organisation' which would place them under the 'strike monger' and the 'unscrupulous man' who used men 'as tools to make him the labour dictator of Dublin'. Murphy warned:

> Now, we are aware of all that is going on. We know perfectly well the people, and the number of people, who are taking an active part in fomenting this strike. What is demanded of you is that you are to bow down before this gentleman; you are to answer his call and obey his command. (Voices—'We never will.') I am here to tell you that this word of command will never be given, and if it is, that it will be the Waterloo of Mr Larkin.[27]

He had heard that a number of hot-headed young men had been attempting 'to coerce, by force and threats, other men in the service to join' this 'gang of city roughs'. Men who were guilty of such conduct were to be summarily dismissed and they could 'go to Mr Larkin for their pay'. No strike had achieved anything for the men except misery in his thirty years' experience:

A strike in the Tramway would, no doubt, produce turmoil and disorder, created by the roughs and looters, who were in evidence not so long ago; but what chance would the men, without funds, have in a contest with a company who could, and would, spend £100,000 or more to put down the terrorism which is being imported into the labour conditions of the city? You must recollect, when dealing with a company of this kind, that every one of the share-holders, to the number of six or seven thousand, will have three meals a day, whatever happens. I don't know if men who go out on strike can count on this.[28]

He was a fair employer, and whatever might be said about the working conditions in the firm, 'it is as good a job of its kind as is to be had in this country'. Efforts had been made in the past among his employees to form a union. All attempts had failed, perhaps because the men did not consider a union either necessary or beneficial. However, 'owing to the recent increase in the cost of necessaries of life—which is not as large as it is commonly represented'—the company was prepared to make concessions to the men. He hastened to add that these concessions had nothing to do with the 'claims of the agitator'. All uniformed men were to get 1s per week increase. The men in their first service year who did not get a day's leave in twelve would be granted the day from the time they started, making 30 full days' leave in the year. The cost of these changes to the company would be £2,250.

On 13 August, strike rumours were so strong in the city that the tramway company was forced to issue a public statement:

The directors are well aware of the attempts being made by James Larkin to foment disturbance among the men which, however, have met with little success. The company have no apprehension of any trouble with their employees, and are prepared to meet any emergency that may arise.[29]

On 18 August, the ultra-Unionist *Daily Express* assuaged the fears of Dublin tradesmen about the possibility of a tramway strike during the high point of the social year—Horse Show Week. The following day the situation grew very much worse. Murphy, after holding a meeting in the dispatch department of the *Independent*, discovered that about half the hands were transport union members, and 'forestalled a possible strike by paying off the men'. On 21 August, he dismissed about 100 men in the parcel service of the tramway company for the same reason. The men were told:

As the directors understand that you are a member of the Irish Transport union whose methods are disorganising the trade and business of the city, they do not further require your service. The parcels traffic will be temporarily suspended. If you are not a member of the union when the traffic is resumed, your application for employment will be favourably considered.[30]

A form was issued to the motormen and conductors to be signed and returned to inspectors. It read: 'should a strike of any of the employees of the company be called for by Mr Larkin or the ITGWU, I promise to remain at my post and to be loyal to the company'. Murphy was determined to rout 'Larkin's dupes', as he described transport union men.

First Larkin moved against the *Independent*. Pickets were placed on the dispatch department. Newsboys refused to handle the paper and delivery vans were attacked throughout the city. Larkin then urged the newspaper wholesalers to boycott the *Independent* and the sister paper, the *Evening Herald*. When Charles Eason (one of the biggest wholesaler distributors in the city) refused to co-operate with Liberty Hall, 35 of his delivery staff walked out. Meanwhile, in the tramway company there were further signs of unrest among the men. The directors were forced to issue a denial of reports that they had received demands from Larkin. What was more, they would not consider any communication from Larkin or his emissaries. On 24 August, Murphy was still insisting that 'no demand has been made on behalf of the transport workers' union and there is no issue between the employees of the tramway company and the board of directors'. He brushed aside questions from newsmen about advertisements which had been appearing daily in the press urging any firm that had difficulty recruiting 'loyal' hands to contact the tramway company.

There was a certain ambiguity in Murphy's position. Since the tramway company had refused on principle to treat with Larkin or his emissaries then how was it possible to know that Liberty Hall had made demands? In fact, the tram men had specific grievances which they expressed at ITGWU headquarters on 22 August. They sought 30s a week all round; one day off in every eight instead of one day in every ten; time and a half for Sunday work; and that the weekly payday be a Friday. But since the demands were put forward on behalf of the men by the ITGWU, Murphy would not listen. Larkin was left with little alternative but to call a strike.

On Saturday, 23 August, the tram men met again at Liberty Hall to discuss what could be done to pre-empt the threatened spate of dismissals. William O'Brien recalls the meeting:

Finally, it was decided to have a ballot of those who had joined and, in order to keep the numbers from the company, each section was placed in a different room in Liberty Hall. I was in charge of one section although at that time I was not a trade union official nor a member of the Irish Transport and General men . . . Those I had in my charge voted unanimously for strike. The numbers were kept secret. The company would be very anxious to find out how the land lay. The son of one of the officials of the union was given a red-hand badge with a fictitious number of the ballot with which we went to the *Freeman's Journal* and bargained for ten shillings for it, and after some bargaining this was given to him.[31]

The false numbers which appeared in the press were 837 votes to 147 in favour of strike.[32]

It was first thought that the strike would take place the following day at 3 p.m., but nothing happened, and the *Daily Express* was quick to point out that the tramway strike bid was a 'fiasco'. Larkin quickly discounted these premature feelings of relief when he told newsmen that he had been mandated by the men to act when and how he pleased in the situation that had arisen. The *Irish Times* editorial writer took Larkin at his word and he urged the tram men who 'are cheerful, hardworking and intelligent' to process their grievances in 'an orthodox fashion'. In that way 'they will have the support of citizens on their side'.[33] The editorial writer, however, neglected to attach proper importance to the unpalatable fact that the tramway company had declared war on the ITGWU and victimised its members. The question was not *if* but *when* an all-out strike would take place.

Larkin was determined to win as much union support as possible before he dare move. In an effort to gauge the mood of his followers, he led a procession through the city. At a meeting in Beresford Place afterwards, he told the crowd:

Mr Murphy had said that the tramway company will not run cars after darkness falls in the event of a strike, and that the Lord Lieutenant had given him an undertaking that the forces of the crown would be used to enable the company to carry on its business and to keep the peace. The Earl of Aberdeen, that good loyal Presbyterian, had not given the forces of the crown to the Catholic workmen who got beaten in Belfast or to the men who were being attacked in Derry. I tell the Earl of Aberdeen that he is lighting a spark in Dublin to-night that will take many buckets of Scotch broth to put out. There are men left in Ireland yet. Mr Murphy says there will be no strike. I tell Mr Murphy that he is a liar. Not only is there to be a strike on the trams but as the Earl of Aberdeen has been good enough to guarantee Mr Murphy all the forces of the Crown, he had better get them ready because we are going to win this struggle no matter what happens.[34]

Tramwaymen Strike

Larkin was true to his word. On Tuesday, 26 August, shortly before 10 o'clock some 200 motor men and conductors left their cars in the street without warning:

> In a short time Sackville Street was in a state of seething excitement. As trams arrived from various directions, drivers and conductors belonging to the transport union stepped off; the conductors gave up their boxes and all donned red-hand badges amidst cheers from a crowd of sympathisers. The cars driven by men who were not members were held up and in a short time the entire street from College Green to the Pillar was lined with trams. As quickly as possible, officials of the company sought to relieve the congestion by having them sent to the sheds or down the Abbey St line. This had to be done through the medium of inspectors, mechanics, etc., and the men who remained loyal. But it was not till about noon that the congestion was appreciably relieved.[35]

The confusion was all the greater because of the thousands of country people who were in the city to attend the Horse Show. The ITGWU move was calculated to cause maximum disruption of the transport system in an effort to conceal their weakness in numbers. Larkin did not hope for a total stoppage, for he had only a minority of tram men behind the move to strike. The older men in the company were not prepared to throw up their jobs and pension rights without a very good reason. Liberty Hall could guarantee neither security nor success against Murphy so they stood by the company as loyal employees. However, Larkin's dramatic tactic created the illusion that the stoppage was more widespread than it was in reality.

Murphy was quick to see the reasoning behind the move. He claimed that the strike had been broken within half an hour, only 150 out of 750 tram men answering the clarion call of Liberty Hall.[36] Larkin countered by pointing out to the hostile citizens of Dublin that his action was prompted by the unprovoked sacking of transport men, who were union members from the parcel department of the tramway company, long before any demands had been served on the directors by the men. He accused 'Murphy and other gentlemen of having made £160,000 in 16 years out of a private monopoly and at the expense of the ratepayers'. He added that 'the tramway slaves of Dublin work 12 hours a week longer than the Belfast tram men and receive 20 per cent less wages'. He demanded the reinstatement of the dismissed men, unconditionally improved wages, shorter hours and the right of appeal against the secret reports of inspectors.

On the evening the strike broke out a mass meeting of the men was held at Beresford Place. William O'Brien, as president of the DTC, presided, and was pessimistic about the outcome of the present dispute. But Larkin was ebullient: 'We can smash the Tramway Company in a few days, if the same determination and spirit exists as was seen today,' he said enthusiastically. It was not a strike, it was a lockout of men who had been 'tyrannically treated by a most unscrupulous scoundrel'. He added defiantly:

> Police brutality has been shown to-night. I advise the friends and supporters of this cause to take Sir Edward's advice to the men of Ulster. If Sir Edward Carson can call on the people of Ulster to arm, I will call upon you to arm. Sir Edward Carson told the people of Ulster that they had a right to arm. If they have a right to arm, the working men have an equal right to arm themselves so as to protect themselves and if at every street corner there is a hired assassin ready to kill you, then you should arm. I don't offer advice which I am not prepared to adopt myself. You know me, and you know when I say a thing I will do it . . . I think I must be right too in telling you to form a provisional government in Dublin. Whether you form a provisional government or not, you will require arms, for Aberdeen has promised not only the police, but the soldiers, and my advice to you is to be round the doors and corners, and if one of our class should fall, then two of the others must fall for that one. We will demonstrate in O'Connell Street. It is our street as well as William Martin Murphy's and if John Redmond will take to the streets of Dublin, then so will we; we are fighting for bread and butter, and we will hold our meeting in the streets, and, if every one of our men falls, there must be justice. By the living God if they want war they can have it.[37]

Councillor Thomas Lawlor and the trade unionist, William Partridge, both mild men in debate, were equally unguarded in their speeches to the same meeting. Lawlor said that if they were going to be arrested in the streets for doing nothing, 'then, by heavens, we shall go to jail for doing something. Go forth to-morrow and increase your ranks. Understand that the whole trade union movement is at your back'. Partridge claimed that the men supporting Larkin were not only prepared to go to prison, but to lay down their lives if necessary. He threatened that the home of Martin Murphy and the houses of fellow shareholders in the tramway company would also be picketed. There was, on the surface, unanimity in the labour camp.

The press was also unanimous in its condemnation of the strike. The *Daily Express* described the dissident tram men as 'dupes' and urged them to 'learn sense'. The *Irish Times* regarded the dispute as the work of agitators:

> We understand that the majority of the strikers were among the youngest and least experienced of the company's servants. It is possible to feel some pity for them in the plight to which their folly has brought them. We can only regard as public enemies the men who deliberately organised the strike and used the unfortunate strikers for their wicked purpose. The thing was reckless and wanton to the last degree.[38]

The *Freeman's Journal*, the most sympathetic of the dailies to the workers' cause, feared that 'Mr Larkin is too much obsessed with the personality of Mr Murphy. Mr Murphy is not everybody, even in the chamber of commerce'.

The media had been very much misled, however, if it thought that the strikers were the willing or unwilling dupes of a labour conspiracy. Grievance, not ideology, was the motor force of the dispute. One conductor, a young man who had been with the company for seven years, explained his position to the press:

> When I saw a number of men gathered about, men who were a long number of years in the company's employment and who have wives and families, I did not see why I should not take my stand in the fight with them, seeing that I am single and have no one but myself to look after.
> 'Were you induced, or in other words, intimidated into leaving your work today?'
> No, I simply could not work seeing old men idle and I not doing anything to help them out.[39]

Intimidation was certainly used on tram men but it was not as widespread as public opinion found it convenient to believe. The employers were not deterred from believing that the movement afoot in the city bore a frightening resemblance to continental socialism:

> Betterment of the workers' conditions was a mere stalking-horse for a far-reaching scheme of red republicanism, in which the elimination of the capitalist by a drastic process had a conspicuous place. In fine, the movement had the worst qualities of syndicalism with the added drawback of a personal ascendancy based on the skilful exercise of an elaborate system of moral and physical terrorism.[40]

The trade unionists were not so much revolutionary as the employers were reactionary. Larkin's speeches were certainly bellicose and contained fulminations against the excesses of the capitalist system. But basically the dispute was about recognition of a *bona fide* trade union. The attack on the principle of combination was what drove trade unionists of differing degrees of moderation to defend the onslaught on the ITGWU and, in so doing, defend their own labour organisations from similar attacks by employers in the future.

Larkin wanted a quick victory but did not get his way. The trams were still running and Murphy found it quite easy to get replacements for the strikers. The transport union estimated that between 700 and 800 men were out but the tramway company put the number as low as 200 conductors and motor men, and about 140 in the parcel service.[41]

Liberty Hall sank lower in the estimation of the public when the strike spread to the shipping companies which handled parcels for Eason's. Under the 28 May agreement between the ITGWU and the shipping lines, Larkin had agreed to give a month's notice before taking industrial action, and he put up a weak defence. 'When an army rebels, what is the commander to do?' he pleaded, tongue in cheek.[42]

The *Leader* expressed the unsympathetic mood of many nationalists to the whole affair:

> The Irish public are heartily sick of strikes and rumours of strikes and the sympathetic strike is an unworkable policy. Labour of all classes and degrees bound together in sympathy and ready to put its full force on in any dispute is merely the class war; it is bad economics, bad sense and unworkable. We have no liking for the organised sympathetic strike.[43]

Meanwhile the tramway strike seemed to be falling flat on its face. *The Times* correspondent wrote: 'the tramway strike has had no effect on the attendance of the (Dublin) Show. The total figures are the biggest for five years. The total for this year is 56,740, compared with 51,118 in 1912'.[44] Unionist feeling in the city was confident that the tramway strike had failed utterly. The leader writer in the *Daily Express* stated rather flippantly:

> The threats of Mr Larkin have had the effect of giving an extra fillip of excitement to Horse Show week, and provided the general public with a burningly interesting topic of conversation—and that is all . . . The mountain's labour, and an absurd mouse is born.[45]

This was true to a point, but then the authorities made an error of judgement. Larkin, P. T. Daly, William O'Brien and Councillor Lawlor were arrested and charged:

> Having on the 26 August at Custom House Square, Beresford Place, been guilty of the crime of seditious libel and seditious conspiracy in agreeing and acting together for the criminal purpose of disturbing the public peace and raising discontent among His Majesty's subjects, to wit, the working classes of Dublin, the police forces of the Crown and the soldiers of the Crown, and for the purpose of exciting hatred and contempt of the Government, and for the purpose of inciting to murder; also that they and each of them about the time and place aforesaid were guilty of the crime of the publication of seditious words, and that they and each of them together with other persons, did at the place aforesaid unlawfully assemble with the intent to carry on the unlawful purpose aforesaid.[46]

The three specific charges were: seditious speaking; seditious conspiracy to hold meetings, and unlawful assembly.

The accused were brought before a divisional justice and returned for trial to the next Commission. All were allowed bail after giving an undertaking not to hold any illegal meetings or to use any inflammatory language in the interim. This new tough line with the strikers was continued when the authorities proscribed a labour demonstration planned for Sunday, 31 August. Meanwhile the Dublin Employers' Federation Limited met behind closed doors to discuss this industrial unrest and it was decided to call a general meeting of all members to put certain plans into action.[47]

Fortunately for Larkin the new hard line by the authorities provided just the fillip the strikers needed to revive their flagging spirits. At a meeting in Beresford Place, Larkin threw caution to the wind and burned the proclamation banning the Sunday meeting in O'Connell Street, called the Lord Mayor a coward, and demanded an all-out rent strike to last until the tram men had won better conditions. His speech was as insulting to the authorities as it was defiant:

> I care as much for the King as I do for Swifte the Magistrate (the justice who had proscribed the meeting); people make Kings and people can unmake them; and what the King of England has to do with stopping the meeting in Dublin I fail to see. I never said God Save the King but in derision. I say it now in derision. If they are going to stop the meeting at the dictation of William Martin Murphy, then I say that for every one of our men that falls, two must fall on the other side . . . Remember, if they

are going to use the weapon of starvation there is food in the shops and clothes in the shops and hungry men want food and clothes. There is coal on the banks, and cheerless homes want fires in the grates and a man who is faced with hunger wants bread. I promise to pay no more rent and you pay no more rent, and see how William Martin Murphy will go on.[48]

James Connolly who had travelled from Belfast to speak at the meeting was no less defiant; the Dublin employers had declared war on their employees, he said. About the banned meeting, he added, all he would say was, 'Come to O'Connell St and see who will hold the meeting. Despite the King's proclamation they intended going there and he hoped they would attend in thousands.'[49]

The following morning Connolly was arrested on an incitement charge. Partridge was picked up by police later, and both appeared before Justice Swifte, who sat especially to hear the case on Saturday afternoon. Partridge was given bail after he agreed to keep the peace, but Connolly obdurately refused to co-operate with the justice: he refused to recognise the jurisdiction of the King's law in Ireland. On the question of the O'Connell St meeting, Connolly advised people to hold no meeting but to 'be there'. That was a method, he explained to the justice, which had been found necessary not only in Ireland but in Britain, 'when they were brought face to face with the organised resistance of the capitalist class'. He wanted the labouring classes to be allowed the same right of free assembly as Carson was allowed in Belfast and Redmond in Dublin.

There was one law for the rich and another for the poor, he added. There was no question of creating 'any mischief' in the streets and he disavowed any intention to use force because the working class did not have superior numbers; but if they had the force to exercise their right to O'Connell St, he would advise the people of Ireland to make themselves masters of their own country. Justice Swifte was neither impressed nor amused, and he had Connolly taken to the cells.

Meanwhile, Larkin had not heard of the arrests and was working as usual in Liberty Hall during the morning. William O'Brien who had finished work early in the North Dublin Union was cycling to Liberty Hall to get the latest news on the strike situation when he met Sheehy Skeffington. O'Brien was told of the arrests and of the warrant out for Larkin. He cycled to Liberty Hall, found Larkin upstairs giving an interview to the German socialist magazine, *Vorwarts*, oblivious of the fact that the police were out looking for him. With the help of a trusted cab driver, Larkin slipped out a back door and was driven to Countess Markievicz's home in Rathmines.

O'Brien returned to Liberty Hall to find the place besieged by police.

Inside the hall were about fifty people, mostly men who had come to pay their union dues. No ITGWU official was present except P. T. Daly and he was not much of a man to handle a crisis situation, according to O'Brien. Larkin's brother, Peter, was also there. Throughout the city, police and rioters clashed and there was every reason to think that the situation was getting out of hand. O'Brien telephoned the trades hall in Capel Street to discuss the deteriorating security problem. Tom Foran (ITGWU) told O'Brien that Larkin had been in touch with him to arrange for a hearse and coffin, in which he hoped to travel to the proscribed meeting, to be sent to Countess Markievicz's home. O'Brien dismissed the idea as 'humbug'. After further discussion it was agreed by some members of the DTC executive to transfer the meeting to another street in order to avoid a bloody confrontation with the police.[50]

The DTC president, Tom McPartlin (Amalgamated Society of Carpenters and Joiners), backed the moderate course of action strongly. He was not prepared, in the present climate of violence and disorder, to provoke a confrontation with the police, who appeared in a particularly ugly mood after days of unrelieved duty without any additional pay. Peter Larkin was the only one present who wanted the plans for the meeting to continue unchanged, but he had no support in the hall. Finally, O'Brien said he would take responsibility for issuing a statement transferring the meeting to a venue less likely to provoke bloodshed.[51]

After further discussion about the choice of venue it was decided to seek the advice of the police. A union messenger brought Inspector Willoughby, accompanied by a number of detectives and uniformed DMP, to Liberty Hall. O'Brien asked the inspector if the union could hold the meeting in Beresford Place. After consulting the authorities, Willoughby said that the proclamation indicated O'Connell Street or its vicinity; thus Beresford Place was precluded. Croydon Park, the ITGWU recreation centre in Fairview, was suggested as a compromise and considered acceptable. O'Brien penned the cancellation notice and telephoned it to the Press:

> In view of the action of the police in brutally batoning defenceless people in all parts of the city last night, and their openly expressed intention of repeating this conduct on Sunday, it has been decided by the strikes committee, in the interests of peace, to abandon the proposed meeting in

O'Connell Street, and to ask all transport workers and friends to assemble in Beresford Place at 12 o'clock today and march to Croydon Park, Fairview.[52]

In order to get the workers to follow the instructions of the strike committee[53] it was decided to station well-known trade unionists on outside cars in front of Liberty Hall, where the crowds flocking to O'Connell Street would see them. As the rioting continued in the city throughout the evening, news of the decision reached Larkin. He opposed the 'countermanding order' and sent a messenger to the offices of the *Freeman's Journal* in Princes Street with a statement for immediate publication but it first appeared in the stop press edition of the *Evening Telegraph* on Sunday, under the headline 'The Alleged Letter from Mr Larkin':

At ten minutes to three this morning a letter puporting to be from Mr James Larkin was brought to the *Freeman* office by a messenger riding a bicycle. It has reference to the O'Connell Street meeting. The messenger furnished his name but disclaimed any identification with Mr Larkin's organisation. He was not in a position to inform us from what address the letter was written, having, he said, pledged his word to Mr Larkin on that score. Though pressed to give the information in the strictest confidence, he refused to add anything except a vague indication of Mr Larkin's whereabouts at the moment. The following is the letter referred to: 'I have been informed that you have been instructed that there will be no meeting to-morrow in O'Connell Street. I desire to inform you that I, James Larkin, intend to hold a meeting at all costs, no matter what the opinion of other labour men may be; and if any person notified you to the contrary, he or she has done so without my authority. Yours in seclusion, Jim Larkin.[53]

Differences between trade unionists are most easily identifiable at times of extreme crisis. Quite obviously, Larkin was not prepared to pull back from the brink. He thought it best to carry on as planned. Otherwise, it would be a sign of weakness on the part of trade union leadership, providing very bad example for the rank and file. The strike committee, who were in a better position than Larkin to judge the situation on the ground, felt that the cost would be too high were thousands of irate trade unionists to crowd O'Connell Street the following day.

A number of important conclusions can be drawn from this decision. Was it the action of revolutionaries or syndicalists to consult a police inspector as to where it would be legally possible to hold the proscribed meeting? Was it the action of extreme leftists to defy Larkin and change the venue of the meeting in the interests of peace? O'Brien, who finally issued the statement to the Press, represented the Dublin socialist wing of the unions and was regarded as such by his contemporaries. Yet he chose to de-escalate the unrest at a time when a tailor-made opportunity for bloody confrontation presented itself. This move certainly vitiated the myth, strongly believed by employers, that the essence of the trouble in Dublin was due to the hybrid ideology of socialism and syndicalism.

The decision was not out of tune with the feelings of the men on the subject. Many workers did not support Larkin *per se*. They supported the men of the transport union and stood with them in defence of the principle of combination. Murphy had launched an attack on the hard-won right of the worker to combine and join the union of his choice. No trade unionist, not even the most moderate of men, could tolerate such an unwarranted intrusion by an employer. This point was put quite eloquently by a labourer, John Lyons. Writing to Archbishop Walsh, he said:

> The Dublin workers are strongly of the opinion that notwithstanding this disclaimer (that Murphy was not opposed to trade unionism) and those who act with him are desirous of breaking up trade unionism, and consequently although many of them (workers) disagree with Mr Larkin and his methods, they consider themselves forced in self-defence, to uphold the transport workers' union, as its defeat would encourage Dublin employers to crush the tradesmen of every degree and reduce them to a condition of slavery which they have been struggling for years to escape from.[55]

However, the trade unionists' support for the ITGWU did not extend to holding provocative public meetings which were liable to end in bloodshed.

During the first week of the tram strike there were persistent rumours that the police were not entirely happy with the way they were being treated by the authorities. Many of the DMP were called upon to do extra duty without adequate compensation or remuneration. On 22 August, the *Daily Express* reported alleged disquiet in police ranks:

> Grave unrest exists in the ranks of the DMP on account of the extra duties they are asked to perform. Inquiry, however, goes to show that the statement is absolutely without foundation.

The rumours persisted, however, and the security forces in the city were severely over-stretched by the industrial troubles. They were forced to guard the offices of the *Independent*, the premises of Charles Eason, and to provide an escort for newspaper delivery vans twice a day. Shortly before the tram strike began, 60 DMP pensioners and 5 elderly RIC men were sworn in to act as jailors.[56]

To withdraw men from the tensions of sectarian rioting in the North and throw them into the fray of industrial turmoil without a break was not prudent on the part of Dublin Castle. Furthermore, to keep the DMP on extended tours of duty without adequate compensation was even less advisable. Even under normal circumstances relations between the police and the transport union were strained. Moreover, the weekly attacks made by the *Irish Worker* on the baton-wielding 'bullies' who lounged at street corners and intimidated passers-by left a residue of resentment among the DMP which could only be vented with a vengeance in a riot situation.

On Saturday, 30 August, the police had to cope with five serious disturbances: in Ringsend, where the power station of the tramway company was situated; in Brunswick Street, where an *Independent* van was attacked; there were clashes in Beresford Place, Talbot Street, Marlborough Street, Earl Street; but the most serious battles took place on Burgh Quay and Eden Quay, where an over-wrought police force were guilty of the most brutal excesses and two deaths were caused. One of the dead was a transport union member named James Nolan. An inquest found that the deceased had died from a fractured skull and the evidence was too conflicting to say by whom the blow was administered. There was no doubt, however, in the minds of the workers as to where the blame lay. John Byrne, also a transport union member, died a few days later from head wounds received from the same source. In all, about 200 civilians and 30 constables were reported to have been treated for injuries received in the fracas.[57]

A 'Bloody Sunday'

Sunday, 31 August, broke in bright sunshine and soon O'Connell Street filled with the usual Sunday crowd of worshippers and strollers. At about eleven o'clock a force of 5 superintendents, 9 inspectors, 23 sergeants and 274 constables, of whom 72 were members of the RIC, took up positions along O'Connell Street. Every measure was to be taken to thwart the arrival of Larkin in any section of the 616-yard long street. Police presence in the area was not diminished in size by the plans to change the venue of the sign-posted meeting to Croydon Park. The police were there in strength but did their best to keep a low profile.[58]

Meanwhile, a large crowd had been gathering at Liberty Hall since about ten o'clock. About 36 brakes were lined up outside and members of the Irish Women Workers' Union were about to leave on an excursion to the Glen o' the Downs. The brakes were driven up Eden Quay, into O'Connell Street and around the Parnell monument with the occupants singing 'A Nation Once Again' while others hissed and hooted at passing tramcars. They then left for their picnic in festive mood. A reporter, walking down the quay after watching the brakes depart peacefully, saw a grim reminder of the previous night's fighting:

> Evidence of the fierceness of the encounters with the police were to be seen along Eden Quay in the pools of blood and smears of dry blood on the roadway and footpaths.[59]

At Liberty Hall the workers were beginning to move off for Croydon Park, led by P. T. Daly and William O'Brien who were riding on outside cars. About 15,000 men set out at one o'clock on the march, which passed off without incident. Despite that, the authorities continued to concentrate the main body of the police force in the O'Connell Street area. It is possible they felt the march might be a diversionary tactic to let Larkin slip through a weaker force. Apart from the many Sunday strollers, between 300 and 400 men had gathered near the GPO to wait for him, his brother, Peter, among them.[60]

At about 1.30, half an hour after the marchers set out from Liberty Hall, an 'elderly' man accompanied by his 'niece' passed unsuspectedly into the Imperial Hotel which was owned by William Martin Murphy. The couple had two rooms, reserved in the name of Donnelly. The stooped figure was assisted up the stairs by the young girl, onto the first floor, and into the smoking room. Moving swiftly at this stage, he quickly opened the french windows and stepped onto the outside balcony which overlooked O'Connell Street. There Larkin shouted to the crowded street that he had kept his promise. He made no attempt to address the crowd and simply stepped back inside again to await the arrival of the police.

His sudden appearance had caused great excitement among the crowd standing near the GPO and they surged across the street. Police cordoned off the hotel, and as Larkin was being led out, flanked by two DMP men, the carriage of Countess Markievicz drove up and stopped across the road. Then, according to one reporter:

> The countess called for cheers for Larkin and led on the cheering herself. A body of police immediately surrounded the car and ordered the driver into Princess St. He did not obey immediately, and a move was made by the police to drag him off his vehicle.[61]

As the car was surrounded by police 'the countess rushed over to greet Larkin and was struck down'.[62] The cheering for Larkin grew louder and the crowd rushed the police cordon twice. A third time the crowd surged forward and were again turned back by a now jittery police force; a stone crashed through a plate glass window of Clery's, the drapery store situated under the imperial hotel. 'Before one realised the situation,' according to one journalist, 'a baton charge was in progress'.[63] The correspondent of *The Times* felt that an order for the charge was given because police feared that the crowd would attempt to rescue Larkin from their custody.[64] Some of the constables charged in a line from O'Connell Bridge, while others charged across the street from the hotel, driving people into Princes Street, where another force of police was stationed. Caught between two lines of baton-wielding policemen the crowds panicked, many people were trampled underfoot and then beaten where they lay. 'For a few minutes a scene of terrible excitement and violence prevailed . . . men and women were beaten indiscriminately,' wrote the *Evening Telegraph* under the emotive headline, 'Charge on inoffensive onlookers.'[65] According to the *Daily Express*, a paper never noted for its labour sympathies:

> People sped in all directions to get out of danger but the throng was so dense that those in the immediate proximity were unable to avoid the punishment meted out to them. The crowds were dispersed towards O'Connell Bridge, and a section was driven into Princes Street where they encountered another force of police and between the two fires there were numerous casualties. People lay prone in the street in all directions, many of them bleeding profusely, and others being temporarily stunned. An old woman was knocked down and an elderly man was rendered unconscious by a baton stroke. One youth who was rather prominent had to run the gauntlet of half a dozen police through Princes Street and he received several strokes in flight.[66]

In a letter to the *Irish Times,* Count Markievicz said such scenes had only been rivalled in history by the Russian bloody Sunday of 1905—somewhat of an exaggeration. A Liberal MP, Handel Booth, who was in Dublin for the Horse Show with his wife, saw the scene from his bedroom window in the Imperial Hotel. He wrote:

> The noble street was in the hands of the most brutal constabulary ever let loose on a peaceful assembly. Up and down the road, backwards and forwards, the police rushed like men possessed. Some drove the crowd into the streets to meet other batches of the Government's minions wildly striking with truncheons at every one within reach. In escaping, many ran the gauntlet until the third or fourth blow knocked them senseless . . . kicking the victims when prostrate was a settled part of the police programme.[67]

As news of the baton charge spread throughout the city, rioting broke out in a number of areas, and police further raised the temperature by entering working class homes, assaulting people and breaking up furniture. Yet there were many who did not feel that the police had acted improperly. The secretary to the Archbishop, Father M. J. Curran, wrote to Dr Walsh in England describing the events:

> I saw the scenes in Brunswick St. The women, and even the young girls, were simply barbarian maniacs, yelling and practically threatening the police and tram men with their fists. I could only compare it to the pictures of the French revolution. Meanwhile the trams ran regularly and the men are acting splendidly—though they admit they are nervous.[68]

A Dalkey priest also wrote to Dr Walsh on the same subject:

> We never had such weather in Ireland. In fact, folk are beginning now to desire a little 'bad weather'. Everything looks well and promises well, except the miserable business in Dublin. It is indeed a blue lookout for Home Rule. Serious people must think. In a free country a man dare hardly call his life his own and must whisper under his breath. I am afraid we Irish are very liable to tyranny . . . Saturday's work was bad but you will see from the papers that Sunday's was worse—not however to me, who see our only hope of salvation in the policeman's baton—in the decision of the government to keep the peace at any cost. Larkin wants what he calls 'revolution'.[69]

The *Daily Express*, despite the objective reporting on the incidents in its news columns, gave unqualified support to the police:

> Fortunately the policy of leaving the fomentors of violence and intimidation in full possession of the central thoroughfare of the city for a Sunday afternoon did not commend itself to the responsible authorities, and the attempt to hold the meeting in Sackville Street was declared by

the strike committee to have been abandoned. The announcement was, however, too late and too vague to prevent the assemblage of large crowds, who were only too easily brought into conflict with the large force of police on the spot.[70]

The *Irish Times* also supported firm action and felt that the tough role adopted by the police had paid off:

We believe that the present tyranny has received its death blow and that the dupes will soon return to the normal sanity of the Irish working man. But all such question of reform and all such thoughts of better wages must be postponed until it has ceased to be possible for self-styled champions of labour to support anarchy in the workshop with riots in the streets.[71]

The indignation of the *Independent* knew no bounds:

Citizens of Dublin who would not have the red flag of anarchy upreared in their midst must think seriously of what the events of the week-end portend. A deliberate attempt is being made to establish a reign of ruffianism in the city. Out from the reeking slums the jail-birds and the most abandoned creatures of both sexes have poured to vent their hatred upon their natural enemies, the police. Strikers there are amongst them. But the legions of the work-shy have not, we may be sure, emerged from their hiding place to put up a fight for any claims of labour, legitimate or the reverse. They are out for devilry and loot.[72]

One of the few people who made any effort to understand the origins of the trouble was the editor of *Irish Homestead*, George Russell, or AE as he was popularly known. Contemptuously discounting the existence of a syndicalist plot in Dublin as the figment of an overheated imagination, he asked sarcastically where were the occupied factories, the barricades. the blazing turned-over trams—actions associated with libertarian communism. So far as he could gather from the *Irish Worker,* Labour had no policy, no idea of the future:

. . . and the tendency to substitute a rage for a policy is helped by the monstrous conduct of the authorities in Dublin who by the liberty they gave the police brutally to beat the brains out of innocent onlookers who had gathered in the streets for no lawless purpose, had done more sharply to divide the classes in Ireland than anything which has happened for half a century.[73]

Official sources claimed, and public opinion agreed, that the riots had their origins in organised attacks on the police. Get rid of the agitator and root out his organisation and peace would be permanently restored. But AE thought differently:

It seems to us, reading the letters in the press, and comments on leading articles on the situation, that the only policy which seems to occur to most people is to suppress labour and its organisation. Get rid of this or that organisation, imprison its leaders and things will go along peaceably as before. That is a vain hope. Larkin is not the cause of labour discontent. He is the product of it himself. Something better will have to be done than denounce labour attitudes as socialism or syndicalism . . . labour is as guiltless of the charge of being socialist or syndicalist as Mr Murphy himself . . . the labour movement in Ireland at the moment is at present nothing else than a passionate discontent with present conditions of wages, housing and employment. When a patient is in a delirium his yells and struggles may be stifled by gags and a bandage, but these are no cure. The ostrich is reported to hide his head in the sand when pursued. There are hundreds of thousands of human ostriches in Dublin.[74]

AE was accurate in his analysis. The labour movement, divided over where to hold the proscribed meeting, was more united than ever before as a result of the baton charge. Larkin, who had his authority undermined while he was in hiding by the moderating influences of William O'Brien and other craftsmen, was suddenly placed at the head of a united force of workers, courtesy of Dublin Castle. Father Curran wrote to the Archbishop[75] about this swing to the general secretary of the transport union who was facing charges after his dramatic appearance on the Imperial Hotel balcony:

The disorder here has grown very seriously since Saturday. It is no longer a question of a tram strike. It is simply the scum of our slums versus the police. Unfortunately the mob have the sympathy of the working classes and nobody helps the police. I think it is a scandal that the military have not yet been utilised. It would free the hands of the police immensely if the soldiers were stationed on the principal thoroughfares . . . It is really surprising to see how much support Larkin commands among the artisans. Even the printers who refused to come out on strike at his command are very largely (loyal) to him . . . The workmen have gone mad over Larkin and will do almost anything for him, even respectable carpenters and bricklayers.[76]

8 Lockout

On 30 August, 1913, trouble broke out at Jacob's factory where 3,000 people were employed. The dispute arose when a man operating a lift refused to handle flour that had been brought under police protection from Shackelton's mills, Lucan, where there was a strike in progress. The men were dismissed and transport union workers walked out in solidarity. However, on Monday the majority of the hands returned to work only to find that the firm had posted a notice saying that it was reluctantly compelled to shut the factory for some time. Maintenance men were also to be locked out.

A fitter, Patrick Kenny, left the following account:

> The men in the department in which I was employed for the past 14 years (maintenance) returned to work on Monday the same as usual, and when the notice was posted, the shop stewards of the two societies, Steam Engine Makers and the Amalgamated Union of Engineers, had an interview with the foreman, Mr William Long, and requested him to find out if the notice affected our department. He sent for the shop stewards some time after and told them that the firm had decided to retain the apprentices and two junior hands to do repairs and the remaining were to be locked out . . .He told them it had been decided to close the entire factory for some time.[1]

Jacob was quite emphatic, like most of his fellow employers, that he had no objection whatever to trade unionism; many of the skilled workers in his business were union members. In fact he would welcome a union among his own work people, but he was determined that no member of the transport workers' union should enter the factory again 'not if I have to sell the coat off my back in the struggle'.[2]

Later, when the factory continued to operate on a limited production with 1,700 hands, efforts were made to take back the maintenance men on acceptable grounds: they were asked to sign a document renouncing the transport union, do electrical work, and take the place of engine drivers.[3]

Jacob's was not the only factory to take action against their men on the day after the O'Connell Street baton charge. At the tramway works, in Inchicore, 250 men were locked out when one worker refused to repair a tram damaged by stone-throwing. At Leixlip, mill workers were dismissed when they refused to dissociate themselves from the transport union. Later, dockers refused to handle goods for Jacob's factory. And when Potters and Sons, North Wall, sacked members of the ITGWU all the coachbuilders on their staff downed tools in sympathy. In the evening, as rioting continued in the city, the chamber of commerce met and carried a resolution of thanks to the president, William Martin Murphy, 'for the energetic manner in which he had dealt with the present labour unrest in the city'.[4] In his reply, Murphy criticised unnamed employers for breeding 'Larkinism' through neglect of their men. Yet the solution he proposed to end industrial turbulence in the city was the routing of Larkin and the Liberty Hall union. Murphy had become as obsessed with the personality of Larkin as Larkin had become with that of the tramway boss:

> I have seen for a long time that the head of this labour agitation in Dublin has been aiming for a position that was occupied some time ago in Paris by a man who was called 'King' Pataud, who was able to hold up the whole business of the city by raising his little finger. That man was driven out of Paris, and the other man will be driven out of Dublin shortly.[5]

The present dispute had nothing to do with wages or working conditions, he told his audience. It was far more sinister than that and Larkin had to be stopped. Employers would have to be prepared, he added, to face trouble and loss of money in the struggle, but like any other business risk, in the end an employer would find he would save money, and he would be relieved from perpetual irritation and interference. Moreover, he said, the fight against Larkin was not so difficult after all. The prospect of a long struggle held much more terror for the employer than the strike itself:

> An employer who had never been up against a strike was terrorised at the prospect. When the strike actually took place the employer had to get his back to the wall, and the workman had fired his last cartridge. The employer all the time managed to get his three meals a day, but the unfortunate workman and his family had no resources whatever except submission, and that was what occurred in ninety-nine cases out of one

hundred. The difficulty of teaching that lesson to the workman was extraordinary.[6]

The next day, 2 September, the Dublin Coal Merchants' Association locked out about 1,500 men. The merchants were apologetic about their action. They stressed that they had no objection to their employees 'being members of any union acting in a lawful and reasonable manner', but as the ITGWU 'would not allow its members to deliver coal to certain firms, they were compelled to decline to employ men belonging to the union'.[7] Meanwhile, the trams were running regularly but a great many had their windows smashed as they passed through working class areas. Father Curran informed the Archbishop:

> The Dublin United Tramway Company's receipts for Horse Show week only went down by a fifth and the net increase of receipts to date for the year is very big. Certainly as far as the trams are concerned the strike is a decided failure. Everywhere you see trams with new motor men and conductors in training. Some are guarded by a policeman, but the service runs freely on the chief lines.[8]

The employers were determined to press home the initiative and teach the workers a lesson. On 4 September, the majority of the city's employers agreed to follow the action of the coal merchants and some other city firms:

> ... this meeting of employers, while asserting its friendly feelings to trade unionism, hereby declares that the position created by the Irish Transport and General Workers' Union (a union in name only) is a menace to all trade organisations and has become intolerable.[9]

Within days, the following document was handed to thousands of workers to be signed immediately and returned to their respective employers:

> I hereby undertake to carry out all instructions given me by or on behalf of my employers and further I agree to immediately resign (*sic*) my membership of the Irish Transport and General Workers' Union (if a member) and I further undertake that I will not join or in any way support this union.[10]

The Cork Employers' Federation voiced its solidarity with the firm action being taken in Dublin, where the conditions under which business has been conducted for a considerable time, 'owing to the bad and dangerous advice given to the workers would, if not discontinued, in time make it impossible to carry on trade in Ireland'.[11]

Within days the decision began to take effect. On 6 September, the staff at Dixon's soap works were locked out along with about

1,000 members of the United Labourers' Union. On 11 September, the Farmers' Association dismissed their hired hands. The same day, nearly 800 carters were locked out for refusing to handle 'tainted' goods.[12] When timber yard labourers refused to deliver goods on 22 September they were locked out, bringing the number of workers affected to roughly 20,000. However, the port was still open although it continued to operate under considerable difficulty. The largest employer in the city, Arthur Guinness, remained comparatively unaffected. Large drapery stores were still open to the public, but with few exceptions the city's commercial life suffered badly. The building trade was brought to a standstill, while many businesses could only operate under police protection. The stock exchange reflected a sudden loss of confidence in trading. One financial journalist suggested rather optimistically on 1 September that he was pleased things were coming to a head, for when they are at their worst they mend.[13] A month later no change had taken place and there were 'scarcely a dozen and a half transactions recorded' and . . . 'in all directions intense dullness prevails'.[14] As reports of stagnation on the Dublin stock exchange continued to be reported daily, Murphy's hopes of a quick and decisive victory over the transport union dwindled. Signs that the battle would be a long, drawn-out one manifested themselves when powerful English unions pledged support.

Britain: Trade Unions Find Support

The British Trade Union Congress met in Manchester the day following 'Bloody Sunday'. Standing orders were suspended to allow an emergency motion to be passed calling for an immediate inquiry into the behaviour of the police. The proposer of the motion was James Sexton, an implacable opponent of James Larkin. He was quick to assure delegates that he had no personal reason to love some of the men in prison but that the matter in hand was so grave that it rose above petty personalities. It might be said, he added, that two blacks did not make a white, but the black of James Larkin and James Connolly, if it was black, was white compared with the hellish blackness of Sir Edward Carson and other members of the Commons. Another delegate, Ben Tillett, felt that it was probably Murphy who had indirectly given the order to charge with drawn batons in O'Connell Street. They had got to realise that their future disputes would be conducted with bloodshed and that armed force would be used by the government. The man who had got pluck enough to strike must have in mind not merely the cessation of labour but the right to use a firearm, he added.[15] In the wave of emotion which swept over congress, the innate hostility felt by many delegates towards the random and undisciplined strike tactics of Larkin was swept aside by a common revulsion to government irresponsibility and police hooliganism.[16] On 6 September, the *New Statesman* put its finger on the real feelings of paid trade union officials towards Larkin and his arbitrary action, which was so destructive of labour discipline:

> One may detest Mr Larkin worse than Marat or a nearer parallel— Babeuf . . . but at the present crisis, no socialist, no trade unionist, no democrat, can hesitate for a moment in ranging himself on Mr Larkin's side . . . With Larkinism, fortunately or unfortunately, the cause of Trade Unionism in Ireland is for the moment bound up. If Larkin goes down, it will be a victory for the employers who claim to dictate to their workers to what organisation they shall or shall not belong.

The British TUC was left in little doubt as to where its allegiance lay after hearing a rousing speech from the president of the DTC, Tom McPartlin, who had travelled over with two other strike committee members to enlist the support of their cross-channel colleagues. A delegation led by the veteran socialist Kier Hardie arrived in Dublin on 4 September in time to join the two-mile-long funeral cortege of James Nolan. A black-bordered notice had been posted throughout the city asking citizens to attend the funeral of a man 'who died at the hands of the police'.[17] Later, the mild-mannered Kier Hardie told a mass meeting that 'John (*sic*) Nolan had been butchered in the street in the interests of sweated labour'.[18] An effigy of Martin Murphy was to be found dangling from a noose in a number of working class streets.

The workers were in mourning again on Saturday, 6 September, when John Byrne, the second victim to die as a result of baton injuries, was buried. The city's chronic housing problem was brought, quite tragically, to popular attention when a tenement house in Church Street collapsed killing eight people. The victims were buried on the same day as Byrne. One person who had lost his father and son in the disaster told how he had to crouch under a huge beam for over five hours as the rubble tumbled down around him.[19] There was a public outcry when it was learned that the corporation had passed the same building as structurally sound only two months before. The incident added fuel to the fire of social grievance and rendered the industrial problem even more intractable.

A peace conference, under the auspices of the Lord Mayor, met on 5 September to discuss a settlement and on 8 September, the parties met for a second time at the Shelbourne Hotel, but talks broke down because no agreement could be reached on the reinstatement of locked-out transport union men. The other major stumbling block was the failure to provide adequate guarantees for the employers against the possible outbreak of future disputes. The guarantee of the British TUC was not adequate, and the 'masters resolutely declined to entertain any proposal which would leave them as before at the mercy of the irresponsible autocracy of Liberty Hall'.[20]

Kier Hardie and his associates returned to England convinced that the employers were primarily responsible for the trouble in Dublin. They were determined to give all the indirect support they could to the dispute but there was a general reluctance to contemplate any direct action. They had been left in little doubt as to what the employers' federation intended:

> The plan of the employers is simple—starve the men out; throw as many of them as possible on the paysheets of their respective unions, and especially the transport union, until exhaustion of funds makes it impossible for them to hold out . . . Mr Murphy is, in our opinion, much the most dangerous man now living in Ireland. He is infinitely more dangerous than poor Captain Craig with his bad speeches and worse rifles.[21]

The Dublin workers were sure of receiving British funds and food. They were less sure of more tangile and more direct help from their cross-channel colleagues.

Both Connolly and Larkin were still in prison on 8 September and the running of the lockout was thrown onto the shoulders of the DTC executive. Four days later, Larkin was released on bail. Connolly, who had been on hunger strike since 6 September, was let out the following day. Both men found a united labour movement and were given a hero's welcome. However, unity was based more on opposition to the repugnant action taken by the employers than it was rooted in positive support for Larkin and his use of the sympathetic strike technique.

The debates in the DTC reflected the nature of the support. The ITGWU claim for recognition as a *bona fide* union was demanded by delegates but faced by what Tom McPartlin described as an effort to starve the workers into submission, the majority on the council were not prepared to call a general strike. On the motion of Nathaniel Rimmer (ASRS), the council debated the issue in a heated fashion. McPartlin felt that it was all a matter of tactics and it was his personal opinion that a general strike was quite hopeless. Mr Lennon of the Mineral Water Operatives' Union felt that such a move could only provoke friction between the unions themselves and after a long debate the motion was defeated by 29 votes to 8. A less contentious suggestion, proposed by Tom Murphy (Carpet Planners' Union) that no trade unionist should work with anyone who signed the employers' pledge, was adopted. The council also proposed to urge unions to levy skilled workers 1s per week and unskilled men 6d a week.[22]

Unions responded generously to the call. The Dublin Metropolitan House Painters agreed to pay the 1s per head levy and voted £10 to the ITGWU besides. Moreover, the painters' forbade its members to travel on tram cars during the dispute. Members were also instructed not to use scaffolding or other materials brought to jobs under police protection.[23]

The bricklayers' union committee heartily pledged 'the moral and financial support of this organisation to the Irish Transport Workers' Union and wish(ed) them a full measure of success in their struggle'.[24] Bricklayers were forbidden to work on a tram company job in Dalkey and members in the Dublin area were levied at the rate of 3s per week and 1/6d in provincial branches. A lot of this money went towards paying 'migration' aid to bricklayers leaving for England to find work. Those in benefit were to receive £1; 12s was to be paid to members over three and under nine months in arrears; and 8s was to be paid to rejoiners and those over nine months in arrears.[25]

The bakers' union, Bridge Street, also voted financial support but was upset about supplies of bread coming from Belfast and other places for the locked-out workers. It felt that bread supplies should be manufactured in Dublin by union labour.[26] The Drapers' Assistants' Association was not directly affected by the lockout but many members gave up their spare time to work in Liberty Hall distributing food, etc.

If any trade union official was inclined to support the radical policies of Larkin, it was the DAA general secretary, Michael O'Lehane, yet he followed the line of DTC council moderates on the sympathetic strike issue:

> We have no desire to become involved at the moment in this dispute, but our members must absolutely refuse to perform work which belongs to others and which they would not be asked to perform if no dispute

existed . . . In conclusion may we suggest to our members, more especially to those who are not resident in Dublin and who are not perhaps so conversant with the pros and cons of the present dispute in the capital, not to take up a too partisan attitude. Whatever the merits or demerits regarding the origin of the dispute may be, our sympathies and support must go out to the thousands of workers and their families who are at present in need of our assistance.[27]

The lockout and the disputes which led up to it probably caused the greatest upheaval within the Dublin Typographical Provident Society. The *Independent* dispute affected the printers directly and they incurred the wrath of Larkin when the DTPS executive refused, at the request of Larkin, to ask its members to come out in support of the transport union men. The ITGWU's appeal was regarded as unreasonable by the printers, who felt that there was a danger, if the *Independent* chapel took action, of the whole trade being locked out by the Master Printers for breach of agreement.[28] However, the most radical chapel in the DTPS, Thom's, wanted to follow Larkin's request to strike:

> Owing to the present labour unrest caused by the action of Mr William Martin Murphy, we, the members of this Chapel, call upon the Executive of our Society to withdraw all members of the DTPS from the *Independent* office, and any other offices where trade unionism is affected.[29]

However, the Combined Newspaper Chapels, joined by other jobbing houses, opposed withdrawal of labour. Then the DTPS council, in consultation with the Printing and Kindred Trades' Federation, opposed the Thom's chapel motion, although they were 'in thorough sympathy with every onward and upward movement entered into by all classes of workers'. Printers were bound by signed contract to give or receive two weeks' notice before terminating employment or going on strike. And as there was interchange of copy, etc. between all 'fairly' worked newspaper offices, the closure of the *Independent* would mean the closing of all offices. Moreover, since there were transport men in practically every office in the city such a dispute would set a precedent, 'thus rendering ourselves liable to strikes from no more than a sympathetic standpoint'.[30] Applied to its logical conclusion, such a course of action could force printers out of work even if only an employer's 'farm labourers or any other employees' were locked out, the council thought.[31] Practically the entire trade took part in a ballot on the issue on 10 September, with 629 voting for the council motion and 228 supporting the Thom's chapel motion. It was a significant minority, but even the hostility of the *Irish Worker*, resulting from the decision, did not deter the printers from contributing generously to the strike fund.

The majority of Dublin unions were not prepared to throw their men out of work either to take part in a general strike or in a sympathetic strike. However, they were prepared to support the ITGWU by contributing funds and refusing to work with 'tainted' goods. The same held true, even more so, for cross-channel unions. Officials just did not want to get involved beyond the level of raising money or collecting clothes. However, this did not prevent some men at Liverpool, belonging to the London and North Western Railway Company, refusing to handle goods which had been diverted from Holyhead due to the Dublin lockout. These men were suspended and immediately some of their colleagues struck in sympathy.[32] There were 1,600 out as a result of the initial refusal to handle 'tainted goods' which were bound for Dublin. J. H. Thomas, MP, the assistant secretary of the newly-formed National Union of Railwaymen, which incorporated the larger railway unions, denounced the action of his men from London:

> If we are to direct you—and there is a tendency to direct us in every tinpot dispute—we ask that you shall not fritter away your power in this or that dispute. Our position as railway men is unique, and I am absolutely and emphatically opposed to what is called the sympathetic strike, because in the first place there is no dispute which can possibly happen but what in some way or other you as railway men must be involved. Neither is it fair . . . to be dragged into every dispute without either your union officials or your organisation being consulted.[33]

The NUR executive later joined Thomas in repudiating the sympathetic strike. Railway companies, the NUR argued, were compelled by statute to carry all goods without discrimination. A delegation from Dublin later met the executive and it was agreed to give preferential treatment to Dublin but the Liverpool strikers were ordered back to work.[34]

By the end of September there were over 20,000 men out of work in Dublin, and 14,000 of these had to be given strike pay from the central lockout fund. By November, 10,017 ITGWU men were being paid 5s per week; Irish Women Workers' Union members, numbering 1,000, were receiving 4s strike pay; 475 bricklayers, 70 plasterers, 20 amalgamated painters, 400 amalgamated carpenters, 30 stonecutters, 7 paviors and 1,000 builders' labourers were also getting 5s a week strike pay.

Larkin, meanwhile, was travelling throughout England whipping up support for his plan to impose a total economic blockage on Dublin. Nobody could deny the justice of his case but he was rapidly making enemies and testing the loyalty of his most trusted friends by his utterances. He was appealing over the heads of British trade union officials to the rank and file to follow his policy of the sympathetic strike.[35] Yet in spite of Larkin's irregular practices and his unconcealed contempt for many of the most respected, powerful and prominent union leaders, they were prepared to tolerate his foibles for as long as was humanly possible, and dedicated themselves to rallying financial support for the beleagured strikers of Dublin. The TUC voted £5,000 to the struggle and the *Daily Mail, Daily Mirror* and the *Herald* collected funds.[36] On 27 September, the food-ship 'Hare' arrived in Dublin and members of the DAA spent their half day dispensing food to ticket-holders. A week later the food-ship 'Fraternity' arrived.

Meanwhile, Father Curran was still trying to convince the Archbishop, who had not returned from Paris, that the strike was the fault of the workers:

> The general body continue defiant and obstinate on the question of tainted goods. They are obsessed with Larkin and are convinced they are going to win and that their unions are strong and better circumstanced than the employers. It is useless talking to them and nothing will convince them but that the whole thing is a plot of 'William Martin Murphy' to put down the working man and an effort of the employers to pull down wages and to destroy trade unionism. Their view of tainted goods is regarded as sacrosanct and their optimism pathetic. It is really amusing to draw the unfortunate dupes out on the principles underlying the dispute and the conversation always gets turned at inconvenient points onto the police or William Martin Murphy. It's all due to William Martin Murphy, William Martin Murphy.[37]

Father Curran explained that while the craft unions did not call out their men, 'most of the men in these societies went out of their own accord when trouble arose over labourers in a particular firm'. As a result the strike was beginning to hit hard and storekeepers and merchants find it almost impossible to get goods delivered. Dr Walsh, however, was not in agreement about Murphy, as evidenced by a further letter from Curran:

> I do not quite see how Your Grace considers that M(urphy) has made such a blunder. The only people he 'locked out' were some of the dispatch hands of the *Independent* and the parcel men on the trams.

The motor men, conductors, and powerhouse men were called out by Larkin . . . I can quite see that the locking out of the last, as well as the parcel men of the trams is technically an undiplomatic 'move' but public opinion, I mean 'the man in the street' kind of person, thinks he was wise in forestalling Larkin, choosing his own time and even Larkin himself has admitted his hand was forced before he wished . . . But tram strike now occupies a very backward position. The issues raised by the subsequent troubles have quite overwhelmed M's position.[38]

Curran was obviously defending a weak case which the Archbishop, though ill at the time, had opposed. The difficulty was that he was not in Dublin to exercise his influence over the dispute when it was in its early stages and before it had got out of hand completely.

The Board of Trade Inquiry

The authorities made an eleventh-hour bid to end the dispute towards the end of September. George Askwith who had been successful in averting a bus strike in London earlier in the month, was given the task by the Board of Trade. Sir Thomas Radcliffe Ellis, secretary of the Mining Association of Great Britain, and J. R. Clynes, MP, chairman of the Gas Workers' and General Labourers' Union, Isaac Mitchell and H. F. Wilson were the members of the team. A court of inquiry was decided upon 'as preferable to an attempt by a single Englishman to intervene in the welter of the revolution'.[39] The hearings, which began on 29 September, were held in public despite the workers' request to proceed in camera. Neither party refused to come before the court but the team soon realised that 'no settlement was meant. Mr Murphy was out for a fight to the finish'.[40] Larkin conducted the case for the trade unions and Tim Healy took the employers' brief. The sessions were well attended but workers were in no sense in the majority:

The audience, whilst mostly Larkinite, is not working class. They are mainly people who dwelt in the suburbs of art and literature. Many of them are angry at Mr Murphy for having driven Sir Hugh Lane's collection of French pictures out of Dublin and Mr Larkin is a new 'thrill'. It is fine to hear Mr Larkin say, 'If I were an atheist, I shouldn't deny it.'[41]

The hearings were charged with emotion as Healy and Larkin argued their respective cases and cross-examined witnesses. Larkin 'abused his best friends in Ireland, descending to personalities'. Yet under his questioning Jacob admitted that his firm was paying boy learners of fourteen 5s, and girls of the same age 4s, and from the manager of the British and Irish Steampacket Company the hearing learned that the wages of its labourers had risen since the activity of the union began in 1909 from 24s to 27s for sixty hours to 30s all round.[42] Tom McPartlin proposed a basis for negotiations consisting of the reinstatement of all workers; the withdrawal of existing notices of dismissal; an undertaking for two years by the unions that employers submitting the conditions to a permanent joint trade board should be exempt from sympathetic strikes; and that every dispute should be dealt with by this board before the declaration of a strike or lockout. Three leading English trade unionists also gave evidence. Mr Havelock Wilson and Mr Gosling argued the justification of Larkin's actions in view of the special conditions in Dublin, while Mr Williams of the National Transport Workers' Union threatened a 'sympathetic strike' among British workers handling coal for Ireland. It was the trade unions who were prepared to concede ground as the McPartlin plan suggested. Askwith's findings indicated that 'grievances of considerable importance have existed'. More importantly, the employers' form which forced workers to resign from the ITGWU was forcefully condemned:

> Whatever may have been the intention of the employers, this document imposes upon the signatories conditions which are contrary to individual liberty and which no workman or body of workmen could reasonably be expected to accept. We understand that many of the workmen asked to sign this or similar documents were in no way connected with the Transport Workers' Union, and we think it was unfortunate that they should have been brought into the dispute. It will be obvious that the effort to secure signatures to such a document would be likely to create a maximum of ill-feeling.[43]

The workers were also criticised for the use of the sympathetic strike which was disruptive of trade in the city. Askwith urged the setting up of a conciliation board based upon a Canadian plan. There was also laid down a method as proposed by the industrial council, for deciding and dealing with questions of breach of agreement.[44]

The inquiry drove a further wedge between workers and employers by emphasising the cleavage between the two sides in public, although the trade unions were prepared to accept the findings as a basis for further discussions with the employers. The *Spectator* felt that the reason for Askwith's success in England as a conciliator rested on the fact that the British were able to compromise but that in Dublin there 'was no habitual love of compromise. On the contrary, the very word itself is anathema to the majority of Irishmen'.[45] This certainly held true for the employers, who rejected the recommendations on the grounds that they did not offer an 'effectual solution of the existing trouble'.[46] A statement said the employers 'were much more concerned to put an end to present difficulties than to consider problems relating to future problems'.[47] Askwith commented in disgust that the only guarantee the employers desired 'was to show that they could beat both Larkin and 'Larkinism'.[48]

In a further statement the employers' counsel, Tim Healy, urged the ITGWU to reorganise on 'proper' lines. New officials should be appointed who had the approval of the British Joint Labour Board. Only then would the employers consider withdrawing the document and give recognition to the 'new look' transport workers' union.

Despite a bellicose speech by Larkin in London, in which he cried, 'to hell with contracts', public opinion shifted onto the side of the workers. *The Times* said the employers had 'played into the hands of the agitator and given substance to the charge that they care for nothing but money'.[49] While the *Independent* continued to predict confidantly that Larkin was about to meet his Waterloo,[50] the *Irish Times* modified its position and sought a quick settlement, arguing that British trade unionists should go guarantor for the general secretary of the transport union.[51]

Responses from private citizens were even stronger than the media. AE addressed an open letter to the 'masters of Dublin' whom he described as 'uncultivated men', 'bad citizens', with a false concept of themselves as 'altogether virtuous and wronged'. He called the employers' demands 'preposterous and impossible', continuing:

> We read in the Dark Ages of the rack and the thumb screw. But these iniquities were hidden and concealed from the knowledge of men in dungeons and torture chambers. Evening in the Dark Ages humanity could not endure the sight of such suffering, and it learnt of such misuses of power by slow degrees, through rumours, and when it was certain it razed its Bastilles to their foundations. It remained for the twentieth century and the capital city of Ireland to see an oligarchy of four hundred masters decide openly upon starving one hundred thousand people, and refusing to consider any solution except that fixed by their pride.

His attack produced all the greater impact because it was so uncharacteristically bitter and uncompromising:

> You, masters, asked men to do that which masters of labour in any other city in these islands had not dared to do. You insolently demanded of those men who were members of a trade union that they should resign from that union, and from those who were not members you insisted on a vow that they would never join it. Your insolence and ignorance of the rights conceded to workers universally in the modern world were incredible, and as great as your inhumanity . . . If you had between you collectively a portion of human soul as large as a threepenny bit, you would have sat night and day with the representatives of labour, trying this or that solution of the trouble, mindful of the womem and children who at least were innocent of wrong against you. But no. The men whose manhood you have broken will loathe you and will always be brooding and scheming to strike a fresh blow. The children will be taught to curse you. The infant being moulded in the womb will have breathed into its starved body the vitality of hate. It is not they—it is you who are blind Samsons pulling down the pillars of the social order. You are sounding the death knell of autocracy in industry.[52]

Another man to resent deeply the ruthlessness of the employers was Archbishop Walsh who had just arrived back in Ireland. Although he was far from well, Aberdeen wrote urging him to intervene in the dispute since all else had failed. Walsh replied:

> How any competent commissioner, to say nothing of a man who is known to be an able lawyer (and in addition, an expert in matters of trade union and labour disputes), could have conducted an inquiry in such an extraordinary position, I have to regard as an absolute riddle. In any case, the labour leader has an exceeding strong case . . . I must say that on the merits of the case generally, my sympathies are altogether with them (the workers) and I trust that the outcome of the present case will be a radical change for better in the position of employed in Dublin.[53]

The Archbishop's favourable attitude towards the workers was taken up in other quarters where support for employers had prevailed. The Citizens' Peace Committee, composed of many prominent public figures, was disbanded and a pro-transport union group set up called the Dublin Civic League. The employers were clearly on the receiving end of a lot of damaging criticism which gave the workers of the transport union a unique opportunity to turn the tables on their opponents.

Larkin was still determined to force the leaders of the British unions to call out their men in sympathy with their Dublin colleagues, although all the signs indicated that he had no hope of succeeding.

On 10 October, speaking in London to a friendly audience, he proceeded to attack the ILP, the Nationalists and the Unionists in the most vitriolic terms. 'As for the Labour Party,' he said, 'they could wrap themselves up in cloth tomorrow and they would be just as useful as the mummies in the museum . . . you have only got to look at them, that's enough.'[54] He compounded his error by singling out individual trade union officials for special condemnation. The veteran socialist, Philip Snowden, 'had never done a day's manual work in his life', he said.[55] Larkin was testing the patience of even his closest friends by the undiplomatic tone of his language. Yet despite the violence of his attacks on the British trade union hierarchy, financial support for the Dublin lockout was on the increase from England. The Miners' Federation, at its annual conference at Scarborough, voted £1,000 a week, and the carpenters' union subscribed £1,500 a week. Larkin realised that the English labour commitment to Dublin was largely an emotional one and that the plentiful supply of funds was likely to dry up after the initial wave of sympathy had passed. He was pushed into demanding more direct action in Britain. A request for a sympathetic strike was not unreasonable, given the extraordinary circumstances prevailing in Dublin, but the tone and manner in which the plea was put forward was unwittingly calculated to provoke a strong reaction among even the most radical elements of the BTUC and antagonise even the most sympathetic.

Even more damaging for the workers' campaign was the bizarre and abortive attempt to alleviate the suffering of children affected by the lockout by sending them on holiday to England. The plan originated in London when Dora Montefiori, a well-off social worker, and an American, Lucille Rand, met Larkin and discussed the plight of the lockout families. Although conceived in good faith, the whole project exhibited a curious insensitivity and deficient awareness of the strong religious sentiments of Catholic Dublin. Many prominent clergymen made no secret of their views of Larkin and his methods. One of his most implacable enemies was a Father Condon OSA, of Thomas Street. His pulpit was used as a platform for an anti-transport union crusade:

> I will say that, in my humble opinion, the working-men of Dublin are being urged to adopt a policy and methods which if followed, will inevitably lead to social disaster, to economic ruin and to the setting up of a tyranny which will be as galling as the worst form of political despotism which has cursed our land. But how, I ask, can a priest continue

silent when the flock committed to his spiritual teaching is exposed to pernicious doctrines preached from press and platform, when the leader whom a Christian people are invited to follow proclaims himself a revolutionary, denies the right of ownership, declares solemnly that the doctrines of socialism are in harmony with the teaching of the Catholic Church, and sets up for himself the arrogant claim of divine commission to preach to Christian men and women the gospel of discontent? This is what the leader of industrial revolt in the city is reported to have done.[56]

Father Condon made the practical suggestion to set up a rival union for the God-fearing transport men to join, and his sentiments were echoed in the columns of the *Irish Catholic* and received widespread support. He did much to antagonise the workers in his congregation, the men being too incensed by the priest's criticisms that a local employer (or foreman) was forced to write to the Archbishop complaining about the damaging influence of the sermons on his employees' faith:

> I am very sorry to trouble you but I would be very glad if you will look into the following matter. There is a Father Condron or Condon of Thomas St chapel who has been saying things for a good while past to the detriment of James Larkin, the man who is fighting the lock-out. And as I have a good many employees under me and as this priest's talk is making them very bitter against priests in general (and most of them are good-living Catholics), they tell me if he holds a meeting on Sunday with a man named Byrne, as he threatened, they will all say things and ask him to mind his religious duties . . . Things are quite bad enough without the clergy helping the poor to lose their faith.[57]

In this climate of recrimination and tension, the scheme to find foster homes for the children of strikers was launched, but as soon as Archbishop Walsh heard of the plan he wrote to the press condemning the move in unusually undiplomatic language:

> The Dublin women now subjected to this cruel temptation to part with their helpless offspring are, in the majority of cases, Catholics. Have they abandoned their Faith? Surely not. Well, if they have not, they should need no words of mine to remind them of the plain duty of every Catholic mother in such a case. I can only put it to them that they can be no longer held worthy of the name Catholic mothers if they so far forget that duty as to send away their little children to be cared for in a strange land, without security of any kind that those to whom the poor children are to be handed over are Catholics, if indeed are persons of any faith at all.[58]

A letter from a Liverpool Catholic helped confirm the Archbishop's fears about the danger to the children's faith and morals:

> I have read your letter in the paper here and you have done a great service to the Catholic people of Dublin by warning them against sending any of their children to England. I can tell you that many of the children would never see their parents again, the homes they would be invited to here are the homes, not of Catholics, but of anti-Catholics, socialists, and various bigoted sects who would do anything to rob a Catholic child of the true faith. Orange people here would take the children for spite to destroy their faith. I will give you an instance. Stephen Walsh, MP for the Ince division of Lancashire (labour member), was in a Catholic industrial school, and brought up a Catholic until he was 16 years of age. He was then boarded out in the colliery districts, and living with Wesleyans, he became a Wesleyan, and local preacher, etc., etc., and Liverpool has other such cases. For God's sake don't let a single child leave Dublin. Surely Catholic mothers in Dublin cannot be so inhuman. The strike will soon be over. If the Catholic mothers of black '47 kept the faith, surely they can do so now.[59]

Mrs Montefiori arrived in Dublin with her colleague, Mrs Rand, only to be greeted by a growing storm of protest in Catholic circles. A letter was sent to the Archbishop explaining some of the facts of the scheme. Up to 21 October, 350 offers of working class English homes for Dublin boys and girls between the ages of four and fourteen were made. Most of the parents applying sent a reference if they did not belong to a trade union. Many had sent money towards travelling expenses and declared that they were Irish and Catholic. A Plymouth working class organisation wrote asking that 40 children be sent, and five mothers to look after them. The children were to be housed in large centres. Their names were to be given to the local parish priests and they were to attend local Catholic schools.[60]

Even these assurances were not sufficient to convince the clergy that the plan was not an attempt to proselytize the Catholic children of Dublin. A small party of children left for England on 22 October. The next day 50 more children were marched to Tara Street public baths where they were washed and dressed in brown jerseys with their names and destinations stitched on the backs. The proceedings were interrupted by the arrival of two priests from nearby Westland Row parish. They appealed to waiting parents to withdraw permission for allowing their children to be sent abroad. The confusion reduced many of the 'deportees', who were aged from seven to eleven years, to tears, or as the *Daily Express* phrased it, they 'loudly proclaimed the fact that they did not want to go to

England to become English children'.[61] In the general confusion the two ladies managed to take 15 of their charges to Westland Row station and board the 1.15 to Kingstown. The priests and some ladies gave pursuit. Boarding the train at a station further down the line, they insisted on sitting in the same carriage as the 'deportees'. By the time the train had reached Kingstown, ten of the boys were admitting that their parents had not given permission for the trip and were returned to the city. The depleted band boarded the *Scotia* and was followed by one of the priests who dashed up the gangplank demanding the name and destination of each child. Before the ship sailed, a woman who had concealed herself on board had grabbed two more of the children and dragged them to 'safety' with the help of willing sailors. The first round clearly went to the clergy; from the trade union point of view the Kingstown venture was a fiasco.

Reaction to the scheme in the Press was somewhat hysterial. The *Tablet*, expressing the views of many well-to-do Dublin Catholics, felt that the souls of the deported children would become the 'proper prey of benevolent theorists'. An editorial in the 1 November issue congratulated the restraint of Irish mothers:

> To the vast astonishment of benevolent British philanthropists Irish mothers explained that they would rather see their little ones dead in their arms than sent to homes where their faith would be imperilled.

The indignation of the *Tablet* was only surpassed by the panic-stricken *Toiler,* a workers' weekly edited by the old enemy of Larkin, J. P. McIntyre of the Workers' Union. Under the headline 'English Revolutionary socialists capture Irish Catholic Children', the paper began a leader in its usual vituperative style:

> Murder will out. And now at last the game of the Larkinite Socialist Syndicalists stands self-exposed . . . (They are) attempting to undermine and destroy the Catholic faith of the rising generation. The 'curse of Cromwell' so bitterly remembered as a phase in Ireland will, in future, pall into insignificance when the Irish workers look back on the 'curse of Larkinism'.[62]

However, Larkin was undaunted by the fulminations of the clergy and the Catholic press. He supported the venture and said that the religion which could not stand two weeks' holiday in England had not very much bottom or very much support behind it. The priests who had stopped the children 'were a disgrace to their cloth'. He launched a further attack on the clergy in general:

Tell the clergy to come down off that fence, and, if it is necessary, pull them down. It is as necessary for their own good as it is for yours that they be honest. Teach them that their business is not Mammon but God. Time and again the Church has to be reminded of that elementary fact; they forget their origin, and then the Church becomes the most debased and debasing lie under the wide heavens. In Ireland today the Church is a lie . . . we will learn that they are making us pay too high a price for the privilege of being called the Isle of Saints.[63]

Despite the opposition, children were still sent abroad for a holiday. As they departed, rival crowds stood on the docks singing 'Cheer up Larkin' to the tune of 'God Save Ireland' while others sang 'Ave Maria' and 'Faith of our Fathers'. Handbills were circulated among the crowds, strongly reinforced by members of the Ancient Order of Hibernians. One such handout read:

Fathers and Mothers of Catholic Dublin—Are you content to abandon your children to strangers, who give no guarantee to have them placed in Catholic or Irish homes? You may never see them again. Kidnappers and soupers are at their deadly work. There is no excuse for exiling your children. Provision has been made in Dublin for all classes of distress amongst them. No city has ever been so disgraced.[64]

The Dublin Children's Distress Fund was swiftly set up to provide Catholic assistance for the starving children on 27 October. The Christian Brothers offered to take eighty boys, while Countess Plunkett agreed to house and feed some girls. The Irish National Pilgrimage to Lourdes donated £2,000 from their surplus fund for relief purposes.[65] It was also claimed that parishes in the city were looking after poor children. In Marlborough Street, Westland Row and City Quay, 1,280 breakfasts were given daily to children attending school. The number of breakfasts being given out had risen to 2,450 in October 1913; nearly 1,400 were being given dinners. In another parish 400 children were being clothed each year; 315 in another; 519 in another; and 780 in yet another. On 28 October, a special collection was held in all churches of the diocese for the relief of distress.[66]

Neither the Catholic Church nor the transport union had benefited from the 'deportation' scheme. It was as ill-conceived as it was ill-timed and it died in a welter of recrimination and confusion. Most damaging of all, the unprecedented reaction provoked by the incident wrested the initiative won as a result of continuing employer intransigence from the transport union, leaving the anti-lockout campaign in a much weaker position as far as popular public support was concerned. Stephen Gwynn wrote to the Archbishop on 29 October describing his feelings on the likely outcome of the trouble:

> These idiot women have developed a situation which gives victory to the employers in a demand that they shall dictate to the employed the form of organisation and persons to run it. A victory of this sort means infinite trouble in future.[67]

Larkin Stands Trial

Larkin appeared before Mr Justice Madden on 27 October, charged with sedition, incitement to riot and incitement to robbery with violence in a speech prior to 'Bloody Sunday'. His chances of a fair trial were remote, particularly following the incident with the children, for even in less emotional times he had not exactly enjoyed a good press. The *Toiler* which, even according to Arnold Wright, was 'a monument of scurrility and vituperation', had gone furthest systematically to try to destroy Larkin's character through lies, innuendo and insinuation.[68]

In one edition a bogus certificate was produced professing to prove that Larkin had been a member of the Baconsfield Lodge (no. 337) of the Independent Orange Order.[69] Another issue carried pictures of both Larkin and James Carey (the secretary of the bricklayers' union who informed on the Invincibles in 1882), and intimated that perhaps they were one and the same person or possibly close relatives. The headline read: 'Was Larkin at the scene of the Park Murders? a thrilling story.'[70] The same story enjoyed widespread popularity and 'by request' it was re-run in three issues. This was the lowest form of journalism and some of the other papers were little better even if somewhat more cautious because of the laws of libel. If the Press had a low opinion of Larkin, he had a correspondingly low opinion of journalists:

> We wonder if the press of Dublin have a shred of decency left. If so, there is still a suitable bed left for the repose of their dirty foul carcasses. We refer to the residual tanks of the Pigeon House sewerage works. Surely for their carnival of lying during the lock-out they deserve eternal rest. What mendacious, brazen-faced monsters they are.[71]

Larkin's sentence was predictably severe. He was given seven months' hard labour for sedition. Criticism of the move was not long in coming from all sides of the political spectrum. The *Spectator* felt that Larkin had been condemned on the antiquated charge of *lese majeste.*[72] The normally staid *New Statesman* said that the prosecution was one of those 'extraordinary administrative ineptitudes that make us wonder whether after all the anarchist is not right in his view that all governments are necessarily bad'. It was only at Dublin Castle, thought the *New Statesman*, that such a clumsy political mistake could be perpetrated:

> At the very moment when peers and Privy Councillors are exulting in treasonable utterances in Ulster, and openly making preparations to 'levy war against the King', when everyone is asking to what lengths the Government intends to allow them to go, Dublin Castle decides to prosecute for sedition, not Sir Edward Carson and his 'gallopers', or the organisers of the 'guarantee fund' which is to make treason cheap, but a trade union leader in the midst of an embittered labour dispute, in which the Special Commissioner of the Board of Trade has found that the workers are largely in the right. Does Mr Birrell—for it is he as the chief secretary who sanctions a prosecution for action—really mean to convince every workman in this country (and every elector in North Bristol) that the justice that he has sworn to administer 'indifferently' winks quite so shamelessly with one eye?[73]

The indignation of people at the judgment was far greater than the Liberal government ever imagined. On 1 November, a meeting was held at the Albert Hall, organised by the *Daily Herald* to press for Larkin's immediate release.[74] There were no fewer than 40,000 applicants to attend the meeting, which was addressed by Ben Tillett, George Bernard Shaw, and AE. The majority of those present pledged themselves to attend every meeting addressed by a Liberal Minister and heckle until Larkin was released. The pledge was kept.

The case was the subject of 'prolonged consideration' in cabinet in November—only three days after a serious by-election reverse for the Liberals—when a large majority of Ministers regarded Larkin's prosecution as 'impolitic and unnecessary and calculated to do more harm than good'. The Chancellor of the Exchequer and the Attorney General commented 'on the way the jury was "packed" and on the tone in which the prosecution was conducted by the Irish Law Office'.

The Cabinet noted that Larkin had been acquitted of the two more serious charges of inciting to larceny and riot. Ministers unanimously agreed that the seven-month sentence was 'grossly excessive' and recommended to the Ministers concerned in Dublin to determine 'the precise amount of reduction'. Larkin was released a week later.

The Citizen Army

At the Albert Hall meeting, Shaw counselled the workers of Dublin to arm without delay:

> Now if you put the police on the footing of a mad dog, it can only end in one way—that all respectable men will have to arm themselves. (A voice: 'With what?') I would suggest you should arm yourselves with something that would put a decisive stop to the proceedings of the police. I hope that these observations will be carefully reported. I should rather like to be prosecuted for sedition and have an opportunity of explaining to the police exactly what I mean by it.[75]

This was not the first time that the beleaguered workers of Dublin had been called upon to arm for the purpose of self-defence. The partisan behaviour of the DMP towards the locked-out men resulted in many cases of intimidation and harassment which were reported in the *Irish Worker*. From Larkin's early days in Dublin there had been calls for men to carry cudgels or hurleys, particularly on the occasion of a strike. For example, during the carters' strike in 1908, Councillor Sheehan advised a meeting of workers to come to meetings armed with sticks.[76] Larkin often echoed these views, and in the militaristic climate of November, 1913, the threats and advice were actualised.[77] Connolly, who was put in charge of the lockout campaign while Larkin was in jail, called on the workers to arm on 14 November. Plans were set in train by Captain Jack White. The son of the 'defender of Ladysmith' was educated at an English public school, commissioned at Sandhurst, and won the DSO fighting against the Boers. Returning to Dublin he set out to champion the cause of the underdog. The lockout afforded him a real opportunity to put his military talents at the disposal of the workers.[78] At a meeting in Trinity College in the rooms of Revd R. M. Gwynn, during a meeting of the Civic League, White recalls moving a resolution in favour of drilling the strikers.[79] Paradoxically, what has been termed the 'first Red Army' held its first meeting in a bastion of unionism, in the rooms of a clergyman and had among its first enthusiastic founders a pacifist named Sheehy Skeffington. However, the presence of Gwynn, Skeffington and other moderate men indicates the early thinking behind the establishment of the organisation. It was set up as a workers' vigilante or defence force although it soon enjoyed the somewhat pretentious title of the 'Irish Citizen Army'. In *Forward*, Connolly explained the genesis and reasons for the ICA:

As a protection against brutal attacks of the uniformed bullies of the police force, as well as a measure possibly for future eventualities arising out of the ferment occasioned by Carsonism in the North, we are organising a citizen army and are drilling every day.[80]

Connolly was certainly aware of the potential of such a body once it had been properly trained and drilled. But 'future eventualities' were far from the mind of many of the founders. Gwynn felt later that the 'title army was then not intended to suggest military action, but merely drill on military lines to keep unemployed men fit and self-respecting'.[81] Even Captain White, although he was to claim later that he had founded the 'first Red Army in Europe' was the first to admit in 1913 that he was training a vigilante force.[82] The conduct and general demeanour of the workers during the lockout seemed to have offended his sense of order and discipline. It seems that he felt the only way to build a successful general workers' union was to organise it along military lines. In December 1913 he wrote:

Drill is nothing but the science of natural combination and, especially in the case of unskilled workers where standards of education are not high, is the best and perhaps the only foundation on which to build the capacity for mutual competence in an industry or enterprise. A military or semi-military organisation, with its accompaniments of order, punctuality and willing obedience, is the best possible basis for industrial organisation.[83]

The scheme was endorsed by the trade union leadership and supported by the rank and file, but it would be misleading to suggest that the ICA was, as it was constituted in 1913, anything other than a vigilante force. It was an army without arms. There were certainly very few of its members whom one could describe as social revolutionaries without rifles.[84]

The employers were playing a waiting game with the locked-out men and it seemed to be paying off. Connolly, with Larkin in jail, was forced to escalate the strike in the vain hope of bringing Murphy and his colleagues to the conference table. He made an effort to seal off the port and stop all supplies of fresh goods and supplies reaching the shops and businesses in the city. A short time later some transport union men were dismissed from Guinness's brewery for refusing to handle a consignment of goods for James's Gate. Connolly could do little to protect the brewery men since a general unwillingness existed among their colleagues to have anything to do with Liberty Hall.

About 1,000 men were idle as a result of the total stoppage of work in the port and the shipping companies brought in about 300 'scabs' from England. However, but for passenger traffic to Holyhead, the port was paralysed, and Dublin was described as 'a city of the dead'.[85] Archbishop Walsh made two pleas for peace talks in the Press, but each was turned down by the employers although the workers, and Harry Gosling of the BTUC in particular, were anxious for a quick end to the dispute which had crippled the commercial life of the city and driven thousands of men and their families to the point of starvation.

Larkin was freed on 13 November and urged an immediate general strike throughout Britain. Three days later he spoke at a mass meeting in Manchester, launched a scathing attack on the Nationalist Party,[86] and redoubled his demands for direct intervention in the lockout by British unions.[87] Meanwhile, the BTUC parliamentary committee spent two days considering what action it should take, but was so badly divided that it was decided to hold a special meeting of congress on 9 December.[88] Funds for Dublin continued to flow into union headquarters: between 25 September and the end of October money subscribed amounted to £38,000; towards the end of November the figure had reached £56,000, while the *Daily Herald* appeal had sent £2,000 to Dublin. However, Larkin was inclined to dismiss these generous contributions somewhat offensively as money from the 'official gang'.[89]

Even the cautious planning of the British trade unionists could not prevent Larkin's appeal for radical action winning converts. George James, a driver at Llanelly on the Great Western line was dismissed for refusing to handle 'tainted goods' from Dublin; another driver followed his example and was meted out the same treatment. Soon others followed and the strike spread to Swansea, Neath, and eventually to Cardiff, halting mineral traffic in the area. The National Union of Railwaymen refused to sanction the men's action and the strike was declared unofficial. Finally the railwaymen capitualated and returned to work without winning the reinstatement of the two dismissed drivers. Larkin, who represented 20,000 men trying to live on 5s strike pay a week (if they were lucky), heaped scorn on the assistant general secretary of the NUR, J. H. Thomas.[90] Not everyone shared Larkin's desire to prolong the dispute. Even certain members of the Dublin Chamber of Commerce wanted a quick settlement. Much to the embarrassment and annoyance of the larger and more bellicose employers in the city, a motion was submitted to the DCC condemning the actions of the ITGWU and urging:

> That this meeting, whilst determinedly opposed to the principle of sympathetic strikes with their attendant disastrous effect to employers and workers, are of the opinion that the employers in the interests of peace and goodwill ought to withdraw the agreement they had asked their workers to enter into in respect of the Irish Transport workers' union which the workers consider infringes their personal liberty.[91]

The sentiments behind the motion, proposed by Richard Jones and W. Lee, reflected the irritation felt by small employers whose businesses were suffering most from the industrial disturbances. There were 400 members in the employers' federation and over 700 members in the chamber of commerce. The motion reflected a division between the two bodies. However, the federation lobby was made up of the city's wealthiest employers and was therefore by far the stronger. A prominent member of the DCC who would not attend the crucial meeting wrote advising that any public talk along those lines 'would be most hurtful to the interests of the employers and it would be far better to meet the resolution with a direct negative and with as little discussion as possible'.[92] It was decided, on Gamble's advice, not to debate the contentious motion. In fact, the employers had managed to close ranks quite successfully and were capable of dealing with any recalcitrant colleague in a harsh manner. Any businessman who re-employed a 'Larkinite' without first having him sign the requisite form renouncing Liberty Hall, etc., put his livelihood in jeopardy. This was the opinion, at least, of a coachbuilder named James J. Lalor who wrote to the Archbishop:

> Now with the other employers. I was sent for by Mr Begley and Son, Van and Carriage Works, 5 to 12 Harmon Row, Dublin, as a bodymaker and I agreed with his terms but on finding out that he had locked a man out with a family I could not see my way to work unless he took back the man. This man's wages was 16s a week helping a smith and Larkin got his wage raised to £1 per week and in a week or so the man was locked out for no reason except that he belonged to the union. He had a boy who was serving his time as a bodymaker doing this man's work though the lad was only on his 2nd year. I said to Mr Begley: 'Do you call that fair or right to have that boy helping a blacksmith while you are keeping that man out coming up to the month of Christmas?' 'Well,' he says, 'what do you want me to do, take back the man? Will you take him into your society?' I said no, we could not. Ours is a skilled trade and when we were on strike we did not support him, and only Larkin did so the man

might starve. Larkin gave him 10s a week for 6 weeks. 'Surely,' I said, 'you would not ask the man for to throw over the union that stood by him when no won (*sic*) else would. Well, he says, if I were to take him back I might shut up for I would be boycotted among the employers. Talk, he says, about a sympathetic strike with the workers, why it is not in it with the employers. But I will see what can be done and if it goes to a show of hands I will put up my two hands. Well, I says, when you take back this man, I will start to work for you and if you don't, well, I will starve along with him. I may say I called again on him and he said there was not a chance unless the man gave up the union. Well, I said, he won't do that and that's why the British trade unionists are helping us. Well, he says, we are out to smash it.[93]

Lalor said he had seen one man sacked who had over 40 years' service with the one firm. He was now 13 weeks out of work and was convinced that some of the 'masters would give in only they are afraid of the big ones'. The same employer (Begley) had told him that if a ballot was taken it would be settled 'in an hour'. Begley was bankrupt while Murphy was still able to run his trams. The employers stood firm and stood together; whatever divisions existed were kept behind closed doors. The same could not be said for the workers.

Dublin Splits with the British TUC

As a sign of Liberty Hall's good faith, the ITGWU offered to open the port provided the shipping companies agreed not to handle goods for Guinness's brewery and Jacob's biscuit factory. The offer was turned down.[94] A delegation from the British Labour Party and the TUC was in Dublin on 4 December, and after some difficulty Arthur Henderson MP managed to arrange a meeting with the employers. The conference lasted from 6 p.m. on Saturday to 6 a.m. the next day. The British delegation acted as intermediaries. The workers agreed to abandon the sympathetic strike; ensure that no strike would take place without a month's notice, and that a strike be preceded by a ballot.[95] However, the employers would not meet the trade union demand to reinstate all locked-out men. There were obvious difficulties with the latter since, even if they wanted to, the employers had taken on new men and would be reluctant to sack them if they had proved their worth. However, the strike had also seen the introduction of motor lorries in large numbers leading to 'the displacement of labour by machinery'.[96] The employers were also not happy with the strength of the guarantee ruling the future behaviour of the ITGWU, and wanted a total surrender or nothing.

The meeting broke up without fixing any date for future talks. Later in conversation with Sheehy Skeffington, the Dublin correspondent of the *Daily Herald,* William O'Brien spoke of the tension between the British and the Dublin trade unionists. The following day, Skeffington wrote in his report: 'We wonder what truth there is in the rumour current in Dublin that the British delegation tried to jockey the Dublin men into an unfavourable settlement.'[97] The remark was ill-timed since the BTUC special conference was due to take place a few days later and there existed sufficient ill-feelings between the various parties besides complicating matters by allowing a deliberate leak about the situation to get into the Press.

On 9 December, some 600 delegates representing 350 affiliated trade unions, with a combined membership of 2.5 million workers, attended the meeting in Farringdon St Memorial Hall, London. Larkin, Connolly, O'Brien, and Tom McPartlin represented the lockout committee. Arthur Henderson opened the proceedings by moving the adoption of the report of the delegates to the Dublin Conference. It was unworthy to suggest, he said, that they had taken a course of ignoring the local men and actually proceeded to discuss the terms of settlement rather than lay out the basis for negotiations. Uproar followed when he added that efforts were being made to prejudice the officials present. When order was restored, he dealt with the contentious matter of reinstatement. He said that they had urged the local committee to look seriously at the situation to see if they could turn the corner and that was why he had been accused of trying to 'jockey' the local men. That was the sort of reward one got from one's own.[98] Mr Gosling followed and said that the only way to get around the question of reinstatement was to get rid of Mr Murphy because the 'employers' federation in Dublin was Murphy from top to bottom and the employers had either got to pull Murphy down and get a reasonable settlement or dissociate themselves from him'.[99]

James Connolly tried to repair the damage done by Henderson's opening speech. He agreed in substance with the Labour MP that there had been much needless recrimination on both sides. An attempt was being made by the employers to split the labour movement and he felt that the comrades from England had made a mistake in staying so long with the employers. But no suspicion of the genuineness or good faith of the British delegates had entered their minds, and he still felt that the split could be healed. The report was adopted and the first crisis was overcome. Before the conference opened, the *New Statesman* had warned the delegates to be gentle with Larkin:

> We hope, however, that British trade union leaders as well as rank and file, will remember that Mr Larkin is a fighter and not a diplomatist and that nothing he may say or do can lessen the importance to the whole trade union world of a victory in Dublin.[100]

It was difficult to see how a stand-up fight could have been avoided but when the attack came on the transport union leader it was from a most unlikely source. The syndicalist, Ben Tillett, who had written some weeks earlier that he 'would be proud to stand in the position of Jim Larkin' proposed the following motion:

> That this conference deplores and condemns the unfair attacks made by men inside the trade union movement upon British trade union officials; it affirms its confidence and its belief in their ability to negotiate an honourable settlement if assured of the effective support of all who are concerned in the Dublin dispute.[101]

W. C. Anderson seconded the motion and launched an attack on Larkin. The ITGWU leader's unfounded charge at an earlier meeting that Havelock Wilson had introduced blackleg labour into Leith gave grist to the mill of his opponents. Wilson stood up to defend himself against such baseless charges. He said that he had begun in the trade union movement over thirty-six years ago and he had not been kicked into it (cheers). Larkin, he said, had made great blunders from the beginning of the dispute; if he would only recognise his mistakes even now it would be better for Dublin and for the trade union movement. In his experience, he had never seen such a state of affairs as had existed in Dublin in the last three months. He had been called a scab and a renegade because he had privately tried to impress a little common sense into the heads of those who had mismanaged affairs in Dublin, Havelock Wilson added. J. H. Thomas, who had spoken earlier in the debate, jumped up to say that he would not be slandered or libelled, 'not for fifty Larkins'.[102] The chairman later called Larkin to the rostrum amid cheers and booing but, angered by the remarks of the previous speakers, the latter had lost all sense of tolerance and cohesion. He began:

> 'Mr Chairman and human beings,' and the phrase seemed to provoke resentment. Mr Larkin replied to the outcry by saying: 'I am not

concerned whether you allow me to go on or not; I can deal with any of you at any place you like to name and if you are not going to give me the opportunity of replying to those foul lying statements it would only be what I expect from you.' (Laughter and uproar)[103]

The speech had a disastrous effect on whatever chances the Dublin delegation had of getting radical measures accepted by congress. The Tillett motion was passed, with only six votes against. Continued financial support was voted to the victims of the lock-out. It was also agreed that the Joint Labour Board seek a meeting with the employers at an early date. This indicated a resounding defeat for the Dublin men, for any approaches made in the future should have come from the employers since it was they who broke off the last round of talks by refusing to accept the ITGWU's good faith. Any initiative by the men would indicate a weakening of their position before employer firmness.

Some of the British trade unionists recognised this danger and tried to avert disaster by proposing an amendment advocating a general strike. J. Jones of the gasworkers' union spoke strongly in favour of the move, and was supported by S. J. Davis who urged union officials to 'give up this tom-foolery' and do something to justify their position as labour leaders. But Mr Shaw of the silkweavers' union was quick to warn delegates of the dangers of syndicalism and the amendment was lost by 2,280,000 votes to 203,000. Before the congress broke up, James Connolly intimated that while the men in Dublin could not alter the terms of the resolutions passed, he could not guarantee that they would be deemed acceptable. This final act of defiance by Connolly was very much an empty gesture. The locked-out workers were in no position to split with London. They really had to accept the majority view no matter how unpalatable it might be.

The Workers Sue for Peace

There was nothing the Dublin men could do to prevent the meeting with the employers taking place. It was now an open secret that the workers were running out of steam, and that the sting had gone out of their campaign. The first tangible sign of the dwindling strength of the workers came when Havelock Wilson ordered the members of his Sailors' and Firemen's Union back to work without delay on the condition that the employers withdraw their 'yellow' document.[104] Before the peace conference had time to convene, the employers recognised that their siege tactics had paid dividends. Martin Murphy had generaled his colleagues through the most serious days of the dispute. His plan was well devised, and there was absolutely no need for compromise.

When the conference assembled on 18 December, it had before it as a basis of discussion a number of proposals drawn up by the Joint Labour Board of Great Britain. The terms arrived at were once again fully acceptable to the workers' delegations from Dublin and London. The conditions were as follows:

(1) That the employers should withdraw the circulars, posters and other forms of agreement known as the employers' agreement.

(2) That the unions as a condition of such withdrawal should abstain from any form of sympathetic strike pending the establishment of a wages board by 17 March, 1914.

(3) That no member should be refused employment on the grounds of his or her association with the dispute, and that no stranger should be employed until all the old workers were re-engaged.

(4) Finally, that all cases of old workers not re-employed on 1 February, 1914, should be considered at a conference to be held on 15 February, 1914.[105]

Nothing had changed. The same insurmountable obstacles stood in the way of progress. Employers declined to give any guarantees on reinstatement beyond the vague and weak assurance that 'as far as their business permits they will take on as many of their former employees as they can make room for'.[106] Capitulation was the price demanded of the workers at the beginning of the lockout and that had finally been achieved, at some considerable cost to the employers.

Popular support for the protracted dispute was on the wane in Britain. By the end of December the BTUC was finding it increasingly difficult to make the necessary weekly cash payments to the beleaguered lockout committee. On 1 January, £2,773 3s was sent to Dublin and £2,835 13s was sent the following week. However, the secretary of the TUC, Charles Bowerman was forced to warn the lockout committee on 8 January:

> The committee find themselves face to face with the fact that the response to the appeal—which until recently was magnificent—has weakened considerably, and they have therefore instructed me to inform

you and your colleagues of the strike committee that unless more generous and general response is made than has been the case during the past few weeks, it will be impossible after the present week to continue the weekly remittance to your committee.[107]

Bowerman and James Seddon visited Dublin two weeks later to explain their difficulties in getting money for the lockout and to see if an eleventh hour settlement could be brought about. They returned to London disappointed with the unfruitful outcomes of their trip. On 29 January, Bowerman wrote to say that 'there appears little hope that the supply can be extended beyond the present week'.[108] In March, a further £800 was sent and £1,200 the following month. After that funds dried up completely. Dublin had lost the battle and the blame for the failure was placed squarely on the shoulders of the British trade union leadership by many of the locked out men. Larkin was bitterly disappointed with his cross-channel colleagues. Speaking at a rally in Birmingham on 25 January, he quoted a speech made by Ramsay MacDonald where he referred to Samson pulling down the pillars of the temple. 'I only hope,' added Larkin, 'that when he does pull them down all the trade union leaders may be underneath the ruins.'[109] The final break with the leading English radical trade unionists came when he was expelled by the National Federation of Transport Workers for failing to supply evidence to support his charges against Havelock Wilson over the sending of scab labour to Leith.

The transport union was finding it almost impossible, by mid-January, to prevent members returning to work on whatever terms they were offered. About 200 ITGWU men were reinstated by Messrs Mooneys on the understanding that they would handle all goods addressed to the bakery.[110] Despite a ballot by dockers, seamen and firemen employed by the City of Dublin Steam Packet Company, who voted not to return to work, 14 men went back on 9 January, agreeing to work alongside free labour. On the same day, the crews of two steamers belonging to the same company signed on and a restricted service was resumed. By 19 January, 600 ITGWU men had gone back to work with the shipping companies with the consent of the union executive.[111] Other men were taken back by the Port and Docks Board, Hammond Lane Foundry and some of the coal yards.[112] A few days earlier, Larkin had advised his men to return to work wherever possible without signing the tainted goods pledge, yet while some employers recognised the folly of objecting to having ITGWU men on their staff and took back their old employees irrespective of their affiliation to Liberty Hall, others sought to humiliate the defeated workmen by forcing the signing of the 'yellow' contract. On 1 February, the 1,500-strong United Labourers' Union agreed to return to work on condition:

> That none of its members remain or become in the future a member of the Irish Transport Workers' Union. Its members will take no part in or support any form of sympathetic strike; they will handle all materials and carry out all instructions given them in the course of their employment. Further, they will work amicably with all employers, whether they be unionists or non-unionists.[113]

The skilled trades in the building industry fared little better. As part of a new agreement, later in the year, between the Master Builders' Association and the Amalgamated Society of Carpenters and Joiners, it was accepted that:

> Carpenters and joiners shall not refuse to work the materials given them by their employers. They also agree not to take part in or support any form of sympathetic strike, and further to work amicably with all workmen who are not belonging to their own trade, whether they are members of a trade union or not.[114]

By the end of January the labour dispute was practically over in the port area. 'Traffic along the quays,' reported the *Irish Times*, 'is gradually resuming its normal state, and everywhere signs of renewed activity are noticeable.'[115] As the business life of the city returned rapidly to normal, there was little doubt as to which side had scored a decisive victory. Nobody was aware of this fact more than the hundreds of ITGWU men who applied for assisted passages to England and Scotland in the first four months of 1914. The Dublin Number 1 branch, which acted as the central executive for the transport union, gave the £1 allowance to victimised men who wanted to travel to Glasgow to find work.[116] The committee even received pleas to pay the rents of some men who were threatened with eviction. Lapsed members, probably hoping to get assisted passage at a later date, often had their arrears remitted by a quarter.[117]

The ITGWU was in a critical financial position and orders were given to cut down on all expenditure and overheads. A sub-committee was formed to advise on economising. There were complaints that even the committee was not taking any interest in the running of the union. The finances of Liberty Hall were low but the morale of the members was even lower. Beaten to the ropes in the lockout, many of the luckier men were forced back to work on the most humiliating terms while the more active and militant members were forced to take the emigrants' ship. The ITGWU was literally fighting for survival.

Perhaps the most severe blow to trade union pride was administered by the Dublin electorate. Ten prominent union leaders stood on a 'lockout' ticket in the municipal elections but no significant gains were recorded by labour. The fledgling labour party's strength in the corporation remained a mere seven out of eighty. The Nationalist Party, or 'baton party' as the *Irish Worker* termed it, had lost no ground despite its somewhat equivocal stand on the lockout.[118] The forces of labour were in disarray and in positive retreat. Temporary disenchantment with Liberty Hall leadership among the trade union rank and file afforded no real answer for Labour's disappointing showing. The harsh fact had to be faced, by both Larkin and Connolly in particular, that initial trade union militancy exhibited during 1913, was only transitory. It had never been translated onto a more permanent political footing.

After the results became known, Archbishop Walsh, wrote a surprising letter to Lorcan Sherlock:

> Allow me to congratulate you and the voters of your ward on the notable victory gained . . . over a combination of influences which, in addition to the havoc they have wrought in the industrial world of Dublin, have done no little harm in blunting if not deadening the moral and religious sense of not a few among the working population of our city.[119]

Whatever about the loss of 'moral and religious sense', many of the workmen shared the Archbishop's view about the havoc wrought in the industrial world of the city. Externally, trade union leaders supported the official line that the lockout had been betrayed by the British TUC but the post mortem continued behind closed doors. James Larkin, who had been playing a very active role in the administrative side of the transport union for a number of months, was elected president of congress in June 1914, the first president since its foundation in 1896 to come from a non-craft union. He gave a brilliant speech in which he claimed victory despite the most ruthless tactics adopted by an 'organised, unscrupulous capitalist class', and advocated the establishment of 'one, big union'.[120]

While the 1913 lockout was fast becoming part of trade union mythology, the chamber of commerce was celebrating what was clearly, to the employers, a great victory under the generalship of Martin Murphy. The ITGWU was 'an anarchist organisation' which 'masqueraded as a trade union'.[121] The demands put forward by Liberty Hall could not have been given in to unless the employers 'were prepared to surrender the management of their business to the dictates of the leaders of the workers'.[122] According to the DCC Annual Report:

> There could only be one termination to such a situation and that occurred during the early months of the year, when the workers gradually and in sections returned to their employment under agreement and conditions, which it is hoped will have the effect of preventing such disastrous occurrences in the future.[123]

As a token of the chamber's esteem for the work performed by Martin Murphy, all 'the prominent members of the commercial community as well as many others' joined a committee to subscribe towards a testimonial for the owners of the *Independent*, and other cities and places in Ireland also contributed. Martin Murphy was presented with his own portrait, by William Orpen, in February 1915, and a replica, executed under the supervision of the same artist, was hung in the chamber's meeting room in Dame Street. In the presentation address, he was praised for his untiring service to the commercial life of the city:

> When the recent labour troubles in Dublin arose the stand taken by companies which you preside over, and your services on the employers' executive committee, have saved the city from a peril that threatened to destroy the industrial enterprise of the metropolis as well as the rest of the country.[124]

But while Murphy was enjoying the plaudits of his contented colleagues there were obvious signs of unrest and dissatisfaction within the labour camp. Sean O'Casey writing under the byline 'Shellback' in the *Irish Worker*, intimated that there were strong indications that all was not well within the upper echelons of the ITGWU and the DTC. It was hinted that Larkin was thinking of leaving the country. His departure, far from being regretted, would bring a sigh of relief from trade unions who use 'sane' methods of compromise and conciliation, wrote Shellback. There were those who opposed Larkin 'as open enemies or two-faced jade-like friends'. Shellback continued rather acidly that Larkin stood for a new phase of combination which threatened the very existence of officialdom and that was the real basis of opposition to him. His departure promised the bureaucrats 'a new lease of life and a continuance of their salaries'.[125]

An obvious clash developed between those who were struggling to run the union in the most difficult circumstances, and Larkin, the ideologue who was attempting to develop a new dimension to traditional trade union philosophy and have it implemented irrespective of the administrative difficulties and expense. On 19 June, Thomas Foran was forced to call a special emergency meeting of the ITGWU Number 1 Branch to discuss 'a very extraordinary letter' tendering the general secretary's resignation. Foran had tried to persuade Larkin to change his mind but with no success, and the meeting resolved to 'wait on Larkin at Croydon Park and try to prevail upon him to change his mind'. Failing that it was agreed to appeal to him to meet the general body of members 'and leave the decision in their hands'.[126] At Croydon Park, on 21 June, Larkin refused to withdraw his resignation, nor did he spare the feelings of his audience the following evening at a meeting in the Ancient Concert Rooms, when he explained the reasons for his decision. There was a certain amount of discipline, honesty and loyalty wanting in their ranks. Those men who shouted and cheered the loudest at meetings were among the men who sold out the union in the past. He spoke of differences of opinion among the strike leaders and of interference with his work and plans for the future, and regretted that he had found the ITGWU committee apathetic and disinclined to carry out its responsibility. He had proposed to set up a medical clinic in Liberty Hall; establish a dental surgery for members; employ a full time family nurse; and start an open-air school in Croydon Park for mentally-retarded children. 'They would have no more of that damnable thing called charity from Lady Aberdeen,' Larkin added. Moreover, he claimed to have the support of eminent gentlemen and doctors for the scheme. The greatest stumbling-block to the fulfilment of these objectives, however, was the union committee which seemed over-concerned with the collecting of funds, forgetting that such social schemes were 'an essential part of their work'. The committee disapproved of certain of his suggestions simply because they failed to grasp 'the spirit of the work'. Added to this, the Countess Markievicz could tell the meeting of the horrible language to which she had been subjected 'by creatures who claimed to be members of the union'. His sister, Delia, had been attacked and insulted going home at night. All these things would amount to nothing, he added, if he had found the members taking an active part in the affairs of the union. Some men, he said, were skulking in back streets afraid to come and talk with him. He was not ashamed of them although he knew they might have done wrong by force of economic circumstances.[127]

Foran rose to support Larkin despite the criticism which was levelled at him in the speech. He was followed by James Connolly, P. T. Daly and Thomas Partridge. A motion was carried 're-affirming the confidence of the members in Jim Larkin and their fidelity to his leadership, and pledging themselves to carry out his ideas for the uplifting of their class and country'. The letter of resignation was then burnt amid 'indescribable scenes of enthusiasm'.[128] The crisis was over for the moment but the central problem remained. At the next Number 1 Branch meeting on 23 June, B. Conway asked the ITGWU general president to write to Larkin to ask what powers the committee had after the Ancient Concert Room meeting. It was felt that whatever executive powers the committee had, had been removed by the sweeping terms of the resolution giving Larkin unlimited and possibly absolute power.[129] This was very much an angry reaction to Larkin's direct attack on the parsimonious attitude of the committee, and was quickly brushed aside, but some of the members did not forget what they considered an unjustified and imprudent assault on the integrity of men who were attempting to carry out the difficult task of rebuilding the administrative structures of the ITGWU without any constructive assistance from the general secretary. While the tension mounted, other events occurred which dealt an even greater blow to trade union strength and morale.

On 4 August, the United Kingdom of Great Britain and Ireland went to war with Germany, a decision which met with a mixed reception within the Irish trade union movement. In the North the response was clear cut: men rallied to the banner and joined the ranks. Tom Johnson, the future leader of the Irish Labour Party, was not opposed to trade unionists enlisting, but in the South the response was a little more complex. Trade union officials, influenced by Connolly, opposed working class participation in what was considered to be a capitalist and imperialist war. Yet their opposition did not deter thousands of Dubliners, craftsmen and general labourers included, from responding to the call of Kerry-born Field Marshall Kitchener, to enlist in the fight to save small nations, and by the end of the war practically half a million Irishmen had served in the army while some 50,000 of them fell in battle.[130] Among those who served and those who were killed were thousands of Dublin workers representing every sector of industry in the city. Trade unions, particularly the amalgamateds, gave men leave of absence from their trade and exempted them from having to keep up the payment of union dues. Many employers also released their workers, agreeing to hold their jobs for them. Richard Gamble told the DCC on 7 September:

> In the first place they could encourage the able-bodied youths to enlist for service, and so enable the military authorities to put a sufficient army in the field. It should be impressed on those who are able to serve that if they do their duty their employment will be kept open for them; but on the other hand, if they stay at home they run just as great a risk of losing their employment through destruction of the trade of the country.[131]

Connolly called this 'economic conscription', but there was a greater degree of willingness to fight on the part of the men than he was prepared to admit. The employers of the city, 'who had agreed to assist in every way the efforts being made to obtain recruits for His Majesty's forces', were less blunt in their methods than Connolly thought. Patrick Leonard, JP, told a meeting of the DCC that it would be absurd for the head of any business house to go among his men and say 'you must enlist'. There were several ways, however, of achieving the end. Leonard encouraged the use of a military band playing rousing marching music, presumably during working hours. In his neighbourhood a company of volunteers had the use of a hunter so that its members might learn how to mount and ride. The recruiting drive in Ireland paid dividends, whatever the methods used to recruit the men were, and while there is no evidence available to support the view, nevertheless it is possible to postulate that a substantial number of the ITGWU rank and file joined up.

The Dublin trade union movement which had looked so healthy and set for expansion in 1913 was weak and disorganised within the space of twelve months. All efforts to revive the transport union and restore it to its former strength had failed. The intervention of the great war was untimely as it was destructive of any hopes the labour leaders cherished for pursuing the fight for working class rights on an industrial plane. The centre of interest was switched swiftly to a different form of direct action—armed revolution.

The founding of the Irish Volunteers in November 1913 had demonstrated the willingness of Irishmen to answer the call to arms in defence of their country. The ICA had also illustrated that same enthusiasm although in a less dramatic way. Indeed, long before 1913, many workers had opted to join the nascent radical nationalist movement. If anything, the lesson of the lockout proved to them the deficiencies of industrial action, and the decline in trade unionism which set in after the rout drove the lesson home still further. Many workers began to accept the view that industrial progress could only be achieved in the wake of Home Rule.

Connolly, who was deeply depressed by the disintegration of the Social Democratic movement in Europe before the tocsin of war, was the most vocal and and outspoken convert to the ubiquitous forces of nationalism. He felt that he had no alternative but to work to bring the trade union movement into the mainstream of national politics, otherwise labour organisations risked isolation and losing an opportunity of exercising maximum influence on the forces which were likely to shape the future structure of Irish society. Connolly was deeply conscious of the dangers of a potential alliance with men who did not attempt to conceal their contempt for the aspirations and methods of the workers, but egalitarian considerations would have to wait. The labour rank and file were less conscious of the snares which might result from joining forces with the nationalists. In fact, many were unqualified supporters of the separatist movement, quite content to leave questions of social justice to some future date when Irishmen would be masters of their own destiny. They were swept into the nationalist mainstream, and the labour movement was simply not mature enough to withstand the pressure.

Meanwhile, all was not well within the ITGWU. A row had developed over the behaviour of Delia Larkin, and it appeared to the union president, Thomas Foran, that she 'was out to cause trouble and disruption among the members'. He explained how she had broken the lock on the Liberty Hall piano while refusing to pay rent for its use. Larkin refused to intervene in the dispute or to attend a committee meeting to discuss the matter, and Delia Larkin was then ordered by the committee, that 'in the interests of the union she should look for some other premises to carry out the work of the Women Workers' Union'. Larkin wrote to the committee saying that he was calling a general meeting of the members over the piano incident, and the committee then resigned en bloc. The crisis was resolved promptly, but the friction between the committee and the general secretary remained. A month later, Larkin left for

America on a short lecture tour, his motives for taking the trip being probably more psychological than political.[132]

'No one,' he said, before he left, 'under God's sun knows what I have gone through.' For six years he had been condemned by the Press and from the pulpit. He had been given harsh jail sentences on two occasions, involved in a number of libel cases and debarred from sitting on the corporation. Despite all this he had worked indefatigably to build up the transport union only to see his work in ruins after the lockout. He was a disappointed man, disappointed with the results of his work and the reaction of his collagues to defeat. But psychology only goes part of the way to explain why Larkin left on a trip which was, after all, meant to be a short lecture tour. In fact the conflict within the ITGWU went far deeper than a clash of personalities. The dispute was, in essence, a difference of opinion over the very nature of trade unionism. For Larkin, a union represented something more than a friendly society which protected workers at a time of industrial unrest or at any other time of personal distress. It was an organisation with a wider social function which transended the more traditional view of labour organisations: it was a mini-welfare state. But after the failure of the lockout the necessary emphasis in the union was on retrenchment rather than on experiment. Besides, there existed a very real danger of the ITGWU failing completely. All this hardly created an atmosphere conducive to the introduction of new ideas. Moreover, a growing lobby at Liberty Hall seemed anxious to place the union on a more orthodox footing. James Connolly, who was appointed temporary general secretary in 'Big Jim's' absence, was not the ideal person to correct this tendency towards conservatism. Connolly was then far more interested in the revolutionary nationalist movement and saw trade unionism as the working class structure most capable of organising Labour's contribution to that struggle. But even had Connolly wished, it is doubtful if he could ever have set the remnants of a labour movement on any other course in the wake of the outbreak of war.

Behind the scenes, the transport union was hoping to discard its old image of Larkinite waywardness and don a more conventional uniform, indistinguishable in method or outlook from the older and more settled craft bodies. A similar path had been travelled by the 'new unions' of 1889 and the ITGWU was undergoing the same process of normalisation in 1914. William Martin Murphy could have no objection to the outcome. The transport union had been through its radical phase. Besides Larkin's friction with his colleagues, he sensed the new mood which encouraged a more cautious approach to industrial conflict, and felt that there was little he could do to combat the shift towards a more moderate approach. With feelings of bitterness and disappointment he went abroad and on his return in the 1920s this 'normalisation' tendency had run its course.

Conclusion

'Failure' is perhaps too harsh a term to describe the outcome of an industrial struggle which had imposed so much hardship, suffering and humiliation on all classes of workers in Dublin. But for the men who lost their jobs in the four-month-long lockout and were 'blacked' by employers because of their support for the ITGWU there was no other term. Indeed, many transport union men had time to reflect on their bitter experience in cities across the channel where they had travelled to find jobs and make new homes for their families. There, at least, they were able to enjoy the anonymity of an impersonal metropolis and thus avoid victimisation. Others enlisted in the army at the outbreak of war often more out of economic necessity than because of any grandiose sentiment related to the need 'to fight for small nations'. In the trenches they had ample opportunity to dwell upon the hectic, hungry days of 1913.

Yet even the totality of suffering imposed (employers would say 'self-imposed') upon the men and their dependants does not outweigh the singular achievement of the trade union movement. The ITGWU had survived with the active support of apprenticed labour. Certainly after the lockout, the union was almost bankrupt, the leadership divided and the rank and file drifting away in large numbers; but no matter how dispirited the men of Liberty Hall were after the collapse of resistance, they could take solace in the fact that their battle-scarred union had come through the fray ready to regroup and take issue with employers again, albeit in less militant fashion. The struggle had rocked the union to its foundations and its organisation was in ruins, yet the ITGWU survived. The reputation of the stormy petrel, James Larkin, was less fortunate. The gifted orator, the mover of masses and the demagogue, was of little practical assistance to men engaged in crisis management. The temporary absence of Larkin in America, at such a crucial moment in the union's history, symbolised the underlying shift in leadership-style and the diminished radicalism of the new men.

If Larkin's reputation was on the wane in 1914, the leader of the employers, William Martin Murphy, was the toast of the Chamber of Commerce and genteel Dublin besides. He had led the employers in a decisive and ruthless manner, and in these circles there was little doubt who had been responsible for what was clearly interpeted as a victory. In Orpen's portrait he is portrayed as an ascetic-looking, white bearded patrician. Frail and somewhat delicate, he sits looking wistfully into the middle distance.

This was not how he was seen by the members of the ITGWU among whom his image was less that of the patrician than the predator. During the lockout, he had been hung in effigy in the backstreets; 'murderer' Murphy was the phrase on the lips of Dublin's poor. They were encouraged in that view, incited would probably be more apt, by the vituperative style of the *Irish Worker*. Cartoonist Ernest Kavanagh penned a series of savage drawings showing Murphy as a vulture, perched on the gate pillar of his home at Dartry Hall, watching over the corpse of a worker crumpled on the ground below under which was written lines from Byron: 'The Demon of death spread his wings on the blast, And spat on the face of the poor as he passed' (6 September 1913). A few weeks later the same cartoonist shows a ghoulish employers' leader gloating as he is surrounded by the skeletons of workers and their families who have starved to death during the lockout. The imagery of the *Irish Worker* was as crude as its language was extreme, and the paper personalised the conflict in a manner which was as singularly unfair to Murphy as *Independent* editorials were to Larkin. Journalism sunk to an all-time low in both papers on numerous occasions during the industrial unrest, and such strident writing did little to cool tempers or bring about reconciliation.

In fairness, Murphy was neither patrician nor predator. He was a self-made man, whose character was shaped in the rough and tumble of the building trade. He was autocratic but not impervious to the demands of employees. Smooth industrial relations were a prerequisite for success in business. Paternalism and authoritarianism secured good results and Murphy perfected the art of 'kindly' coercion. He could be as tough on bad employers as he was on unruly trade unionists, for both threatened the smooth running of trade.

However Murphy chose not to sustain his moderation in the face of what he considered to be intolerable and highly personalised provocation by Larkin and his transport union which was out to 'wreck Irish industry and bring about social revolution'. At least, that was how Murphy read the situation. He accepted Larkin at his word. The difficulty was that he lost his sense of balance during the lockout and allowed the industrial conflict to deteriorate into a bitter personal conflict with the leader of the transport union. For Murphy, the defeat of Larkinism meant the avoidance of socialist revolution. Indeed, it is possible that the employers' leader was not so convinced of that fact in private as he was in public. It was clear, however, that the greater the advances made by the transport union the greater would be Murphy's headaches in the future caused by the militancy of the recently organised and the poorly paid.

In the heated climate of 1913 Murphy might have been forgiven for confusing rhetoric and reality. Perhaps his confusion was genuine, although he might also have been operating in an opportunistic fashion and have been out to weaken the transport union while exploiting the fears of his fellow employers regarding a left wing takeover. If he ever had a sense of balance he lost it in 1913. His attempts to defeat the transport union, the alleged agent of social revolution in the capital, were not unsurprisingly interpreted by workers as an attack on their basic right to combine and join the union of their choice. Murphy's main weakness was to believe that Larkin *was* the ITGWU. That was not the case, and the radical social and political philosophy of 'Big Jim' was not necessarily shared by other members of the ITGWU. The owner of the tramway company did not attempt to outflank his main rival by appealing to the moderates. He saw the need for a decisive and humiliating victory over the union which had done so much to advance the demands of the lower paid in such a short time. His tactics were ruthless and pre-emptive, and Murphy cleverly took advantage of the wild language of Larkin. In so doing, he strengthened the unity of the transport union.

The ruthlessness of the employers' federation towards the general workers had repulsed many craftsmen. The indiscriminate attack on the fundamental principle of combination shattered their confidence in the powers of negotiation. General and apprenticed labour alike were seen to be entitled to the protection of the trade union movement. However, the acceptance of the need to extend the application of the right to combine had not come overnight. The progressive trade union legislation of 1906 which gave protection to pickets, the growing awareness of Catholic social teaching among workers, the spread of socialist doctrine, the dissatisfaction with

British institutions evoked by advanced nationalism, all combined to force a more radical approach to industrial problems. Leadership in that direction was provided by Michael O'Lehane and the Drapers' Assistants Association. Both he and the trade union movement generally grew less tolerant of injustice in the industrial sphere and more conscious of their corporate power to challenge the abuses which employers had enshrined almost to the level of inalienable rights. An injury to one was felt to be the concern of all.

In this context, it is both misleading and inaccurate to suggest that one man was solely responsible for creating and dictating the character and development of trade unionism in the city. If anything, Larkin was the catalyst that galvanised the general workers into action. His popular appeal was due in no small part to his skills as an orator, organiser and socialist, but the men he had come from Liverpool to unionise were not lacking in courage or militancy as had been evidenced by their behaviour during the coal strikes in 1890. What non-apprenticed labour in Dublin lacked was not militancy but leadership. In effect, Larkin proved the right man for that job. Moreover, he arrived in Dublin at an opportune moment while the local men were casting around for a leader. So timing, talent and temperament combined in one explosive package to give the Liverpool Irishman the chance needed to push forward the horizons of trade unionism.

The study has brought to the centre of the stage other trade union leaders which has allowed Connolly and Larkin's roles to be interpreted in a different light. The consciousness of the labour movement was not merely an extension of that of the two most prominent leaders who were not themselves united in any common vision of the path to socialism. I have argued that labour unity in 1913 was based on a highly-developed trade union consciousness, but that consciousness was not a revolutionary one, and perhaps this explains the mystery of the social revolution that never was. The revolution was neither betrayed nor was it deferred; it was a left wing option never seriously contemplated by the majority of the leaders of the trade union movement. The trade union movement simply did not go through a revolutionary phase.

Ironically, a statue of the 'disreputable' demagogue James Larkin graces Dublin's main street, standing mockingly only yards away from what was once the Imperial Hotel. It is unlikely that William Martin Murphy will ever be so honoured. Perhaps that is a mistake; both should share the same plinth as monuments to intransigence and the conflicting philosophies which have contributed to the formation of Irish society. In folk memory, Larkin's 'name endures on our holiest page, scrawled in a rage by Dublin's poor'. Yet despite the popular romantic and nostalgic attachment to the promethean figure of 'Big Jim', the philosophy of William Martin Murphy has been the more enduring and influential in the shaping of modern Ireland.

Notes

1. Dublin: A Tale of Two Cities

1. Arnold Wright, *Disturbed Dublin* (London, 1914), p. 15.
2. William Dawson, 'Dublin in 1912' in *Studies*, Vol. IX, Nos 239–40, Autumn–Winter 1971, p. 245.
3. For detailed account of this situation see Leon O Broin, *The Chief Secretary, Augustine Birrell in Ireland* (London, 1969), pp 124–6.
4. S. Shannon Millin, 'Slums, a Sociological Retrospect of the city of Dublin' in *Journal of the Statistical and Social Inquiry Society of Ireland*, read on January 23, 1914, pp 131–2.
5. Sir Charles Cameron, 'How the Poor Live', chapter in *Annual Public Health Report* for 1903, published in 1905, p. 1.
6. L. M. Cullen, *An Economic History of Ireland since 1660* (London, 1972), p. 166.
7. Cameron, *op. cit.*, p. 2.
8. *ibid.*, p. 14.
9. *ibid.*, p. 12.
10. *ibid.*, p. 13.
11. *The Dublin Trade and Labour Journal*, May 1909; The Dublin Trades Council (DTC) were debating the events surrounding the tuberculosis exhibition of 1909 mounted by the WNHA. A number of lectures were delivered, which amused and infuriated trade unionists, urging the workers to eat health foods and spend their money 'intelligently'.
12. Cameron, *op. cit.*, pp 4–5.
13. D. A. Chart, 'Unskilled Labour in Dublin' in *Stat. Soc. Ire. Jn*, read on March 6, 1914, p. 161.
14. Cameron, *op. cit.*, p. 3.
15. Shannon Millin, *op. cit.*, p. 131.
16. *ibid.*, p. 2.
17. Peter Laslett, *The World We Have Lost* (London, 1965), p. 209.
18. 'Ireland's Six Greatest Things in the World' in *The Lady of the House*, Christmas, 1910.
19. *ibid.*
20. 'Dublin and its Industries', *Dublin Chamber of Commerce Journal*, October 1927, p. 31.
21. Wright, *op. cit.*, p. 22.
22. *The Industries of Dublin* (London, 1898), p. 45.
23. Wright, *op. cit.*, p. 19.
24. 'Dublin and its Industries', *op. cit.*, pp 31–3
25. Wright, *op. cit.* pp 24–7.
26. DCC *Annual Report*, 1906, p. 4.
27. *ibid.,* 1918, p. 3.
28. *ibid.,* 1900, p. 15.
29. *ibid.,* 1906, p. 12.
30. The *Irish Times*, c. 1860; cutting in Dublin Typographical Provident Society minute book, May 12, 1860.
31. J. S. Crome, *A Concise Dictionary of National Biography* (London, 1928), p. 164. A biography of William Martin Murphy can be found in the pamphlet, 'Souvenir of Presentation by Staff of Independent Newspapers Ltd', to Dr William Lombard Murphy, 29 July 1941, pp 11–29. My attention was drawn to this document by Gerald

M. Murphy, a relative of William Martin. I have not discussed the rich nationalistic dimension of William Martin Murphy's character—the Irish Parliamentary Party MP, the anti-Parnellite, the man who refused a knighthood and who took such a strong anti-partitionist line in the Irish Convention of 1917.

32. Obituary note signed by 'Abbeyfeale' in *Irish Independent*, June 30, 1919.
33. Crome, *op. cit.,* p. 164.
34. *New Statesman*, October 11, 1913.
35. 'Daily Express' quoted in *Irish Independent*, June 28, 1919.
36. W. M. Murphy, *Wood Quay National Registration Club speech* (1887), TCD pamphlet, p. 4.
37. *ibid.,* p. 21.
38. 'Obituary note', *Irish Independent*, June 30, 1919.
39. Murphy, *op. cit.,* p. 12.
40. William Martin Murphy's will (died 1919), PRO (Dublin) File T5311.
41. *Irish Independent*, August 1, 1919.
42. William Martin Murphy, *Dublin United Tramways Co. (1896) Ltd, Meeting of Motormen, Conductors, & c., held in the Ancient Concert Rooms* on July 19, 1913 (NLI Pamphlet), p. 6.
43. John E. Lyons to Archbishop Walsh, November 30, 1913 (Dublin Archdiocesan Archives, Walsh Papers Laity File, 1913).
44. *ibid.*
45. *Freeman's Journal* obituary of William Martin Murphy, quoted in *Irish Independent*, June 28, 1919.

2. The Old Unions

1. Dublin Typographical Provident Society minutes, July 25, 1865.
2. *Irish People,* December 3, 1864.
3. J. Dunsmore Clarkson, *Labour and Nationalism in Ireland* (New York, 1925), p. 166.
4. J. O. French, *Plumbers in Unity* (Manchester, 1965), p. 27.
5. T. J. Connolly, *The Woodworkers* (London, 1960), p. 23; he incorrectly states that the Dublin carpenters merged with the English union in 1891.
6. *Operative Butchers' Trade Union Report for 1894* (in possession of the Old Dublin Society, and kept in the Civic Museum, 58 William St Sth, Dublin).
7. G. W. Alcock, *Fifty Years of Railway Trade Unionism* (London, 1922), p. 453.
8. *ibid.*
9. The Railway Clerks Association had 9,476 members in 1910; see Sidney and Beatrice Webb, *History of Trade Unionism* (London, 1920), p. 749.
10. A. E. Musson, *The Typographical Association* (Oxford, 1954), p. 240.
11. Lord Mayor to Joseph P. Seales (chairman) and Thomas Halpin (secretary) of DTPS, March 12, 1909, in DTPS council minute book for 1909.
12. DTPS council minutes; undated memorandum, October 1911.
13. *ibid.*
14. Musson, *op cit.,* p. 241.
15. Stucco Plasterers minutes, July 5, 1899 (incomplete minutes).
16. Stucco Plasterers *Annual Report*, 1901.
17. *Irish Builder,* April 15, 1876; letter from Thomas Parker.
18. Henry Pelling, 'Labour Aristocracy' in *Popular Politics and Society in late Victorian Britain* (London, 1968), pp 51–2. See also E. J. Hobsbawm, 'The Labour Aristocracy in Late Nineteenth Century Britain' in *Labouring Man* (London, 1971), pp 272–315.
19. *Bakers' Rule Book*, 1903; see rule 41.
20. DTPS minutes, November 14, 1913.
21. Ancient Guild of Brick and Stone Layers' minutes, December 4, 1912.

22. *Regular Glasscutters, Glaziers and Lead Sash Makers of Dublin rule book, 1906,* Rule XI, p. 4.
23. *Irish Builder,* February 15, March 15, and May 15, 1862.
24. William O'Brien Dairy, 1908 (NLI O'Brien MS 15705).
25. *Irish Builder,* April 15, 1876.
26. *ibid.,* January 15, 1862.
27. *The Bakers' rules,* 1903.
28. Glasscutters' minutes, 1906, Rule XIII, p. 5.
29. *Irish Nation,* April 4, 1909.
30. DTPS *Annual Reports,* 1902; 1903; 1907; and 1909.
31. See Chapter 5; on the brushmakers' strike in 1911. Although no primary sources remain, I suggest that such societies as the plumbers, bleachers and dyers, sugar boilers, mineral water operatives, glass bottle workers, etc., were in a very unsound financial state.
32. *Irish Builder,* April 15, 1876; letter of Thomas Parker.
33. *Bakers' rules,* 1900, p. 7 (NLI).
34. *Regular Glasscutters, Glaziers, and Lead Sash Makers of Dublin rule book for 1906,* Rule XXI, p. 6
35. Bricklayers' minutes, January 8, 1913.
36. United Operative Plumbers' minutes (Dublin lodge), June 16, 1868.
37. *Rules of the National Association of Operative Plasterers,* c. 1900, p. 4.
38. *Evening Mail,* August 21, 1906.
39. *Evening Telegraph,* August 23, 1906.
40. *ibid.,* June 22, 1906.
41. *Undated newspaper cutting of letter from William Partridge and E. L. Richardson,* (NLI, O'Brien MS 15774–5).
42. *Irish Trade Union Congress Report* 1894.
43. Bricklayers' minutes (Quarterly Report), July 1915.
44. Metropolitan House Painter' minutes, July 3, 1912 (PRO, Dublin).
45. Margaret Stewart and Leslie Hunter, *The Needle is Threaded* (London, 1964).
46. *ibid.,* p. 161.
47. *Unidentified newspaper cutting, dated 1903* (NLI, O'Brien MS 15652).
48. Census figures quoted in Louis Hyman, *The Jews in Ireland* (Dublin, 1972), p. 161.
49. See Irish Garment Workers Industrial Union, annual returns to Registrar of Friendly Societies and rule book (Department of Industry and Commerce, Merrion Square, Dublin, file 274T). See also report in *Freeman's Journal,* July 8, 1909. The William O'Brien diaries for 1909 also contain references to the 'Jewish union'.
50. DTC minutes, July 19, 1909.
51. *Irish People,* June 4, 1864.
52. *ibid.*
53. E. J. Riordan, *Modern Irish Trade and Industry* (London, 1920), p. 273. Ironically, the DTPS claimed that the IDA catalogue advertising the trade mark was printed abroad.
54. DTC minutes, October 12, 1908.
55. *ibid.,* October 22, 1900.
56. *ibid.,* December 9, 1907.
57. *ibid.,* February 12, 1912.
58. *ibid.,* March 27, 1911.
59. *ibid.,* October 12, 1908.
60. *ibid.,* March 7, 1912.
61. *ibid.,* November 13, 1905.
62. *Irish Times,* April (?), 1860; quoted in full in DTPS minutes, April, 1860.
63. DTC minutes, February 16, 1896.

3. The Winds of Change

1. J. Dunsmore Clarkson, *op. cit.,* p. 186.
2. 'Presidential address of J. H. Jolly (Printer)', in *ITUC Annual Report*, 1895, p. 11, (NLI pamphlets).
3. Clarkson *op. cit.,* p. 189.
4. *ibid.,* p. 19.
5. *ibid.,* p. 195.
6. James McCarron, presidential address, *ITUC annual report,* 1907.
7. Stephen Dineen, presidential address, *ITUC annual report,* 1906.
8. John Murphy, presidential address, *ITUC annual report,* 1908.
9. Henry Pelling, *Modern Britain* (London, 1964), p. 50.
10. F. S. L. Lyons, *John Dillon* (London, 1968), pp. 176–8.
11. David W. Miller, *The Politics of Faith and Fatherland, The Catholic Church and Nationalism in Ireland, 1898–1918* (Dublin, 1978).
12. *ITUC annual report,* Dublin, 1907.
13. Nannetti speech, *ITUC annual report,* Athlone, 1906.
14. DTC minutes, May 1902.
15. *ibid,* July 27, 1903.
16. Revd P. Coffey, 'The Church and the Working Class' in *Catholic Truth Society of Ireland pamphlet,* 1906, pp 5–6. Dr Coffey was the most advanced Catholic social thinker in the country. His progressive socialistic ideas later got him into trouble with his superiors (see Coffey papers).
17. *ibid,* pp 33–5.
18. *ibid,* p. 20.
19. *ibid,* p. 39.
20. Adolphus Shields, November 11, 1889 (papers in possession of Mrs Vanek, Co Wicklow).
21. *Workers Republic,* June 3, 1900; there is some evidence in the O'Brien papers suggesting that Connolly first saw Ireland as a British soldier.
22. *ibid,* August 15, 1900. The most detailed published account of Connolly's early days in Ireland can be found in Desmond Grieves, *The Life and Times of James Connolly* (London, 1961).
23. William O'Brien notebook (NLI, O'Brien, MS 15,674).
24. William O'Brien, *Forth the Banners Go* (Dublin, 1969), p. 1.
25. *ibid,* pp 2–3.
26. Indenture of William O'Brien, NLI, O'Brien, MS 15,704–1.
27. *Irish Times,* May 5, 1904.
28. DTC minutes, May 9, 1909; O'Brien complained that postal board uniforms were being made in 'unfair' houses. On May 22, he complained that the corporation supplies committee were also giving contracts to 'unfair' houses.
29. O'Brien Diary, July 12, 1909.
30. William O'Brien to James Connolly, December, 1907 (NLI, O'Brien, MS 13,908).
31. Lord George Askwith, *Industrial Problems and Disputes* (London, 1920), pp 88–90.
32. Bernard Shillman, *Trade Unionism and Trade Disputes in Ireland* (Dublin, 1960), p. 14.
33. *ibid,* p. 66; the complete act is cited.
34. Unidentified newspaper cutting, dated March 16, 1908 (NLI, O'Brien, MS 13,952).
35. Handbill, (NLI, O'Brien MS 13,952).
36. *ibid.*
37. *Irish Times,* May 4, 1908.
38. *ibid.*

4. The Drapers' Assistants Show the Way

1. Sidney and Beatrice Webb, *History of Trade Unionism* (London, rev. ed., 1920), p. 503.
2. O'Brien to Connolly, December, 1907 (NLI, O'Brien MS 13,908).

3. E. W. Stewart, *The History of Larkinism in Ireland* (NLI, O'Brien collection LO P92). Larkin is described as the 'mighty Czar of Tyranny Hall', p. 4; P. T. Daly, 'wears alternately the many-coloured political Joseph's coat and the flowing garb of hypocrisy which appears to have descended to him in a direct line from Judas Iscariot', p. 9; William O'Brien was the 'peeler's son' and 'about the most "downey" rascal of a bad lot', p. 14.
4. Clarkson, *op. cit.* pp 165–6, quoting the *First Report of the committee of the Drapers' Assistants Early Closing Association*, Dublin, 1859 (Haliday Pamphlets, 2209:11).
5. *The Drapers' Assistant*, February 1907; a magazine of the trade founded by O'Lehane in 1903. He acted as editor until his death in 1920. Most of the material was probably written by O'Lehane himself. Consequently, references are cited giving month and year only. A complete file of the magazine is in the offices of the Irish Union of Distributive Workers and Clerks, 9, Cavendish Row, Dublin.
6. *ibid.*, February 1907 and March 1920; the latter article is an unsigned obituary for Michael O'Lehane giving a useful and detailed biography of his earlier life.
7. O'Brien Diary, July 1909.
8. *Drapers' Assistant*, August 1918.
9. *ibid.*, March 1920.
10. *ibid.*
11. *ibid.*, August 1918.
12. William Paine, *Shop Slavery and Emancipation* (London, 1912), pp 15–30.
13. DAA Scrapbook: newspaper cuttings and notes on the founding and early days of the union collected in 1901 (in possession of the Irish Union of Distributive Workers and Clerks, 9, Cavendish Row, Dublin). See also *Drapers' Assistant*, April 1907.
14. *ibid.*
15. *ibid.*
16. DAA Annual Delegates Meeting Minutes, 5 December, 1905.
17. DAA *Annual Report*, 1906, pp 3–7.
18. See Irish Union of Distributive Workers and Clerks (70th report).
19. Dublin Silkweaver's Society minute book, 1 August 1863 (records incomplete). Minute book, from 1860 to 1917, in possession of the Irish Union of Distributive Workers and Clerks, 9 Cavendish Row, Dublin).
20. DAA *Annual Report*, 1914, p. 17.
21. *Drapers' Assistant*, March 1904.
22. *ibid.*, April 1908.
23. *ibid.*, April 1913.
24. *Irish Times*, 19 July, 1905.
25. *Drapers' Assistant*, August 1905.
26. *ibid.*, June 1910.
27. *ibid.*
28. William Paine, *op. cit.*, p. 24.
29. Drapers' Assistants' scrapbook, quoting *Bray and South Dublin Herald*, 30 August, 1902.
30. Paine, *op. cit.*, p. 59.
31. *Drapers' Assistant*, December 1912.
32. *ibid.*, September 1912.
33. *ibid.*, October 1904.
34. Paine, *op. cit.*, pp 18–9.
35. *ibid.*, p. 21.
36. *ibid.*, p. 20.
37. *Drapers' Assistant*, October 1913.
38. *Irish Independent*, 13 October, 1906.
39. 'Employees' statement', in *Drapers' Assistant*, November 1906.
40. 'Mr Boyer's statement', *ibid.*
41. 'Employees' statement', *ibid.*

42. *ibid.*
43. *Irish Independent,* 13 October, 1906.
44. *ibid.*
45. *Drapers' Assistant,* November 1906.
46. *Irish Independent,* 19, 20 October, 1906.
47. *ibid.,* 14 October, 1906.
48. *Drapers' Assistant,* November 1906.
49. DTC Minutes, 29 October, 1906.
50. *Drapers' Assistant,* December, 1906.
51. *Freeman's Journal,* 15 January, 1907.
52. *Drapers' Assistant,* August 1907.
53. DTC Minutes, 10 December, 1906.
54. *Drapers' Assistant,* February 1907.
55. *ibid.*
56. *Freeman's Journal,* 24 January, 1907.
57. *Drapers' Assistant,* June 1907.
58. *ibid.*

5. The Rise of the General Workers' Unions

1. See *Censuses of Ireland 1891, 1901 and 1911* giving principal occupations in the city of Dublin.
2. United Builders' Labourers and General Workers' Union. See annual returns of *Registrar of Friendly Societies* (Department of Industry and Commerce, Merrion Sq. Dublin) File 85T.
3. William Martin Murphy, *Address to Dublin United Tramway Staff,* (Dublin, 19 July, 1913) p. 3.
4. Henry Pelling, *A History of British Trade Unionism* (3rd ed., London 1969) p. 97.
5. S. and B. Webb, *The History of Trade Unionism* (2nd ed. London 1920) p. 439.
6. E. J. Hobsbawn, 'General Labour Unions in Britain, 1889–1914' in *Labouring Man, Studies in the History of Labour* (London 2nd ed. 1971) p. 182.
7. Webb, *op. cit.,* p. 439.
8. P. Gregg, *A Social and Economic History of Britain* (London 6th ed., London 1970) p. 392.
9. W. Thorne, *My Life's Battles* (London 1927) p. 144.
10. Pelling, *op. cit.,* pp 93–101.
11. Thorne, *op. cit.,* pp 50–70.
12. J. Sexton, *James Sexton, Agitator* (London, 1936), pp 5–20, 89.
13. *Irish Times,* Sept. 8, 1890.
14. Thorne, *op. cit.,* p. 104.
15. D. D. Sheehan, *Ireland since Parnell* (London, 1921) pp 171–73.
16. Thorne, *op. cit.,* p. 92–3.
17. *Irish Times,* July 1890.
18. Sexton, *op. cit.,* p. 155.
19. *McCormick scrapbook of news cutting.*
20. *Irish Times,* 5 July, 1890.
21. *ibid.,* 2 July, 1890.
22. *ibid.,* 7 July, 1890.
23. George Askwith, *Report on the Government court of Enquiry into the 1913 Lock Out,* quoted in Arnold Wright, *Disturbed Dublin* (London, 1914) p. 269.
24. *Irish Times,* 4 July, 1890.
25. *ibid.*
26. *ibid.,* 8 July, 1890.
27. *ibid.,* 9 July, 1890.

28. *ibid.*, 4 September, 1890.
29. *ibid.*, 8 September, 1890.
30. Thorne, *op. cit.*, p. 142.
31. *ibid.*, p. 144.
32. *ibid.*
33. *ibid.*, p. 142.
34. A. H. Clegg, *General Unions in a Changing Society* (London, 1964), p. 22.
35. Thomas Mann, *Memoirs* (London, 1923) p. 151.
36. Sexton, *op. cit.*, p. 202.
37. *ibid.*, pp 202–3.
38. Mann, *op. cit.*, p. 151.
39. Sexton, *op. cit.*, pp 203–4.
40. George Askwith, *Industrial Problems and Disputes* (London, 1920), p. 113.
41. *ibid.*, p. 111.
42. *New Statesman*, 11 October, 1913.
43. Askwith, *op. cit.*, p. 109.
44. W. Collison, *Apostle of Free Labour* (London, 1913) p. 102.
45. Clarkson, *op. cit.*, p. 216.
46. *Irish News*, 12 July, 1907.
47. Askwith, *op. cit.*, p. 110.
48. R. M. Fox, *Jim Larkin, Irish Labour Leader* (New York, 1957) p. 45.
49. Clarkson, *op. cit.*, p. 218, quoting the *Northern Whig*, 29 July, 1907.
50. Letter from F. H. Crawford, Wilson Street Works, Belfast to Major R. W. Doyne of Aston, Gorey, Co. Wexford, 20 August, 1907, in possession of Stephen Toal, 4 Cathedral Villas, Armagh.
51. Askwith, *op. cit.*, p. 111.
52. *ibid.*, pp 112–3.
53. Belfast Trades Council Minutes, 5 October, 1907.
54. John McAleavey, ITGWU Branch Secretary, Newry. Memo on the 1907 Newry dock strike, p. 14. Copy in the author's possession.
55. *ibid.*, p. 23.
56. *ibid.*, p. 28.
57. *ibid.*, pp 26–32.
58. *Freeman's Journal*, 23 December, 1907.
59. *Irish Times*, 9 June, 1908.
60. *ibid.*, 10 June, 1908.
61. *ibid.*, 10 July, 1908.
62. O'Brien Diary, 12 July, 1908 (NLI, MS 16274).
63. *Irish Times*, 20 July, 1908.
64. Arnold Wright, *op. cit.*, pp 305–6, quoting an extract from the *Board of Trade Labour Gazette*, August 1908.
65. *ibid.*
66. O'Brien Diary, 19 August, 1908.
67. *ibid.*
68. *Freeman's Journal*, 15 September, 1908.
69. DTC Minutes, 20 July–26 October, 1908.
70. *Cork Examiner*, 24 August, 1909.
71. Emmet Larkin, *James Larkin: Irish Labour Leader, 1876–1947* (London, 1965) pp 49—50.
72. O'Brien Diary, 15 November, 1908.
73. *Thom's Directory, 1914*, p. 1383.
74. *Irish Times*, 18 November, 1908.
75. O'Brien Diary, 2 December, 1908.
76. *Irish Times*, 20 November, 1908.
77. O'Brien Diary, 18 November, 1908.
78. Clarkson, *op. cit.*, p. 222.

79. DTC Minutes, 23 November, 1908.
80. *Irish Times,* 20 November, 1908.
81. *Sinn Fein,* 28 November, 1908.
82. *ibid.,* 30 March, 1908.
83. *Irish Nation,* 2 January, 1909.
84. *ibid.*
85. O'Brien Diary, 21 December, 1908.
86. *Irish Nation,* 2 January, 1909.
87. 'Griffith lectured at the central branch of SF on exports during Irish parliament as evidence of prosperity. Edwards (ILP) asked inconvenient questions and was told he was an Englishman.' O'Brien Diary, 5 October, 1908.
88. *Irish Nation,* 2 January, 1909.
89. *ibid.*
90. The Sinn Fein organisation was at a very low ebb, even during its pre-war hayday between 1908–10. However, while people would not join SF, many would share Griffith's thinking about the strike organiser.
91. *Sinn Fein,* 28 November, 1908.
92. O'Brien Diary, 27 November, 1908.
93. *Freeman's Journal,* 30 November, 1908.
94. *Irish Times,* 12 December, 1908.
95. Sir Andrew Marshall Porter and Patrick John O'Neill acted as arbitrators. No fixed minimum rate of wages was set because 'many different rates and incidents of employment prevail' in the firms. Overtime was fixed at six pence after 6.30 p.m. and from 11.30 p.m. to 6.30 a.m. at rate of nine pence an hour. Meal hour and short Saturday was, they thought also impossible to enforce but recommended the employers to follow the practice. The maltsters fared no better. No wage recommendations were made but the system of stopping a 'black shilling' was halted. Maltsters should give, and receive from management, two weeks notice. There was to be no victimisation as a result of the strike. Finally, the arbitrators recommended that a Board of Conciliation be set up. *Text of Award* in Wright, *op. cit.,* pp 308–12.
96. *Irish Times,* 6 September, 1909, letter read by Sexton as evidence at Larkin's trial in Cork.
97. *ibid.*

6. **The Founding of the ITGWU**

1. *Irish Times,* 23 December, 1908.
2. O'Brien Diary, 30 November, 1908.
3. *ibid.,* 29 February, 1908.
4. *ibid.,* 20 March, 1908.
5. *ibid.,* 25 March 1908.
6. *ibid.*
7. O'Brien, *Forth the Banners Go,* p. 55.
8. O'Brien Diary, 24 May, 1908.
9. *ibid.,* 15 July, 1908.
10. *ibid.,* 25 July, 1908.
11. O'Brien, *Forth the Banners Go,* p. 55.
12. *Irish Nation,* 2 January, 1909.
13. *ibid.*
14. *ITGWU Rules for 1909, Preface.*
15. *ibid.*
16. *ibid.*
17. *ibid.*
18. *Cork Examiner,* 10 September, 1909.
19. *Sinn Fein,* 23 January, 1909.

20. O'Brien Diary.
21. *Sinn Fein,* 23 January 1909.
22. ITUC *Annual Report,* 1909.
23. *ibid.*
24. O'Brien Diary, 31 May, 1909.
25. ITUC *Annual Report,* 1909,
26. O'Brien Diary, 3 June, 1909.
27. *ibid.,* 10 June, 1909.
28. The bitterness between Larkin and Harris had grown since the beginning of the year. The latter recognised that he could never compete against the Transport Union and in March offered Larkin to bring in all WU branches in the country under Liberty Hall, on certain conditions, but Larkin refused.
29. *Irish Nation,* 26 June, 1909.
30. *ibid.*
31. *Irish Times,* 20 August, 1909.
32. Sexton, *op. cit.,* p. 206.
33. DTC Minutes, 23 August, 1909.
34. O'Brien Diary, 31 August, 1909.
35. *ibid.,* 12 September, 1909.
36. *ibid.,* 5 May, 1910.
37. ITUC *Annual Report,* Dundalk 1910.
38. O'Brien Diary, 17 May, 1910.
39. *ibid.*
40. *ibid.,* 8 August, 1910.
41. *Freeman's Journal,* 18 June, 1910.
42. O'Brien Diary, 17 June, 1910.
43. *Freeman's Journal,* 15 June, 1910.
44. *Irish Nation,* 25 June, 1910.
45. DTC Minutes, 20 June, 1910.
46. *Irish Nation,* 27 August, 1910.
47. O'Brien Diary, 16 July, 1910.
48. *ibid.,* 8 September, 1910.
49. *ibid.,* 18 December, 1910.
50. *Irish Nation,* 8 October, 1910.
51. *ibid.*
52. Askwith, *op. cit.* p. 274.
53. DTC Minutes, 21 February, 1910.
54. *ibid.*
55. *ibid.,* 7 February, 1910.
56. *ibid.,* 1 March, 1909; 5 March, 1910; 27 February, 1911.
57. Larkin attended an SPI meeting where Fred Ryan gave a lecture on evolutionary socialism which was mainly a criticism of Marxist position. Larkin supported the lecturer and said the majority of Marxian socialists he had met had never read a line of Marx. (O'Brien Diary, 27 March, 1910).
58. *Irish Nation,* 2 October, 1909.
59. O'Brien Diary, 24 August, 1909.
60. ITUC *Annual Report,* 1909. There was no love lost between the Nationalist party and James Larkin. John Dillon, belonging to the progressive wing of the nationalists described him in 1913 as a 'malignant enemy and an impossible man. He seems to be a wild international syndicalist and anarchist and for a long time he has been doing his best to burst up the nationalist party'. (F. S. L. Lyons, *John Dillon, op. cit.* p. 335, quoting Dillon to T. P. O'Connor, 16 October, 1913).
61. Connolly to J. C. Mathreson, 30 January, 1908 (NLI, O'Brien MS 13906(2)).
62. *Irish Nation,* 23 January, 1909.

63. In France, the *Confederation Generale du Travail,* was organised on this basis of a federation of 700 *syndicats.* In Spain, the *Confederacion Nacional de Trabajo,* an anarchist labour federation served the same purpose as its French counterpart although somewhat more effectively.
64. *The Axe to the Root;* quoted by Clarkson, *op. cit.* p. 232.
65. O'Brien Diary, 14 July, 1910.
66. *ibid.,* 18 July, 1910.
67. *ibid.,* 2 August, 1910.
68. *ibid.,* 11 September, 1910.
69. Connolly to O'Brien, 20 September, 1910 (NLI, O'Brien MS 13908(2)).
70. *ibid.,* 11 October, 1910.
71. *ibid.,* 6 July, 1913.
72. *ibid.,* 23 July, 1913.
73. *ibid.*
74. ITUC *Annual Report,* 1911.
75. W. P. Ryan, *The Irish Labour Movement* (Dublin 1919), p. 197. I have not been able to substantiate this claim from any official sources.
76. *Irish Worker,* 27 May, 1911.
77. *ibid.,* 29 July, 1911.
78. DTC Minutes, 6 December, 1909: letter read from Oldham branch of brushmakers' union by Murphy stating that Varian had attempted to recruit men in the area.
79. *ibid.,* 20 June, 1910.
80. *ibid.,* 8 June, 1910.
81. O'Brien Diary, 8 August, 1910.
82. *Irish Times,* 13 July, 1911.
83. *ibid.,* 18 July, 1910.
84. *Irish Worker,* 29 July, 1911.
85. *ibid.,* 1 March, 1913.
86. *Irish Times,* 21 August, 1911.
87. *ibid.,* 14 September, 1911.
88. *ibid.,* 30 August, 1911.
89. *ibid.,* 24 August, 1911.
90. *Irish Worker,* 29 July, 1911; extract from the appeal by the provisional committee of the employers' federation.
91. The members of the provisional committee were: Ed H. Andrews; R. W. Booth, JP; S. P. Boyd, JP; John Brown; William Crowe; H. M. Dockrell; D. Frame; R. K. Gamble, JP; Sir W. J. Goulding; James Mahony; Laurence Malone; Frank V. Martin; Wm M. Murphy, JP; T. R. McCulagh; John McIntyre; J. D. MacNamara; Thos A. Farrell; J. B. Perarso; William Perrin; J. E. Robinson; J. Sibthorne; J. Young; F. J. Fisher; and Wm Wallace, JP.
92. *Irish Worker,* 29 July, 1911.
93. *Irish Times,* 29 August, 1911.
94. DCC Minutes, 21 September, 1911.
95. *ibid.,* 3 November, 1911.
96. *ibid.*
97. *ibid.,* 27 September, 1911.
98. *ibid.*
99. *ibid.*

7. A Bloody Sunday

1. *Freeman's Journal,* 23 March, 1912.
2. In May, 1911, Lloyd George brought the insurance scheme, which Churchill had promised in 1909, before the Commons. The Bill embraced health insurance as well as

unemployment insurance. The scheme was modelled on Bismarck's health insurance scheme for Germany. It was contributory and compulsory on employers and employees, covering all between sixteen and seventy. All workers whose annual income did not exceed £160 were included. Disablement, sickness and maternity benefits were covered. The participants were also to have the services of a GP. However, the plan in outline received a cool reception in Ireland. The Catholic Hierarchy opposed the application of the Act to Ireland (see the *Tablet*, 1 July, 1911). The objections of the bishops were debatable, as far as urban workers were concerned. They felt that under the Poor Law, the Irish were adequately catered for as regards the medical clause of the Act. But the recipients of poor law medicine, who had to accept pauper status, were less than happy with their lot. The bishops also felt that the working of the Act might place 'a heavy burden on many of our small, struggling industries, and would in our opinion, increase unemployment' (*ibid*). The trade unions were also suspicious of the Act at first, but they soon saw its advantages and pressed to have it extended to Ireland without any dilution of its terms (see DTC minutes, 9, 23, October 1911). A union delegation was also sent to London to interview Lloyd George. However, the politicians got their way and the medical clause of the Act was not extended to Ireland, although other sections were. The bishops were not at all displeased with the outcome.
3. Pelling, *Popular Politics and Society, op. cit.*, p. 153.
4. Sligo branch contributions book, 1912 (NLI, MS 7285).
5. Emmet Larkin, *op. cit.*, p. 98.
6. For brief treatment of this subject, see William Logan, *Great Social Evils* (London, 1871). In 1848, Cork had 85 regular brothels in which there were 356 prostitutes. In the city there were also 100 'privateers'. 'The class from whence prostitutes are supplied are generally low class dressmakers and servants; manure collectors who are sent into the street very young have also furnished their quota.' In Dublin, he saw some of the more depraved parts of the town and saw a brothel employing 200 girls. 'Old Hell' was painted over the door (p. 51).
7. DTC Minutes, 25 April, 1900.
8. *Irish Worker*, 9 September, 1911.
9. DCC minutes; presidential address of William Martin Murphy, 5 January, 1914.
10. DCC Quarterly Report, 2 March, 1914.
11. Ian Sharp, *Industrial Conciliation and Arbitration in Britain* (London, 1950), p. 302.
12. *Silkweavers' Logbook* (in possession of the Irish Union of Distributive Workers and Clerks, 9 Cavendish Row, Dublin). Weavers were taken over by this union in 1918.
13. DTC minutes, 7 April, 5 May, 16 June, 1913.
14. Bricklayers' minutes, special meeting, 1 May, 1913.
15. *ibid.*
16. DTPS minutes, 16 August, 1913, 20 February, 1914.
17. Wright, *op. cit.*, p. 307.
18. For further reading on land question in general, *see* Brian O'Neill, *The Struggle for the Land in Ireland* (Dublin, 1934); for a personal account, *see* Patrick MacGill, *Children of the Dead End* (London, 1912).
19. *Freeman's Journal,* 13 August, 1913.
20. *Daily Express*, 18 August, 1913.
21. Wright, *op. cit.*, p. 71.
22. *The Stock Exchange Official Intelligence* (London, 1913), p. 1,600.
23. Jim Curran to Archbishop Walsh (DAA, Walsh papers, Laity file 1913).
24. Anonymous memorandum (DAA, Walsh papers, Laity file, 1913). This source appears to be reliable in many of the charges made against the tramway company and can be corroborated from other sources; see also Clarkson, *op. cit.*, p. 260.
25. *ibid.*
26. Martin Murphy pamphlet, p. 4 (NLI, LO p. 83).
27. *ibid.*, p. 5.
28. *ibid.*, p. 8.

29. Breandan Mac Giolla Choille, ed., *Chief Secretary's Office, Dublin Castle, Intelligence Notes, 1913–16* (Dublin, 1966), p. 38.
30. *Daily Express*, 21 August, 1913.
31. O'Brien, *op. cit.*, p. 52.
32. *Daily Express, Freeman's Journal*, 25 August, 1913.
33. *Irish Times*, 26 August, 1913.
34. *Daily Express*, 25 August, 1913.
35. *ibid.*, 27 August, 1913.
36. *ibid.* and *Freeman's Journal*, 27 August, 1913.
37. *Freeman's Journal*, 27 August, 1913.
38. *Irish Times*, 27 August, 1913.
39. *Daily Express*, 28 August, 1913.
40. Wright, *op. cit.*, p. 121.
41. *Daily Express*, 28 August, 1913.
42. *Freeman's Journal*, 3 and 4 October, 1913.
43. *Leader*, 30 August, 1913.
44. *The Times* 30 August, 1913.
45. *Daily Express*, 29 August, 1913.
46. NLI, O'Brien MS 13,908.
47. Wright, *op. cit.*, p. 154.
48. *Daily Express*, 30 August, 1913.
49. *ibid.*.
50. O'Brien, *op. cit.*, pp 88–90.
51. *ibid.*, p. 90.
52. *Evening Telegraph* (stop press edition), 31 August, 1913.
53. In times of industrial unrest the DTC executive acted as a strike committee to coordinate trade union support for the disputants.
54. *Evening Telegraph*, 31 August, 1913.
55. John E. Lyons, 14 Portland Place, Dublin, to Archbishop Walsh (DDA, Laity file, 1913).
56. *Daily Express*, 23 August, 1913.
57. *Evening Telegraph*, 31 August, 1913.
58. Wright, *op. cit.*, p. 138.
59. *Evening Telegraph*, 31 August, 1913.
60. *Daily Mirror*, 1 September, 1913.
61. *Evening Telegraph*, 31 August, 1913.
62. *Daily Express*, 1 September, 1913.
63. *ibid.*
64. *The Times*, 1 September, 1913.
65. *Evening Telegraph*, 31 August, 1913.
66. *Daily Express*, 1 September, 1913.
67. *Jim Larkin and the Dublin Lock-out* (Workers' Union of Ireland, Dublin, 1964), p. 34.
68. Fr M. J. Curran to Walsh, 31 August, 1913 (DAA, priests file, 1913).
69. Fr Healy to Walsh, 4 September, 1913 (*ibid.*).
70. *Daily Express*, 1 September, 1913.
71. *Irish Times*, 1 September.
72. *Independent*, 1 September.
73. *Irish Homestead*, 13 September, 1913.
74. *ibid.*
75. Archbishop Walsh had been seriously ill and had gone abroad to recuperate, first to England and then to Paris. Few of his replies to Fr Curran remain but it is obvious from the correspondence that the Archbishop was not wholly in agreement with his secretary about the nature and cause of events in Dublin. Curran kept writing, trying to explain away the action of the police and apparently the Archbishop remained incredulous.
76. Fr M. J. Curran to Walsh, 2 September, 1913 (DAA, priests file).

8. Lockout

1. Patrick Kenny memorandum (NLI, O'Brien MS 13, 913-2).
2. *Tablet*, 22 November, 1913.
3. Kenny Memorandum, *op. cit.*
4. *Daily Express*, 2 September, 1913.
5. *ibid.*
6. DCC minutes, 1 September, 1913.
7. *Daily Express*, 3 September, 1913.
8. Fr Curran to Walsh, 2 September, 1913 (DAA, Walsh papers).
9. Wright, *op. cit.*, p. 159.
10. *Freeman's Journal*, 5 September, 1913.
11. *Daily Express*, 5 September, 1913.
12. Fr Curran explained to the Archbishop 'a shocking, but really amusing case of "tainted" goods came under my notice today. I heard the story from one who knows the case first hand. A "scab" died. The society refused to pay for his burial. Two undertakers in turn, who were seeing after the funeral arrangements, refused to go on with the burial, even at extra cost. At last a man was got, and every thing seemed all right, when it transpired that the coffin was "tainted", and the unfortunate corpse had actually to be taken out of the coffin and put in another before the third undertaker could carry out the burial—even a "tainted" corpse can't be buried in a "tainted" coffin'. (Curran to Walsh, 26 September, 1913).
13. *Irish Times*, 2 September, 1913.
14. *ibid.*, 4 October, 1913.
15. *The Times*, 2 September, 1913.
16. This was brought home most forcefully to delegates by some of the best photographic journalism of the decade. The impact of the prints was noted by the Bishop of Ossory: 'pictures are now doing harm all round and this lower depth yet reached by the press is found in its adoption of the picture craze to fire the imagination of the mob'. Bishop Brown to Walsh, 7 November, 1913 (DAA, Walsh papers; Bishops file).
17. *Daily Mirror*, 5 September, 1913.
18. *ibid.*
19. *ibid.*
20. Wright, *op. cit.*, p. 164.
21. *New Statesman*, 6 September, 1913.
22. DTC minutes, 23 September, 1913.
23. Dublin Metropolitan House Painters' Minutes, 8 September, 13 and 14 October, 1913 (PRO, Dublin, uncatalogued).
24. Bricklayers' minutes, 11 September, 1913.
25. *ibid.*, 10 October, 11 November, 1913.
26. Bakers' minutes, 2 November, 1913.
27. *Drapers' Assistant*, October, 1913.
28. DTPS minutes, 25 August, 1913.
29. *ibid.*
30. *ibid.*
31. *ibid.*, 15 August, 1913.
32. *Tablet*, 6 September, 1913.
33. *ibid.*
34. *ibid.*, 15 September, 1913.
35. *Manchester Guardian*, September, 1913.
36. *The Times*, 24 September, 1913.
37. Curran to Walsh, 18 September, 1913 (DAA, Walsh papers, priests file).
38. Curran to Walsh, 27 September, 1913.
39. Askwith, *op. cit.*, p. 262.
40. *ibid.*
41. *New Statement*, 11 October, 1913.

42. *National Review*, 1913, p. 207.
43. Askwith, *op. cit.,* p. 264.
44. *ibid.,* p. 265.
45. *Spectator,* 11 October, 1913.
46. *Daily Express,* 15 October, 1913.
47. *New Statesman,* 11 October, 1913.
48. Askwith, *op. cit.,* p. 267.
49. *The Times,* quoted in the *New Statesman,* 11 October, 1913.
50. *Independent,* 8–15 October, 1913.
51. *Irish Times,* 8–16 1913.
52. *ibid.,* 7 October, 1913.
53. Walsh to Aberdeen (draft letter in bad handwriting), 10 October, 1913 (DAA, Walsh papers, Bishops file).
54. *The Times,* 11 October, 1913.
55. *ibid.*
56. *Tablet,* 27 September, 1913.
57. 'Annoyed Catholic' to Archbishop Walsh, 19 September, 1913.
58. *Daily Express,* 21 October, 1913.
59. 'A Catholic' to Archbishop Walsh, 21 October, 1913 (Laity file).
60. Dora Montefiori to Archbishop Walsh, 21 October, 1913 (Laity file).
61. *Daily Express,* 23 October, 1913.
62. *Toiler,* 25 October, 1913.
63. Undated newspaper cutting (*circa* 24 October, 1913; DAA, Walsh Papers, Laity file).
64. *Daily Express,* 23 October, 1913.
65. *Tablet,* 1 November, 1913.
66. Children's Distress Fund (DAA, *pamphlet* in printed material file), pp 1–14.
67. Stephen Gwynn to Archbishop Walsh, 29 October, 1913 (Laity file).
68. Wright, *op. cit.,* p. 61.
69. *Toiler,* 25 October, 1913.
70. *ibid.,* 27 December, 1913.
71. *Irish Worker,* 4 April, 1914.
72. *Spectator,* 1 November, 1913.
73. *New Statesmen,* 1 November, 1913.
74. *The Times,* 3 November, 1913.
75. *ibid.*
76. *Irish Times,* 4 December, 1908.
77. For detailed account of the origins of the ICA, see R. M. Fox, *The History of the Irish Citizen Army* (Dublin, 1943).
78. Jack White, *Misfit* (London, 1930), pp 20–30.
79. Fox, *op. cit.,* p. 44.
80. *Forward,* 6 December, 1913.
81. Fox, *op. cit.,* p. 45.
82. *Irish Times,* 9 September, 1943.
83. *Daily Herald,* 18 December, 1913.
84. The role of the ICA in the 1916 revolt has often forced historians to over-stress and misunderstand its involvement in the 1913 lockout. It is possible to see behind the ICA the thinking of the Social Democratic Federation, as outlined by a former editor of *Justice,* Harry Quelch. He advocated the Swiss notion of an armed nation rather than a standing army. According to his scheme every citizen was to be trained as a soldier, but no one was to become merely a soldier or cease to be a citizen: 'It means that the flower of the nation shall not be withdrawn from civil life and made to waste some of the best years of its existence in the useless routine and pernicious atmosphere of a barracks' (H. Quelch, *Social Democracy and the Armed Nation,* 1900), p. 6.
85. *New Statesman,* 22 November, 1913.
86. The Nationalist MPs had not distinguished themselves during the lockout. All four men had kept 'a low profile' and refused to take sides with the workers. Stephen Gwynn

wrote on 29 October: 'that nationalist members are afraid to move at this juncture for fear of creating disunion as to the main question (Home Rule); and that the representation of this act itself is in weak hands. Nannetti moribund, Abraham devoid of real connection, Field too eccentric—and Brady new to the work. Clancy is very good but very strongly conservative; Afton (?) no use politically and committed to the employers' (Stephen Gwynn to Archbishop Walsh, 29 October, 1913).

87. *Freeman's Journal,* 14 November, 1913.
88. *The Times,* 19–22 November, 1913.
89. *New Statesman,* 22 November, 1913.
90. *The Times,* 10 December, 1913.
91. DCC minutes, 27 November, 1913.
92. *ibid.*
93. James J. Lalor, RC, to Archbishop Walsh, November, 1913 (DAA, Walsh Papers, Laity file).
94. *National Review,* 1913, p. 225.
95. *ibid.*
96. Thomas Kettle, *The Day's Burden* (Dublin, 1968), p. 122.
97. O'Brien, *op. cit.,* p. 98.
98. *The Times,* 10 December, 1913.
99. *ibid.* At end of the day's proceedings the chairman had received a letter from Martin Murphy repudiating the charges.
100. *ibid.*
101. *ibid.*
102. *ibid.*
103. *ibid.*
104. *New Statesman,* 20 December, 1913.
105. Wright, *op. cit.,* p. 247.
106. *ibid.*
107. Bowerman to O'Brien, 1 January, 1913 (NLI, O'Brien MS 13913-1).
108. *ibid.,* 29 January, 1913.
109. *Irish Times,* 26 January, 1914.
110. *New Statesman,* 2 January, 1914.
111. *Freeman's Journal,* 20 January, 1914.
112. *Irish Times,* 20 January, 1914.
113. *ibid.,* 3 February, 1914.
114. Working Rules for *Dublin District of the Amalgamated Society of Carpenters and Joiners, 1914:* Rule IX, p. 7, (in the author's possession).
115. *Irish Times,* 27 January, 1914.
116. ITGWU No. 1 Branch Executive Minute Book, *see* most entries for first six months of 1914 (NLI, MS 7298).
117. ITGWU No. 1 Branch Executive Minute Book, 7 April, 5 May, 1914.
118. *Irish Worker,* 14 January, 1914.
119. *ibid.* On 6 November, 1913, Cardinal Logue had written to Archbishop Walsh giving his view of the lockout: 'There does not seem to be much prospect of an early settlement of the troubles in Dublin. Judging by the speeches, the Larkinites and their abbettors do not want a settlement. They are working not in the interests of the men but using the unfortunate men for the purposes of propagating and establishing their socialistic and syndicalist principles. As long as they are receiving support from England they will go on without abating one iota of their (positions); and when the support ceases they will leave the men to take the consequences, unfortunate victims of their own folly. It is surprising that the men, many of whom must be intelligent, do not see through the game. If they had an ounce of sense, they would go back to their work and leave the Larkinites to air their theories elsewhere. The real misery will come when the thing collapses and numbers of the men find themselves without employment. Their places will be taken in the meantime by others, and it will be hard to expect the employers to dismiss these men

who stood by them in their need and take back the rebels.

'Another consideration is that this unfortunate business is a greater set back to Home Rule than all the vapourisings of Sir E. Carson. I sympathise sincerely with your Grace in all the annoyance and anxiety this fortunate state of things must cause you. I enclose a trifle for the support of the children. I cannot spare much . . .' (DAA Walsh Papers, Bishops file, 1913). Walsh seems to have been very annoyed about the way the strike ended for the men but he was even more annoyed at the behaviour of Larkin for allowing the affair to end in a welter of personal recriminations in which the clergy were included.

120. *Jim Larkin and the Dublin Lock-out, op. cit.* p. 103.
121. *Irish Times,* 11 October, 1916.
122. DCC *Annual Report,* 1914.
123. *ibid.*
124. *ibid.*
125. *Irish Worker,* 27 June, 1914.
126. ITGWU No. 1 Branch Minutes, 19 June, 1914 (NLI, MS 7298).
127. *Irish Worker,* 27 June, 1914.
128. *ibid.*
129. ITGWU No. 1 Branch Committee Minutes, 23 June, 1914.
130. H. E. D. Harris, *The Irish Regiments in the First World War* (Cork 1968), and 'The Other Half Million', in Owen Dudley Edwards and Fergus Pyle (ed.), *1916 The Easter Rising* (London 1968).
131. DCC Minutes, 7 September, 1914.
132. ITGWU No. 1 Branch Committee Minutes, 5 September, 1914 (NLI, MS 7298).

Selected Bibliography

MANUSCRIPT SOURCES

National Library of Ireland
Dublin Trades Council minutes
Thomas Johnson papers
William O'Brien papers
Adolphus Shiels papers

Dublin Archdiocesan Archives
Archbishop William Walsh papers

Dublin Chamber of Commerce
Council minutes

Trade Union Records
Operative Society of Bakers
Ancient Guild of Brick and Stonelayers
Drapers' Assistants Association
Metropolitan Society of House Painters
Dublin Municipal Officers' Association
Dublin Operative Plasterers
United Operative Plumbers Society
Silkweavers' Records
Amalgamated Society of Slaters
Amalgamated Society of Tailors
ITGWU
Dublin Typographical Provident Society

PUBLIC DOCUMENTS AND OFFICIAL PUBLICATIONS

Annual Returns of Trade Unions to the Registrar of Friendly Societies from 1900 to 1920 (Dept of Industry and Commerce, Kildare St, Dublin).

Parliamentary Papers
The seventeenth report of trade unions 1908–10 XLVII 655 (Cd 6109).
Dublin Disturbances Commission, 1914 XVIII, (Cd 7269).
Earnings and Hours of Labour of Work People of the United Kingdom, Report of enquiry by the Board of Trade, 1910 LXXXIV, (Cd 5460).
Factories and Workshops for the Year 1907, Annual Report of the Chief Inspector, 1908, XII, (Cd 4166).

Housing of the Dublin Working Classes, Report of Departmental Committee of Enquiry, 1913, XXVIII, (Cd 6953).

Enquiry into the Rebellion in Ireland, 1916.

Medical Benefit Under the National Insurance Act to Ireland, Appendices to the Report of the Committee Appointed to Enquire into the Extension, Minutes of Evidence, etc., 1913, XXXVII, (Cd 7039).

Poor Laws and Relief of Distress, Royal Commission. Appendix, Vol. X. Minutes of Evidence with Appendix, 1910, L, (Cd 5070).

Poor Laws and Relief of Distress, Appendix Vol. XIXB. Royal Commission. Report by Mr Cyril Jackson on the Effects of the Employment or Assistance Given to the 'Unemployed' since 1886 as a Means of Relieving Distress Outside the Poor Law in Ireland, 1909, XLIV, (Cd 4890).

Royal Irish Constabulary and the Dublin Metropolitan Police, Report of the Committee of Inquiry, 1914, XLIV, (Cd 7421).

Tuberculosis. Interim Report of the Departmental Committee, 1912–13, XLVIII, (Cd 6164).

OTHER PRINTED SOURCES

Newspapers
Cork Examiner; Daily Express; Daily Mirror; Daily Sketch; Evening Mail; Evening Telegraph; Forward; Freeman's Journal; Independent; Irish Catholic; Irish Freedom; Irish Homestead; Irish Nation; Irish People; Irish Times; Irish Worker; Leader; Manchester Guardian; Sinn Fein; The Peasant; The Times (London); *Toiler.*

Periodicals
DCC Journal; Drapers Assistant; Dublin Review; Irish Builder; Irish Ecclesiastical Record; Irish Rosary; Irish Theological Quarterly; Irish Labour History Journal (Saothair); Lady of the House; National Review; New Statesmen; Spectator; Stock Exchange Official Intelligence; Studies; Tablet.

Published Works
Alcock, G. W., *Fifty Years of Railway Trade Unions,* London, 1922.

Anon., *The Attempt to Smash the ITGWU,* Dublin, 1923.

Anon., *Fifty Years of Liberty Hall,* Dublin, 1959.

Anon., *James Larkin's Ordeal: A Plea for Justice,* 1910, (NLI).

Anon., *James Larkin: Plea to Lord Lieutenant,* 1910, (NLI).

Anon., *Labour War in Ireland: Story of a Great Betrayal. Larkin Versus Cork Employers, Simon Punch, James Sexton, the Alleged Labour Leader, and Others,* 1910, (NLI).

Apter, D. E., and Joll, J. (ed.), *Anarchism Today,* London, 1971.

Askwith, G., *Industrial Problems and Disputes,* London, 1920.

Bagwell, P. S., *Railwaymen: The History of the NUR,* London, 1964.

Beckett, J. C., *The Making of Modern Ireland 1603–1923,* London, 1966.

Bower, F., *Rolling Stone Mason,* London, 1938.

Boyd, A., *Irish Trade Unions,* Tralee, 1970.
Boyle, J. W. (ed.), *Leaders and Workers,* Cork, 1960.
Bullock, A., *Life and Times of A. E. Bevin,* London, 1963.
Bundock, C. J., *The National Union of Printing, Bookbinders and Paper Workers,* London, 1959.
Bundock, C. J., *The NUJ. A Jubilee History 1907-57,* London, 1957.
Cameron, G., *How the Poor Live,* 1905, (TCD).
Chart, D. A., 'Unskilled Labour in Dublin: Its Housing and Living Conditions', *Journal of the Statistical and Social Inquiry Society of Ireland,* 6 March, 1914.
Citrine, N. A., *Trade Union Law,* London, 1972.
Clarkson, J. D., *Labour and Nationalism in Ireland,* New York, 1925.
Clegg, A. H., *General Unions in a Changing Society,* London, 1964.
Clegg, A. H., and Adams, R., *The Employer Challenge,* Oxford, 1957.
Coleman, T., *The Railway Navvies,* London, 1965.
Coleman, T., *Passage to America,* London, 1972.
Collin, J., *Life in Old Dublin,* Dublin, 1913.
Collison, W., *Apostle of Free Labour,* London, 1913.
Connelly, U. J., *The Tragic Week: A Study of Anticlericalism in Spain, 1875-1912,* Harvard, 1968.
Connolly, J. J., *The Woodworkers 1860-1960,* London, 1960.
Connolly, James, *Labour in Irish History,* Dublin, 1920.
Connolly, James, *Labour and Easter Week,* Dublin, 1966.
Connolly, James, *Socialism and Nationalism,* Dublin, 1966.
Connolly, James, *The Workers Republic,* Dublin, 1966.
Connolly, M., S. J., 'James Connolly, Socialist and Patriot,' *Studies,* 1952, Vol. XLI, Nos 163-4.
Corfe, T., *The Phoenix Park Murders,* London, 1968.
Corkery, D., *The Hidden Ireland,* Dublin, 1967.
Court, W. H. B., *A Concise Economic History of Britain,* Cambridge, 1964.
Cox, C. B., Dyson, A. E., (ed.), *The Twentieth Century Mind,* Oxford, 1972.
Crome, J. S., *A Concise Dictionary of National Biography,* Dublin, 1928.
Cruise O'Brien, C., *Parnell and his Party,* Oxford, 1957.
Cruise O'Brien, C., *The Shaping of Modern Ireland,* Dublin, 1960.
Cruise O'Brien, C., *States of Ireland,* London, 1972.
Cullen, L. M., *An Economic History of Ireland Since 1660,* London, 1972.
Cullen, L. M., (ed.), *The Formation of the Irish Economy,* Cork, 1969.
Dangerfield, G., *The Strange Death of Liberal England,* London, 1966.
Dawson, C., 'The Housing of the People, with Special Reference to Dublin', *Stat. Soc. Irel. Ju.,* 27 March, 1910.
Dawson, W., 'Dublin in 1912', *Studies,* Autumn-Winter, Vol. LX, No. 239-40.
Eason, C., 'The Tenement Houses of Dublin: Their Condition and Regulation', *Stat. Soc. Irel. Ju.* 13 December, 1898.
Edwards, O. Dudley, & Pyle, F., (ed.), *The Easter Rising,* Dublin, 1966.

Edwards, O. Dudley, *The mind of an activist: James Connolly,* Dublin, 1971.

Ferro, M., *La Gran Guerra 1914–18,* Madrid, 1969.

Finlay, T. A., 'The Church and the Co-operative Movement', *Record of the Maynooth Union,* 1898–9.

Fitzpatrick, D., 'Strikes in Ireland, 1914–21', *Saothar 6,* 1980.

Fogarty, L, *James Fintan Lalor,* Dublin, 1918.

Fox, R. M., *Jim Larkin, Irish Labour Leader,* New York, 1957.

Fox, R. M., *History of the Citizen Army,* Dublin, 1946.

Fox, R. M., *Louie Bennett,* Dublin, 1957.

Fox, R. M., *Smokey Crusade,* Dublin, 1937.

French, T. O., *Plumbers in Unity,* Manchester, 1965.

Gilbert, B. B., *British Social Policy 1914–29,* London, 1970.

Gillispie, S. C., *A Hundred Years of Progress–Record of the Scottish Typographical Association 1852–1952.*

Goldberg, G. Y., 'The Jewish Community', Thomas Davis Lecture in *Religion and Irish Society Series* (No. 15), 1973.

Greaves, C. D., *The Life and Times of James Connolly,* London, 1972.

Greaves, C. D., *Liam Mellows and the Irish Revolution,* London, 1971.

Green, T. R., *Irish Nationality,* London, 1922.

Gregg, P., *A Social and Economic History of Britain,* London, 1971.

Griffith, A., *Resurrection of Hungary,* Dublin, 1918.

Guinan, J., *The Saggart Aroon,* Dublin, 1905.

Handley, J. E., *The Irish in Modern Scotland,* Oxford, 1947.

Harris, H. E. D., *The Irish Regiments in the First World War,* Cork, 1968.

Henry, R. M., *The Evolution of Sinn Fein,* Dublin, 1920.

Hobsbawm, E. J., *Labouring Men,* London, 2nd ed. 1971.

Hobsbawm E. J., *Primitive Rebels,* Manchester, 1971.

Hobsbawm, E. J., *Revolutionaries,* London, 1973.

Hogan, R. (ed.), *Feathers From the Green Crow, Sean O'Casey 1905–25,* London, 1963.

Hyman, L., *Jews in Ireland,* Dublin, 1972.

Hyman, R., *Strikes,* London, 1972.

Inglis, B., *Roger Casement,* London, 1973.

Kane, R., *The Plain Gold Ring,* London, 1910.

Kee, R., *The Green Flag,* London, 1972.

Kettle, T., *The Day's Burden,* Dublin, 1968.

Kiddier, W., *The Old Trade Unions,* London, 1930.

Krause, D., *Sean O'Casey, The Man and His Work,* London, 1967.

Larkin, E., *James Larkin,* London, 1968.

Larkin, E., 'Socialism and Catholicism in Ireland', *Church History,* Vol. XXXIII, December 1964, pp 462–83.

Laslett, P., *The World We Have Lost,* London, 1965.

Lee, J., *The Modernisation of Irish Society 1848–1918,* Dublin, 1973.

Leeson, R. A., *United We Stand: An Illustrated Account of Trade Union Emblems,* Somerset, 1971.

Lowell, J. C., *Stevedores and Dockers,* London, 1969.

Lyons, F. S. L., *John Dillon,* London, 1968.

Lyons, F. S. L., *Culture and Anarchy in Ireland 1890-1939,* Oxford, 1979.

Lyons, F. S. L., *Ireland Since the Famine,* London, 1971.

Lyons, F. S. L., *The Irish Parliamentary Party,* London, 1951.

MacGill, P., *Children of the Dead End,* London, 1912.

MacGill, P., *Moleskin Joe,* London, 1914.

MacGiolla Choille, B., (ed.), *Chief Secretary's Office Dublin Castle, Intelligence Notes, 1913-16,* Dublin, 1966.

McCarthy, C., *The Decade of Upheaval,* Dublin, 1973.

McCarthy, C., 'From Division to Dissention: Irish Trade Unions in the Nineteen Thirties', *The Economic and Social Review,* Vol. 5, No. 4, July 1974.

Mann, T., *Memoirs,* London, 1923.

Martin, F. X., (ed.), *The Scholar Revolutionary,* Dublin, 1970.

Martin, F. X., (ed.), *Leaders and Men of the Easter Rising,* Dublin, 1967.

Martin, J, *Huelga General de 1917,* Madrid, 1971.

Marwick, A., *The Deluge: British Society and the First World War,* London, 1965.

Marwick, A., *Britain in the Century of Total War,* London, 1968.

Marx, K., and Engels, F., *On Ireland,* Moscow, 1971.

Mayor, S., *The Church and the Labour Movement,* London, 1967.

Mitchell, A., *The Irish Labour Movement,* Dublin, 1917.

Mitchell, A., 'William O'Brien, 1881-1968, and the Irish Labour Movement', *Studies,* Autumn-Winter, Vol. XL, No. 239-40.

Mitchell, B. R., *Abstract of British Historical Statistics,* Cambridge, 1962.

Miller, D. A., *Church, State and Nationalism in Ireland 1898-1921,* Dublin, 1973.

Moody, T. W., 'Michael Davitt and the British Labour Movement 1882-1906', *Transactions of the Royal Historical Society,* 5th Series, Vol. 3, 1953.

Morris, W., *Three Works of William Morris,* Berlin, 1968.

Murphy, W. M., *Address to Woodquay National Registration Club,* 10 January, 1887, (TCD).

Murphy, W. M., *Address to Dublin United Tramway Company Motormen and Conductors,* 19 July, 1913, (NLI).

Murry, P., Electoral Politics and the Dublin Working Class before the First World War', Saothar 6, 1980.

Musson, A. F., *The Typographical Association,* Oxford, 1954.

Nevin, D., *Jim Larkin and the Dublin Lockout,* Dublin, 1964.

Norman, E. R., *The Catholic Church and Ireland in the Age of Rebellion,* London, 1967.

Norman, E. R., *A History of Modern Ireland,* London, 1971.

Nowlan, K. B., (ed.), *The Making of 1916,* Dublin, 1969.

O'Brien, F. Cruise, 'The Independent Labour Party in Dublin', *Leader,* 22 August, 1908.

O'Brien, W., *Forth the Banners Go,* Dublin, 1969.

O'Broin, L., *The Chief Secretary Augustine Birrell in Ireland,* London, 1969.

O'Casey, S., *Autobiography,* London, 1971.

O'Cathasaigh, P. *The Story of the Irish Citizen Army,* Dublin, 1914.

O'Connell, T. J., *A Hundred Years of Progress, The Story of the INTO,* Dublin, 1968.

O'Donnell, M. J.,'Strikes', *Record of the Maynooth Union,* 1911–12.

O'Donnell, P., *There Will Be Another Day,* Dublin, 1963.

O'Neill, B., *The Struggle for the Land in Ireland,* London, 1934.

Paine, W., *Shop Slavery and Emancipation,* London, 1912.

Pearl, C., *Dublin in Bloomtime,* London, 1969.

Pelling, H., *Modern Britain,* London, 1964.

Pelling, H., *A History of British Trade Unions,* London, 1969, 3rd ed.

Pelling, H., *A History of the TUC 1868–1968,* London, 1968.

Pelling, H., *Popular Politics and Society in Late Victorian Britain,* London, 1963.

Pelling, H., *Origins of the Labour Party,* London, 1965.

Plunkett, H. *Ireland in the New Century,* London, 1905.

Postgate, R. W., *The Builders History,* London, 1923.

Purcell, M., *The Work of Matt Talbot,* Dublin, 1972.

Raeburn, A., *The Militant Suffragettes,* London, 1974.

Ransom, B., *Connolly's Marxism,* London, 1980.

Riordan, E. J., *Modern Irish Trade and Industry,* London, 1920.

Roebuck, J., *The Making of Modern English Society from 1850,* London, 1973.

Russell, B. *Roads to Freedom,* London, 1970.

Ryan, W. P., *The Irish Labour Movement,* Dublin, 1919.

Ryan, W. P., *The Labour Revolt and Larkinism,* 1913, (NLI).

Ryan, W. P., *The Pope's Green Isle,* London, 1912.

Sexton, J., *James Sexton, Agitator,* London, 1936.

Shannon, M. S., 'Slums: A Sociological Retrospect of the City of Dublin', *Stat. Soc. Irel. Ju.,* 23 January, 1914.

Sharp, I., *Industrial Conciliation and Arbitration in Britain,* London, 1950.

Shaw, F., 'The Canon of Irish History—A Challenge', *Studies,* Summer, 1972, Vol. No. LXI, 242, pp 117–82.

Sheehan, D. D., *Ireland Since Parnell,* London, 1921.

Shillman, B., *Trade Unions and Trade Discipline in Ireland,* Dublin, 1960.

Shilton, E. H., *Foes of Tyranny, History of Amalgamated Unions of Building Trade Unions,* London, 1963.

Sorel, G., *Reflections on Violence,* London, 1953.

Stankey, P., *The Left and War: The British Labour Party and World War One,* London, 1969.

Stewart, M., & Hunter, L., *The Needle is Threaded,* London, 1964.

Stuart Hughes, H., *Consciousness and Society: The Reorientation of European Social Thought 1890–1930,* New York, 1958.

Swift, J., *History of the Dublin Bakers,* Dublin, 1948.

Taylor, A. J. P., *The Struggle for Mastery in Europe 1848–1918,* Oxford, 1971.

Taylor, A. J. P., *The Trouble Makers,* London, 1969.

Thompson, E. P., *The Making of the English Working Class,* London, 1974.

Thompson, W. J., *The Imagination of an Insurrection, Easter 1916,* New York, 1970.

Thomson, D., *England in the Twentieth Century,* London, 1965.

Thorne, W., *My Life's Battles,* London, 1927.

Thornley, D. 'The Development of the Irish Labour Movement', *Christus Rex,* XVIII, 1964.

Tressell, Robert, *The Ragged Trousered Philanthropists,* London, 1971.

Tuchman, B., *The Proud Tower,* New York, 1970.

Vives, J. V., *Approximacion a la Historia de Espana,* Madrid, 1970.

Walsh, P. J., *Archbishop William Walsh of Dublin,* Dublin, 1928.

Webb, J. J. *Municipal Government in Ireland,* Dublin, 1918.

Webb, S., and Webb, B., *History of Trade Unionism,* London, 1920.

White, J., *Misfit,* London, 1930.

Williams, T. *Magnificent Journey,* London, 1954.

Winks, R. W. (ed.), *British Imperialism: Gold, God, Glory,* New York, 1963.

Woodcock, G., *Anarchism,* London, 1962.

Wright, A., *Disturbed Dublin,* London, 1914.

Unpublished

Boyle, J. W., 'The Rise of the Irish Labour Movement 1888–1907' (Ph.D. thesis, TCD, 1961).

Crowley, M. E., 'A Social and Economic Study of Dublin' (MA thesis, UCD, 1971).

D'Arcy, F., 'Dublin Artisan Activity, Opinion and Organisation 1820–66' (MA thesis, UCD, 1968).

Index